Sociology beyond Societies

In this ground-breaking contribution to social theory, John Urry argues that the traditional basis of sociology – the study of society – is outmoded in an increasingly borderless world. If sociology is to make a pertinent contribution to the undersanding of the 'post-societal' era it must forget the social rigidities of the pre-global order and, instead, switch its focus to the study of physical, imaginative and virtual movements. In considering this 'sociology of mobilities', the book concerns itself with the travels of people, ideas, images, objects, messages, waste products and money across international borders, and the implications these mobilities have for the experiences of time, space, dwelling and citizenship.

Sociology beyond Societies extends recent debate about globalisation, both by providing an analysis of how mobilities reconstitute social life in uneven and complex ways, and by arguing for the significance of objects, senses, time and space in the theorising of global processes.

John Urry is Professor of Sociology at Lancaster University.

International library of sociology
Founded by Karl Mannheim
Editor: John Urry
University of Lancaster

Sociology beyond Societies

Mobilities for the twenty-first century

John Urry

London and New York

First published 2000
by Routledge
11 New Fetter Lane, London EC4P 4EE

Simultaneously published in the USA and Canada
by Routledge
29 West 35th Street, New York, NY 10001

Routledge is an imprint of the Taylor & Francis Group

© 2000 John Urry

Typeset in Baskerville by Taylor & Francis Books Ltd
Printed and bound in Great Britain by Biddles Ltd, Guildford and
King's Lynn

British Library Cataloguing in Publication Data
A catalogue record for this book is available from the British
Library

Library of Congress Cataloging in Publication Data
Urry, John.
Sociology beyond societies: mobilities for the twenty-first century/
John Urry.
p. cm. – (International library of sociology)
Includes bibliographical references and index.
1. Sociology–Philosophy. I. Title. II. Series.
HM585.U77 1999   99–34303
301′.01–dc21

ISBN 0–415–19088–6 (hbk)
ISBN 0–415–19089–4 (pbk)

To Richard Urry

It seems to me that I would always be better off where I am not, and this question of moving is one of those I discuss incessantly with my soul.

(Charles Baudelaire, cited Kaplan 1996: 27)

Our nature lies in movement; complete calm is death.

(Blaise Pascal, cited Bruce Chatwin 1988: 183)

A *self* does not amount to much, but no self is an island; each exists in a fabric of relations that is now more complex and mobile than ever before.

(J.-F. Lyotard 1984: 15)

Contents

Acknowledgements

I am very grateful for the comments and inspiration resulting from recent writing and research collaboration with Greg Myers, Phil Macnaghten, Bron Szerszynski and Mark Toogood (as well as the ESRC for research funding: grant R000236768). I am also grateful for comments on one or more of the chapters or related papers from Nick Abercrombie, Eric Dariér, Anne-Marie Fortier, Sarah Franklin, Scott Lash, John Law, Mike Michael, Doreen Massey, Ann-Marie Mol, Andrew Sayer, Mimi Sheller, Elizabeth Shove, Jackie Stacey, Sylvia Walby and James Wickham.

I have greatly benefited from supervising the doctorates of the following who have been at Lancaster during the 1990s and whose work has in one way or another influenced this book: Christof Armbruster, Bulent Diken, Saolo Cwerner, Monica Degen, Tim Edensor, Kevin Hetherington, Neil Lewis, Richard Sharpley and Kathleen Sullivan.

It should be noted that most of the examples discussed in this book relate to what I call the North Atlantic rim; the point of this reference to an ocean criss-crossed by ships and planes, cables and satellites, should become clear.

I am very grateful for the encouragement for this book from Amy and Thomas Urry.

John Urry
Lancaster, March 1999

Chapter 1

Societies

> At the present moment of history the network of social relations spreads over the whole world, without any absolute solution of continuity. This gives rise to the difficulty ... of defining what is meant by the term 'society' ... If we say that our subject is the study and comparison of human societies we ought to be able to say what are the unit entities with which we are concerned.
>
> (A.R. Radcliffe-Brown 1952: 193)

Introduction

In this book I seek to develop the categories that will be relevant for sociology as a 'discipline' as we enter the next century. I seek to present a manifesto for a sociology that examines the diverse mobilities of peoples, objects, images, information and wastes; and of the complex interdependencies between, and social consequences of, these diverse mobilities. Hence the subtitle of this book – the investigation of mobilities into, and for, the next century.

I show how such mobilities transform the historic subject-matter of sociology within the 'west' which focused upon individual societies and upon the generic characteristics of such societies. I consider how the development of various global 'networks and flows' undermines endogenous social structures which have generally been taken within sociological discourse to possess the powers to reproduce themselves. I interrogate the concept of the social as society and show that, whatever its value in the past, it will not in the future be especially relevant as the organising concept of sociological analysis. I try to develop a new agenda for sociology and make set out a manifesto for its reformulation in its 'post-societal' phase.

The concept of society will in the future be one particularly deployed by especially powerful 'national' forces seeking to moderate, control and regulate these variously powerful networks and flows criss-crossing their porous borders. New rules of sociological method are necessitated by the apparently declining powers of national societies (whether or not we do in fact live in a global society), since it was those societies that had provided the social context for sociological study until the present. If there are no longer powerful societies then I try to establish what new rules of sociological method and theory are appropriate. In particular I elaborate some of the material transformations that are remaking the 'social', especially those diverse mobilities that, through multiple senses, imaginative travel, movements of images and information, virtuality and physical movement, are materially reconstructing the 'social as society' into the 'social as mobility'.

Three arguments might be made against these claims. In the first, it is said that society has never been the key concept in sociology; that has been provided by other notions, such as meaningful action, agency, interaction or world-system. In the second, it is claimed that societies are still powerful entities and that nation-states are able to undertake important actions, both externally and internally, in order to sustain existing patterns of power. In the third, it is argued that since 'globalisation' undermines the very basis of sociology as a separate discipline that loses its central concept of society, so sociology with nothing to put in its place should wither on the vine.

Against these points it is shown that sociology in north Atlantic rim societies has been historically organised around the discourse of 'society' and hence of the conditions which sustain their characteristic structuring (such as functional integration, or social conflict, or base and superstructure). This societal structuring has been bound up with notions of what it is to be a member or citizen of a given national society and of the particular societally guaranteed rights and duties of citizenship.

Second, mobilities on an enormous scale involving diverse technologies and objects do problematise the powers of society. I consider how and to what degree 'social governmentality' is put into question by mobilities organised through complexly organised times and spaces. Analysis is provided of whether such mobilities undermine societal borders and of the degrees and forms of their permeability. Comprehending such mobilities is not straightforward and in part requires the employment of various kinds of metaphor of movement, especially of networks and flows.

Third, these mobilities criss-crossing societal borders in strikingly new temporal–spatial patterns hold out the possibility of a major new agenda for sociology. This is an agenda of mobility. And there is here an irony. Much twentieth-century sociology has been based upon the study of occupational, income, educational and social *mobility*. In some sense British sociology has presumed that the differential rates of upward and downward mobility, within generations and across generations, is the defining question of the sociological enterprise. So to stretch a point – one might say that sociology has always regarded mobility as its 'core business' but in the formulation I develop there are various breaks with this twentieth-century vision of a sociology that is organised around social/societal mobility.

Most obviously, mobility is taken to be a geographical as well as a social phenomenon. Much of the social mobility literature regarded society as a uniform surface and failed to register the geographical intersections of region, city and place, with the social categories of class, gender and ethnicity. The existing sociology of migration is incidentally far too limited in its concerns to be very useful here. Further, I am concerned with the flows of people within, but especially beyond, the territory of each society, and how these flows may relate to many different desires, for work, housing, leisure, religion, family relationships, criminal gain, asylum seeking and so on. Moreover, not only people are mobile but so too are many 'objects'. I show that sociology's recent development of a 'sociology of objects' needs to be taken further and that the diverse flows of objects across societal borders and their intersections with the multiple flows of people are hugely significant. Finally, mobility is predominantly understood in a horizontal rather than the vertical sense common within the social mobility literature. I explore further the fruitfulness of horizontal metaphors as the basis of a reconfigured sociology.

Why, it might be asked, should sociology be the discipline principally concerned with the study of these horizontal mobilities? Does not such a focus imply a post-disciplinary social/cultural/political science with no particular space or role for any individual discipline? Indeed maybe the very industries responsible for these global flows will not need the academy anyway since they can reflexively know (or think they know) what is involved in their particular domain and can themselves interrogate the main processes (albeit researched in-house or in private think-tanks). So why can and should sociology analyse these intersecting horizontal mobilities?

First, most other social science disciplines are subject to much more extensive forms of discursive normalisation, monitoring and policing which make them poor candidates for such post-disciplinary reconfiguration. Indeed theories, methods and data may be literally expelled from such disciplines since they are too 'social' and outside the concerns of that particular policed discipline (see Urry 1995: chap. 2). Second, sociology's discursive formation has often demonstrated a relative lack of hierarchy, a somewhat unpoliced character, an inability to resist intellectual invasions, an awareness that all human practice is socially organised, a potential to identify the social powers of objects and nature, and an increasing awareness of spatial and temporal processes. While all these wreak havoc with any remaining notion of society *tout court*, sociology may be able to develop a new agenda, an agenda for a discipline that is losing its central concept of human 'society'. It is a discipline organised around networks, mobility and horizontal fluidities.

In the rest of this chapter various notions of *society* and their constitutive role in the historical development of sociological discourse are examined. Such notions of society are linked to an examination of borders, mobilities and governance. I discuss a range of ways in which a 'sociology of mobilities' disrupts a 'sociology of the social as society'.

In Chapter 2 I show the importance of different *metaphors* of the social, particularly considering those appropriate for examining various mobilities. I interrogate the metaphors of net/network and of flows/fluids, and contrasts will be drawn with the metaphors of region and structure that have been central to the society concept. Also some consideration is paid to the spatial and temporal organisation of networks/flows and to their complex consequences for what have been historically viewed as societal processes.

In Chapter 3 I consider diverse socio-spatial practices of *mobility*. I consider corporeal mobility and especially walking, travelling by train, car-driving and air travel; object mobility as objects are constituted through mobilities and are themselves mobile; imaginative travel through radio and television and its effects in reconstituting the public sphere; and virtual travel and its connections with communities and corporeal mobility. In each of these mobilities it is demonstrated that there are complex mobile hybrids constituted through assemblages of humans, machines and technologies.

This last point is further developed in Chapter 4 where it is shown that in order to investigate these relationships of humans and things we need to consider the role of the various *senses*, something neglected in most sociology. It is the analysis of the senses that embodies sociological analysis but it is necessary to do this in a way that connects such embodiments to larger-scale cultural processes. Particular 'actants', it is shown, depend upon particular senses, and that mobilities to, and from places, rest upon specific 'ways of sensing'. The changing relationships between the different senses are elaborated.

Chapter 5 is concerned with *time* and especially with outlining and critiquing the distinction between so-called social and natural time. It is shown that apparently 'natural' clock-time is in fact socially produced and yet has exerted a powerful role in the subduing of nature. Examination is then provided of instantaneous time that is implicit within, and in turn transforms, various mobilities that are concerned with the saving of brief moments of time. The social consequences of such instantaneous time are shown to be profound and underexplored within mainstream sociological debate.

In Chapter 6 attention is paid to the nature of *dwelling*. It is considered just what is involved when we say that people dwell within communities, whether given or constructed, and how most forms of dwelling depend upon various modes of real or imagined mobility. Particular attention is focused upon local communities, *bunds*, collective enthusiasms, virtual communities, nations and diasporas. It is argued that the sociological concept of community should be replaced by that of dwelling and dwellingness, many forms of which presuppose diverse mobilities.

In Chapter 7 a critique is provided of existing notions of *citizenship* based upon the national society and the limited rights and duties that that entails. It is increasingly hard to sustain a societal model of citizenship with the development of diverse forms of mobility rights and duties, including those of cosmopolitanism and global citizenship. Such a citizenship is analysed in terms of new practices, risks, rights and duties; these transcend individual national borders. A central role in this citizenship is played by shame as the public sphere is transformed into a 'mediatised' and partially globalised public stage.

In the final chapter an agenda for a *sociology beyond societies* is developed, organised around the distinction between gardening and gamekeeping metaphors. The emergence of gamekeeping involves reconsidering the nature of a civil society of mobilities; seeing how states increasingly function as 'regulators' of such mobilities; dissolving the 'gardening' distinction between nature and society; and examining the emergent global level that is comprised of roaming, intersecting, complex hybrids.

'There is no such thing as society'

I begin with the concept of the social as 'society'. When former Prime Minister Margaret Thatcher famously declared that 'there is no such thing as society', sociologists led the charge to critique her claim. They declared that there is obviously such a thing as society and that Thatcher's claim indicated the inappropriateness of her policies based upon trying to reduce the societal to the interests of what she termed 'individual men and women and their families'.

In this book I shall not install Thatcher as a major figure of individualist social theory (her views were loosely derived from Hayek). But the smug riposte to Thatcher from the British sociological community was not justified. It is actually unclear just what is meant by the term 'society'. Although there is something 'more' in social life than 'individual men and women and their families', exactly what this surplus amounts to is not obvious. Most sociologists would not agree on the nature of this surplus. Yet this is particularly ironic since if sociology does possess a central concept, it is surely that of society (even when alternative terms are used, such as country, social structure, nation or social formation).

First then, I argue that the concept of society has been central to sociological discourse. I then argue that if there is any agreement on the concept of society this is embedded within notions of nation-state, citizenship and national society, working through a 'banal nationalism' (Billig 1995). But then I show that it is this sense of 'nation-state-society' that contemporary mobilities call into question and which suggest that maybe Thatcher was oddly right when she said there is no such thing as society. But she was at the same time quite wrong in that she ignores many 'post-societal' processes that lie beyond individual men and women, including especially those of the global marketplace. She also omits to consider the enduring ideological power of the nation presumably because she would regard this as 'natural' and not 'societal'. I will now expand on these points.

Sociological discourse has indeed been premised upon 'society' as its object of study (Billig 1995: 52–3; Hewitt 1997: chap. 1). This was especially so from the 1920s onwards as sociology was institutionalised especially within the American academy. MacIver and Page's standard *Society: An Introductory Analysis* argues that sociology is ' "about" social relationships, the network of relationships we call society' (1950: v). The radical Gouldner in *The Coming Crisis of Western Sociology* talks of 'Academic Sociology's emphasis on the potency of society and the subordination of men [sic] to it' (1972: 52). In the definitive *The Social Science Encyclopedia*, Shils talks of sociology's knowledge being 'gained through the study of the whole and parts of society' (1985: 799), while Kornblum defines sociology as the 'scientific study of human societies and human behaviour in the many groups that make up a society' (1988: 4). The world system theorist Wallerstein summarises the overall situation: 'no concept is more pervasive in modern social science than society' (1987: 315).

This construction of the discourse of sociology around the concept of society in part stemmed from the relative autonomy of American society throughout the twentieth century. It thus represents a universalisation of the American societal experience. The theorist of the US as the prototypical modern society, Talcott Parsons, defined 'society as the type of social system characterised by the highest level of self-sufficiency relative to its environment, including other social systems' (1971: 8). Such self-sufficient societies are of course empirically rare and generally rely upon their domination of their physical and social environments and on securing that their 'members' performances ... "contribute" adequately to societal functioning' (Parsons 1971: 9).

Wallerstein also argues that no concept is used more unreflectively than that of society (1987: 315). This can be seen by considering the main 'theoretical perspectives' within sociology and by reconstructing the sense of society that they each presume. The perspectives, which are not necessarily similar in organisation, structure, or intellectual coherence, are those of critical theory, ethnomethodology, feminism, functionalism, interactionism, Marxism, structurationism, systems theory and Weberianism (see Urry 1995: 41; Hewitt 1997: chaps 1 and 2). The following sets out the notion of society specific to each perspective:

critical theory	society as forms of alienated consciousness reproduced by the institutions of mass society
ethnomethodology	society as the fragile order displayed by the common sense methods used by members in practical reasoning
feminism	society as the bounded system of social relations within which the interests of men dominate those of women
functionalism	society as the social system in which its various parts are functionally integrated with each other
interactionism	society as the precarious social order negotiated and renegotiated between actors
Marxism	society as the structure of relations between the economic base and the political and ideological superstructures
structurationism	society as the clustering of institutions across time and space which results from drawing on and in turn reproducing certain structural principles
systems theory	society as an autopoietic network of self-regulating and recursive communications organisationally distinguished from its environment
Weberianism	society as the relations between specific social orders and of the unequally distributed social groupings present within each order

Thus there are various senses of the term 'society', each presuming a somewhat different emergent quality at the level of society which is over and above 'individual men and women and their families'. Giddens concludes that society is a largely unexamined term in sociological discourse (1987: 25), while Mann argues that we should abolish the term because of this extensive disagreement and incoherence (1986: 2).

What most of these formulations neglect to consider is how the notion of society connects to the system of nations and nation-states. Billig argues that: 'the "society" which lies at the heart of sociology's self-definition is created in the image of the nation-state' (1995: 53, 10). Interestingly American-based theories of society have frequently ignored the 'nationalist' basis of American and indeed of all western societies. They have typically viewed nationalism as a surplus to society that only needs to be deployed in situations of 'hot' extremism (which supposedly does not describe the 'west'). However, Elias clearly points out that: 'Many twentieth century sociologists, when speaking of "society", no longer have in mind ... a "bourgeois society" or a "human society" beyond the state, but increasingly the somewhat diluted ideal image of a nation-state' (1978: 241; and see Billig 1995: 52–4).

Thus in the following theorisation of society, sovereignty, national citizenship and social governmentality lie at its core. Each 'society' is a sovereign social entity with a nation-state that organises the rights and duties of each societal member or citizen. Most major sets of social relationships are seen as flowing within the territorial boundaries of the society. The state is thought to possess a monopoly of jurisdiction or governmentality over members living within the territory or region of the society. Economy, politics, culture, classes, gender and so on, are societally structured. In combination they constitute a clustering, or what is normally conceptualised as a 'social structure'. Such a structure organises and regulates the life-chances of each member of the society in question.

This societal structure is not only material but cultural, so that its members believe they share some common identity which in part is bound up with the territory that the society occupies or lays claim to. And *contra* the argument of much sociology, central to most such societies is a vernacular nationalism that is part of how people think and experience themselves as humans. There are many features of the banal nationalism that articulates the identities of each society through its mundane differences from the other. These include the waving of celebratory flags, singing national anthems, flying flags on public buildings, identifying with one's own sports-heroes, being addressed in the media as a member of a given society, celebrating independence day and so on (Billig 1995). One might metaphorically characterise this vernacular nationalism as being something like a fractal, the irregular but strangely similar shapes which are found in fragmented phenomena at very different scales of the body social. We could see this self-similarity in the way from each local level right up to the centre of the state, members of a society do similar kinds of things as each other, share similar beliefs, think of themselves as characteristically 'French' or 'American'.

However, it is doubtful if societies could ever be conceived of as entirely self-reproducing entities (see Luhmann 1995, for an autopoietic formulation of society). Sociology has a tendency to treat what is 'outside' the society as an unexamined environment. But no society, even in the heyday of the nation-state earlier this century, has been separate from the very system of such states and from the notion of national identity that mobilises sovereign societies. As Calhoun points out: 'No nation-state ever existed entirely unto itself' (1997: 118). It is through this interdependence that societies are constituted as partially self-regulating entities significantly defined by their banal or vernacular differences from each other. As Wallerstein argues: 'it is futile to analyze the processes of the *societal development* of our multiple (national) 'societies' as if they were autonomous, internally evolving structures, when they are and have been in fact primarily structures created by, and taking form in response to, world-scale processes' (1991: 77). The north Atlantic rim has been constituted as a system of such national societies, with clear boundaries and multiple banal nationalisms that mark each society from the other (Billig 1995; Held 1995; Calhoun 1997). Societies have varied in their degree of boundedness, and especially, as Touraine argues, in the degree to which society has been organised through, and integrated with, a mobilising 'culture'; but without such a societal culture it is hard to determine what are a society's boundaries (1998).

Over the past two centuries this conception of society has been central to north American and west European notions of what it is to be a human being, someone possessing the rights and duties of social citizenship. To be human meant that one is a member or citizen of a particular society. Historically and conceptually there has been a strong connection between the idea of humanness and of membership of a society. Society here means that ordered through a nation-state, with clear territorial and citizenship boundaries and a system of governance over its particular citizens. Conceptually and historically there has been an indivisible duality, of citizens and societies. Rose characterises this model as government from 'the social point of view' (1996: 328). Such societal governmentality has been effected through new forms of expertise, partly based upon sociology as the science of such societies and of the appropriate forms of social citizenship (see Chapter 7 below).

In this account 'society', and its characteristic social divisions of, especially, social class, are strongly intertwined with the 'nation-state'. Mann shows in his massive dissection of the 'rise of classes and nation-states' in the 'west' between 1760 and 1914, that societies, nation and states have been enormously intertwined in their historical development (1993: 737). They developed together and should not be conceptualised as colliding billiard balls existing only in external relations with each another. Mann evocatively talks of the sheer patterned messiness of the social world and of the mutually reinforcing intersections of class and nation, as societies developed their 'collective powers' (as opposed to the distributive powers of person-over-person; see Parsons 1960). He persuasively argues for the concept of collective powers, showing how:

> Western collective power had been revolutionized ... Societies were qualitatively better organized to mobilize human capacities and to exploit nature, as well as to exploit less developed societies. Their extraordinary social density enabled rulers and people actually to participate in the same 'society'.
>
> (1993: 14)

Such collective powers implied a very strong distinction between social governmentality, on the one hand, and what lies beyond society as nature, on the other. This is so whether that pre-social nature is viewed as Hobbesian or Lockean, as brutish or benign (Macnaghten and Urry 1998: chap. 1). The intense conflict between nature and society reached its high point during the later nineteenth-century in western Europe and north America. Nature was viewed as, and degraded into, a realm of unfreedom and hostility to be subdued and controlled. Modernity involved the belief that human progress should be measured and evaluated in terms of the domination of nature, rather than through transforming the very relationship between 'humans' and 'nature'. The realisation of the collective powers of such societies resulted in remarkable increases in the rates of extraction and exploitation of energy.

Sociology as a specific academic practice was the product of this particular historical moment, of an emergent industrial capitalism in western Europe and north America. It took for granted the success of modern societies in their spectacular overcoming of nature. Sociology specialised in describing and explaining the character of these modern societies that were based upon industries that enabled and utilised dramatic new forms of energy and resulting patterns of social life. As such sociology adopted one or other versions of a tradition-modernity divide that implied that a revolutionary change had occurred in north Atlantic rim societies between 1700–1900. These modern societies were presumed to be qualitatively different from the past. This dichotomy of tradition and modernity has been variously formulated: Maine's status to contract, Marx's feudalism to capitalism, Tönnies' *gemeinschaft* to *gesellschaft*, Spencer's militant to industrial society, Foucault's classical to bourgeois ages and Durkheim's mechanical to organic forms of the division of labour.

Sociology was thus based upon the acceptance and enhancement of the presumed division of academic labour stemming from the Durkheimian identification of the region of the social to be investigated and explained autonomously (Durkheim 1952). In a way sociology employed the strategy of modelling itself on biology and arguing for its specific and autonomous realm of facts, in this case pertaining to the social or societal. Until recently this academic division between a world of natural facts and one of social facts was uncontentious. It made good sense as a strategy of professionalisation for sociology since this division provided a clear and bounded sphere of investigation. This sphere was parallel to, but did not challenge or confront, those physical sciences that dealt with an apparently distinct and analysable nature, and which had an enormous head-start in the race for academic respectability and funding (see Macnaghten and Urry 1998: chaps 1, 4 and 6).

There was presumed to be a chasm between nature and society (sometimes conceived of as methodological, sometimes ontological). It was assumed that the natural sciences were just that – 'natural' – and their scientific method had been largely resolved. I am not suggesting of course that all sociologies have been Durkheimian. Other sociologies have on occasions transcended these formulations, arguing that agency, interaction, members' concepts, world system, culture should instead be the key concept. But these have been relatively marginal discourses within the general sociological concern to establish the character of the societal order that is crucially separate from the natural order.

It was also presumed within organised capitalism (1900s–70s Europe and north America) that most economic and social problems and risks were produced by, and soluble at, the level of the individual society. Each society was sovereign, based upon a social governmentality and was separate from nature. The concerns of each society were to be dealt with through national policies, especially from the 1930s onwards through a Keynesian welfare state that could identify and respond to the risks of organised capitalism (Lash and Urry 1987, 1994). These risks were seen as principally located *within* the geographical borders and temporal frames of each society. And solutions were devised and implemented within such societal frontiers. National societies were based upon a concept of the citizen who owed duties to, and received rights from, their society through the core institutions of the nation-state.

Of course this 'societal' model at best only applied to the dozen or so societies of the north Atlantic rim (as well as Japan). And even here the Vatican in Rome partially dominated the domestic policies of a number of 'southern' European countries (see Walby 1996). Most of the rest of the world was subject to domination. It was the societies of the north Atlantic rim which were the colonial powers, having hugely significant economic, military, social and cultural relationships beyond their borders. By 1913, for example, European and north American societies accounted for 90 per cent of world industrial production (Mann 1993: 14). Also one particular national society, Germany, was nearly able to subject most of Europe to its military hegemony. And for much of the twentieth century the most powerful society, the US, has principally functioned as a superpower locked into an escalating diplomatic, political, military, economic and cultural struggle with another massively powerful imperial society, the USSR. I have already noted the paradox that it was within the US that theories of society as bounded, relatively autonomous 'functional' entities were particularly developed.

I have thus shown in this section that the concept of society (whatever the actual term used) has been central to sociological discourse, especially within the US, but that the concept is used in contradictory ways within different sociological perspectives. I argued that if the concept of society does make sense then such societies have to be embedded within the analysis of the *system* of nation-states-societies.

In the next section I consider further this system which contemporary changes have put into question and which suggest that maybe Thatcher was oddly right when she said there is no such thing as society. But that there may not be such a thing as society is not because of the power of individual human subjects, but because of their weakness in the face of 'inhuman' processes of globalisation. Wallerstein points out that: 'What is fundamentally wrong with the concept of society is that it reifies and therefore crystallizes social phenomena whose real significance lies not in their solidity but precisely in their fluidity and malleability' (Wallerstein 1991: 71). I now detail some recent debates about supposed globalisation that demonstrate such a fluidity and malleability of social phenomena.

Inhuman globalisation

In various chapters below I examine the extraordinary array of 'global' processes which appear to be redrawing the contours of contemporary social experience. As a starting point into this literature Table 1.1 sets out some of the main types of globalisation argument.

I shall at times in this book consider all these uses. In the next chapter I develop the last of these as the most fruitful way of comprehending what

Table 1.1 Main forms of globalisation

Strategy	As developed by transnational corporations which operate on a worldwide basis and involving a lack of commitment to the needs of particular places, labour forces or governments
Image	Images of the 'earth' or 'globe' which are used in the advertising of products (airlines for example) and for recruiting people to join groups protesting about threats to the 'global environment'
Ideology	Those with economic interests in promoting capitalism throughout the world argue that globalisation is inevitable and that national governments should not intervene to regulate the global market-place
Basis of political mobilisation	The characterisation of issues as 'global' facilitates the mobilisation of a wide range of individuals and organisations for or against the phenomena in question
Scapes and flows	People, money, capital, information, ideas and images are seen to 'flow' along various 'scapes' which are organised through complex interlocking networks located both within and across different societies (such as the monetary scapes and flows between London, New York and Tokyo)

might be involved in the supposed globalisation of contemporary capitalism. It should also be noted that the term 'globalisation' is particularly confusing since it refers both to certain global processes (from the verb, to globalise) and to certain global outcomes (from the noun, the globe). In this book I use globalisation in the first sense since it will be seen that many of the processes discussed are incomplete and there is nothing approaching a single global economy or society. I ask: are there certain global processes and the partial development of an emergent level of the global; if so how are they to be examined; and what are their implications for the analysis of 'societies'?

A useful starting point is Mann's description of the contemporary world: 'Today, we live in a global society. It is not a unitary society, nor is it an ideological community or a state, but it is a single power network. Shock waves reverberate around it, casting down empires, transporting massive quantities of people, materials and messages, and finally, threatening the ecosystem and atmosphere of the planet' (1993: 11). A number of points are being made here: there is not a unified global society; there are exceptional levels of global interdependence; unpredictable shock waves spill out 'chaotically' from one part to the system as a whole; there are not just 'societies' but massively powerful 'empires' roaming the globe; and there is mass mobility of peoples, objects and dangerous human wastes. In this book I develop the sociological implications of this sketch.

Two very different responses to such a globalisation-thesis can be noted. There are global enthusiasts who see these processes as producing a new epoch, a golden age of cosmopolitan 'borderlessness'. This epoch offers huge new opportunities, especially to overcome the limitations and restrictions that societies and especially national states have exercised on the freedom of corporations and individuals to treat the world as 'their oyster' (Ohmae 1990).

Others describe globalisation not as a borderless utopia but as a new dystopia. The global world is seen as a new medievalism, as the 'west' returns to the pre-modern era (Cerny 1997). The medieval world was characterised by a lack of clear territorial boundaries and 'societies'; there were empires with centres and peripheries with many criss-crossing networks and contested jurisdictions; and there were multiple linguistic communities (see Mann 1986; Billig 1995: 20–1; for a critique of neo-medievalism, Hirst and Thompson 1996: 184). The new medieval global world seems likewise to consist of competing institutions with overlapping jurisdictions and identities. States are being reconstituted as competition-states; and there is an absence of external military threat for many such states and hence a difficulty of the nation imagining itself as one. Various powerful empires such as Microsoft and Coca-Cola are roaming the earth and reconfiguring economies and cultures in their global interests. And there is the growth of competing city-states, such as New York, Singapore, London, Hong Kong, Sydney, Tokyo and so on.

In both the optimistic and the pessimistic analyses, it is *inhuman* objects that reconstitute social relations. Such relations are made and remade through machines, technologies, objects, texts, images, physical environments and so on. Human powers increasingly derive from the complex *interconnections* of humans with material objects, including signs, machines, technologies, texts, physical environments, animals, plants, and waste products. People possess few powers which are uniquely human, while most can only be realised because of their connections with these inhuman components. The following inhuman developments are novel in their ontological depth and transformative powers: the miniaturisation of electronic technologies into which humans are in various ways 'plugged in' and which will inhabit most work and domestic environments; the transformation of biology into genetically coded information; the increasing scale and range of intensely mobile waste products and viruses; the hugely enhanced capacities to simulate nature and culture; changing technologies which facilitate instantaneously rapid corporeal mobility; and informational and communicational flows which dramatically compress distances of time and space between people, corporations and states.

Because of the significance of these inhuman hybrids I do not deploy conceptions of agency that specifically focus upon the capacities of humans to attribute meaning or sense or to follow a social rule. This is not to suggest that humans do not do such things, not to suggest that humans do not exert agency. But they only do so in circumstances which are not of their own making; and it is those circumstances – the enduring and increasingly intimate relations of subjects *and* objects – that are of paramount significance. This means that the human and physical worlds are elaborately intertwined and cannot be analysed separate from each other, as society and as nature, or humans and objects. In various chapters complex mobile hybrids are shown to be of utmost sociological importance.

Also agency is not a question of humans acting independently of objects in terms of their unique capacities to attribute meaning or to follow rules. Rather what are crucial are the ways in which the physical world and artefacts are sensuously experienced by humans. The concept of agency needs to be embodied and I develop this through an analysis of the senses and of the inter-relationships between them. Such senses are not only crucial, as Simmel suggested in terms of the relations of person to person, but also in terms of the relations of people to 'nature' and to technologies, objects, texts and images (see Chapter 4).

If then there is not autonomous realm of human agency, so there should not be thought of as a distinct level of *social* reality that is the unique outcome of humans acting in and through their specific powers. Various writers have tried to develop the thesis of the dialectic of individuals making society and society making individuals (Berger and Luckmann 1967). But such a dialectic would only be only plausible if we mean by society something trivial, that is pure social interactions abstracted from the networks of intricate relationships with the inhuman. Since almost all social entities do involve networks of connections between humans and these other components, so there are no uniquely *human* societies as such. Societies are necessarily hybrids.

Furthermore, we will subsequently see how various transformations of the inhuman weaken the power of societies to draw together their citizens as one, to endow all with national identity and to speak with a single voice. Rose argues:

> While our political, professional, moral and cultural authorities still speak happily of 'society', the very meaning and ethical salience of this term is under question as 'society' is perceived as dissociated into a variety of ethical and cultural communities with incompatible allegiances and incommensurable obligations.

> (1996: 353)

More generally, Laclau and Mouffe show the impossibility of society as a valid object of discourse (1985; and see Barrett 1991). This results from the necessarily incomplete character of every totality. In particular there is no underlying principle which fixes and hence constitutes the relevant field of differences that marks off one society from the other. Employing a Lacanian metaphor, they suggest that social relations are continuously being opened up, the skin is broken and there is an enduring need for a hegemonic filling in or suturing the society together again (Laclau and Mouffe 1985: 88). Such a closure or stitching back of the social is thought an impossibility. It will simply break open somewhere else, the wound will bleed, the tissue will be scarred since the past will remain marking the surface of the 'body social' (in the next chapter I consider some other metaphors of the social).

Laclau and Mouffe thus ask what does stitch together a 'society' when inhuman networks criss-cross it in strikingly new ways at ever-faster speeds? In this book I presume that the classic philosophical–sociological debates as to the respective virtues of methodological individualism versus holism, or in their later manifestations, structurationism versus the dualism of structure, are unhelpful. These debates do not deal with the complex consequences of diverse mobilities; the intersecting sensuous relations of humans with diverse objects; the timed and spaced quality of relations stretching across societal borders; and the complex and unpredictable intersections of many 'regions, networks and flows'. To describe these as either 'structure' or as 'agency' does injustice to the temporal and spatial complexity of such relations. In this book then the ordering of social life is presumed to be contingent, unpredictable, patterned and irreducible to human subjects. Luhmann summarises: 'There can be no "intersubjectivity" on the basis of the subject' (1995: xli).

These points can be illuminated by briefly considering Archer's morphogenetic social theory designed to deal with the 'vexatious' nature of society (1995). She places 'time' at the centre of her 'non-conflationary' social theory based on two main claims. First, the social world is ontologically stratified so that the emergent properties of structures and agents are irreducible to each other and are in principle analytically distinct. And second, structures and agents are temporally distinguishable so that it is possible to talk of the respective emergence of either structure or agency (1995: 66). It is the combination of analytical separability and temporality rather than simultaneity, which are her key realist moves. They provide the basis for examining *morphogenesis*, the radical and unpredictable re-shaping of society that results from the historically emergent interplay between structure and agency. This interplay over time generates an open society which is like itself and nothing else (see Archer 1995: 157, for a diagrammatic representation of the morphogenetic cycle).

However, her examination of the key concept of time is problematic. First, time is analysed separate from space and in that sense goes against the entire thrust of twentieth century science, as well as extensive argumentation within the social sciences. It is a Newtonian conception of time. There is no discussion of the extensive debates in the sociology of time that have revealed the multiple 'times' that constitute social life. Time is seen by Archer as linear, as the fourth dimension, as merely 'before-and-after' (see Chapter 5 below). She treats structures and agents as being in time, as strung out like beads along the fourth dimension. In that sense she does not examine the possibility that time (and space) are themselves powerful 'entities' or that there is an arrow of time, all of which are unconfined within societies. Nor does she consider the position that, although time in itself does not possess powers, there are particular times that do exert such powers. In particular the hybrid of 'clock-time' has been powerfully instrumental (uniquely with other causal processes) in the subjection of the natural world throughout much of the nineteenth and twentieth centuries. Similarly the putative 'end of society' would appear to be on the agenda because of the extraordinary warping of time–space that contemporary global changes are ushering in, changes in which time as instantaneous is a particularly powerful hybrid.

Such a putative 'end of society' would appear to mean the end of sociology. This has been the discipline which, according to Rose: 'ratified the existence of this [social] territory'; as that territory is transformed through the emerging power of these new temporal and spatial topologies, so sociology is 'undergoing a crisis of identity' (Rose 1996: 328; Mol and Law

1994). Likewise Touraine argues that the framework of classical sociology is collapsing because society itself is decomposing; he describes a process of 'demodernisation' and a 'loss of unity of what we still sometimes call societies' (1998).

In particular, if there is not a bounded society then how is it possible to establish the functional requirements that have to be met, in order that each 'society' continues? Without being able to provide those requirements, then a sociological functionalist will be unable to explain either the effects of particular organisations or processes upon the society, or more interestingly, the emergence or the persistence of any such organisation in terms of their functional consequences (Isajiw 1968; Elster 1978). But even if we are no longer 'functionalists', it is hard to see how we can conceptualise certain entities except in terms of their 'functions' in some sense for society. Subsequently I show that contemporary states are to be principally characterised in terms of 'regulation'. But what entity is being regulated and how can that function be specified if there are no longer discrete boundaries to what we call society? I try to establish that new global flows and networks have generated a new functional requirement, for states to regulate their immense consequences. I show that this globally generated functional requirement is transforming states, which move from what I will term an endogenist regulator of peoples à la Foucault, to an exogenist state facilitating, regulating and responding to the consequences of diverse mobilities.

Sociology thus appears to be cast adrift once we leave the relatively safe boundaries of a functionally integrated and bounded society, or of an autopoietic societal system à la Luhmann (1995). There is a theoretical and empirical whirlpool where most of the tentative certainties that sociology had endeavoured to erect are being washed away. This book is about mobilities and this involves the rapid dissolving of the few fixed points that sociology had precariously established over the past few decades. In such a maelstrom of social and intellectual mobility I ask whether any fixed points can remain.

I suggested earlier some factors that might enable sociology to recover from the potential loss of its key concept of society. Such a recovery would stem from certain disciplinary characteristics that might make it particularly suited to the relatively fluid world and horizontal mobilities of the 'global age', characteristics stemming from sociology's rather fluid, amorphous and networked character (Albrow 1996). But there is another issue here. Sociology has always skirted close to the edge of the academy (some would say over the edge) because of its proximity to various social movements. These include the working class and trade union movement, the movement of the professional–managerial class, urban movements, movements of the poor, the women's movement, gay and lesbian movements, environmentalist movements and so on. Each of these has significantly inflected sociology's development within the academy. It is unlikely that 'sociology' will survive if it does not again embody the ambitions of one or more such social movements. This issue is returned to in the last chapter when I consider whether movements for global citizenship might provide the social base for such a revived sociology.

More new rules of sociological method

To conclude this chapter, I set out what sociology's 'rules of sociological method' ought to be for the next few decades (with apologies to Durkheim 1964 and Giddens 1976). I have already shown that 'societies' can only be understood through their relations with other 'societies' – they have over the past two centuries constituted each other. Societies more-over are not necessarily organised around an originating centre, they are partially constituted through objects as well as through subjects, and since their borders are porous it is difficult to specify just what constitutes the edge of any such a society (see Mingers 1995, on such autopoietic systems). Moreover, societies are only one of various emergent levels of social life. They are not the only entities that in some sense or other are self-reproducing in relationship to their environment. More generally, the following sets out the desirable characteristics of what Diken calls the 'more "mobile" theorizing' that will be necessary to deal with the variety of emerging hybrid entities, as well as with so-called societies (1998: 248). In the following I indicate in which chapter(s) I develop each of these rules:

- to develop through appropriate metaphors a sociology which focuses upon movement, mobility and contingent ordering, rather than upon stasis, structure and social order (Chapter 2)
- to examine the extent, range and diverse effects of the corporeal, imag-ined and virtual mobilities of people, for work, for pleasure, to escape torture, to sustain diasporas and so on (Chapters 3 and 6)
- to consider things as social facts – and to see agency as stemming from the mutual intersections of objects and peoples (Chapter 4)
- to embody one's analysis through investigating the sensuous constitu-tion of humans and objects (Chapter 4)
- to investigate the respective and uneven reach of diverse networks and flows as they move within and across societal borders and of how they spatially and temporally interconnect (Chapters 2, 3 and 5)
- to examine how class, gender, ethnicity and nationhood are consti-tuted through powerful and intersecting temporal regimes and modes of dwelling and travelling (Chapters 5, 6 and 8)

- to describe the different bases of people's sense of dwelling, including their dependence upon various mobilities of people, presents, photographs, images, information, risks and so on (Chapter 6)
- to comprehend the changing character of citizenship as rights and duties are increasingly owed to, and derive from, entities whose topologies criss-cross those of society (Chapter 7)
- to illuminate the increased mediatisation of social life as images circulate increasingly fast and with added reach so as to form and reform various imagined communities (Chapter 7)
- to appreciate the increasing interdependencies of 'domestic' and 'foreign' issues and the reduced significance of the means of physical coercion to the determination of the powers of states (Chapter 8)
- to explain changes within states towards an emphasis upon 'regulating' mobilities and their often unpredictable and chaotic consequences (Chapter 8)
- to interpret how chaotic, unintended and non-linear social consequences can be generated which are distant in time and/or space from where they originate and which are of a quite different and unpredictable scale (Chapters 5 and 8)
- to consider whether an emergent level of the 'global' is developing which can be viewed as recursively self-producing, that is, its outputs constitute inputs into an autopoietic circular system of 'global' objects, identities, institutions and social practices (Chapter 8)

This is I hope a brave manifesto for a discipline that is apparently losing its central concept. But maybe some of this is already old hat. The great urban sociologist, Henri Lefebvre, wrote a quarter of a century ago about the importance of new spatial networks and mobilities moving both within and across societal borders. He said that commodities:

> constitute relatively determinate *networks* or chains of exchange within a space. The world of commodities would have no 'reality' without such *moorings* or *points of insertion*, or without their existing as an ensemble ... of stores, warehouses, ships, trains and trucks and the *routes* used ... The initial basis or foundation of social space is nature ... Upon this basis are superimposed – in ways that transform, supplant or even threaten to destroy it – successive *stratified and tangled networks* which, though material in form, nevertheless have an existence beyond their materiality: paths, roads, railways, telephone links, and so on.
>
> (Lefebvre 1991: 402–3; emphasis added)

In the following I examine such stratified and tangled networks of paths, roads, railways and so on. Lefebvre also points out that when we see the dwelling of a house, this can be approached in one of two ways. Either a house can be viewed as stable and immovable with stark, cold and rigid outlines. Or we can see any such house as 'permeated from every direction by streams of energy which run in and out of it by every imaginable route'. As a consequence the image of immovability is 'replaced by an image of a complex of mobilities, a nexus of in and out conduits' (Levebvre 1991: 93).

In the various chapters that follow it is these conduits and the resulting mobilities that are described and analysed. It is argued that the material reconstitution of the social presumes a sociology of diverse mobilities. This book can be seen as a manifesto of such a revived sociological project.

Chapter 2

Metaphors

The feudal ownership of land did bring dignity, whereas the modern ownership of movables is reducing us again to a nomadic horde.

(E.M. Forster [1910] 1941: 141)

Introduction

Much of our understanding of society and social life is based upon, and reflected through, various metaphors. In this chapter the nature of such metaphorical thinking is examined. I suggest that sociological thinking, like any other form of thought, cannot be achieved non-metaphorically. As Sontag argues in *Aids and its Metaphors*, 'one cannot think without metaphors' (1991: 91). And although elsewhere Sontag seems to claim that science can be undertaken without metaphor, much of the history and philosophy of science has shown both the exegetical and the constitutive role that metaphors have played in the development of science.

Metaphor is used here in an inclusive figurative sense, to refer to the wide variety of modes of substitution of one figure into another; such a process suffuses language and meaning. This notion of metaphor contrasts with the original Aristotelian sense where metaphor, as giving a name to a thing that belongs to something else, is specifically distinguished from simile, analogy, synecdoche and metonymy. In contemporary linguistic and post-structuralist formulations metaphor is taken as generally integral to language and constitutive of human subjects. Hawkes summarises: '*All* language ... is fundamentally metaphorical ... Metaphor is a function of *language* ... it is the "omnipresent principle" of all language' (1972: 60).

Lakoff and Johnson further claim that metaphor, the understanding and experiencing of one kind of thing in terms of another, is not only a matter of language. Rather human thought processes much more generally are largely metaphorical (1980: 5–6). They argue that it is impossible to develop thought and existence outside of the many *Metaphors We Live By* (Lakoff and Johnson 1980). The human conceptual system is metaphorically structured and defined. New meanings and realities are dependent upon diverse kinds of metaphorical thinking.

I presume in the following that all human thought, including the specific and abstracted practices of science/social science, involves metaphor. Indeed to seek to establish non-metaphorical thought itself involves forms of metaphorical substitution. I also presume that 'revealing' the metaphorical basis of diverse forms of thought is a major task and goal of social science. Also much theoretical debate consists in effect of the counter-posing of one metaphor against another with a variety of extra-scientific considerations determining the respective success of one metaphor over another.

However, I am not suggesting here that there are no procedures for assessing and evaluating different theories. Relativism, I take it, is a self-refuting position. Metaphors themselves vary greatly in their productivity, both for everyday dwelling and for scientific practice. Assessing the respective productivity of such different metaphors involves complex issues of meaning and interpretation. And this can certainly stretch the assessment of theories beyond the apparently relevant empirical data, beyond what Lakoff and Johnson term the 'myth of objectivism' (1980). However, empirical data, derived from various 'situated contexts', does constitute part of the process by which the appropriateness and fit of different metaphors are to be evaluated and implemented. There are good and bad metaphors and part of what is used to assess such metaphors are various kinds of empirical evidence, although the relationship between evidence and metaphors-as-theories is hugely mediated. More generally though we should consider just what circumstances lead theories to be accepted or rejected, when part of the appeal of any such theory is the metaphor(s) underpinning it. It is necessary to consider how much the development of theory is a matter of evaluating the plausibility of respective metaphors. For example, we should ask how long a good metaphor can preserve a theory from rejection; and what are the bases within the endless flux of social life that lead particular metaphors-as-theories to be, for the present, accepted or rejected.

In this book I seek to develop theories pertaining to social life which depend upon metaphors of network, flow and travel. It is clear that such theories are now more rhetorically persuasive because these metaphors appear to be going with the grain of much contemporary experience, with the perceived sense that global processes are producing a 'shrinking world'. This is particularly the case for many social science academics whose travelling networks flow, and periodically create, curiously intense 'small worlds' (Lodge 1983). Alternative theories that emphasise the enduring power of national societies, such as that of Hirst and Thompson, in turn rely upon the contrasting metaphor of the 'sovereign' nation-state that is enduringly able to resist the global market-place and the flows of international capital (1996).

I return subsequently to such metaphors. For the present we should consider why this power of metaphorical thinking has been difficult to grasp. Why have the social sciences not been more aware that different theories of society entail or presuppose metaphor, that being and thinking sociologically cannot be undertaken outside of metaphor? Partly this is because of the influence of a positivist view of science and the resulting obliteration of the metaphorical thinking that such as a history of the social sciences produces. Lakoff and Johnson argue: 'Objectivism ... misses the fact that human conceptual systems are metaphorical in nature and involve an imaginative understanding of one kind of thing in terms of another' (1980: 194). Analogous to Kuhn's account of the role of textbooks in the rewriting of the narrative of science, so social *science* has tried to disguise its non-scientific roots and origins. It has sought to present itself as having expunged anything that is metaphorical and/or metaphysical and hence outside the certainties of observational science (Kuhn 1962).

In sociology this forgetfulness about its metaphorical past particularly resulted from the widespread critique of functionalism and especially of the 'organic analogy' which underlay functionalist theory (see Isajiw 1968: chap. 5). In this metaphor, most famously articulated by Herbert Spencer, the workings of the social body are regarded as analogous to those of the human body; that as societies develop and grow there is, as with the body, an increase in the structured differentiation of specialised functions. The social body, like the human, is characterised by the interdependence and integration of the separate parts which together effect self-regulation; and that explaining any particular social institution is achieved by showing its contribution to the functioning of the social organism as a whole (Spencer 1893; Peel 1971: chap. 7).

In the 1960s and 1970s many western sociologists argued that this organic analogy was 'false', both as a particular metaphor, and on the general grounds that all metaphorical thinking is mistaken. Methodological individualists, otherwise sympathetic to Spencer's individualist advocacy of *laissez-faire*, argued that any statements about society presuming it to be an organic entity could be reduced to statements about individuals. Positivists advocated a science of laws and facts that were to be entirely tested by rigorous research methods, far removed in their eyes from metaphors of the social or the societal. Advocates of various brands of conflict theory sought to replace the metaphor of society as an organism, characterised by increases of structured differentiation, with analyses of the underlying 'reality' of progressively simplified and conflicting class or authority structures (see Rex 1961: 50, who talks of organic metaphor's 'pernicious' effects).

But in each case the denunciation of the organic metaphor was achieved through developing new metaphors, thus demonstrating that theoretical debate often involves in part the counter-posing of one metaphor against another. Even Spencer's original advocacy of the organic metaphor had itself been developed in opposition to the metaphor of society as a 'mechanism' or 'manufacture'.

In the case of methodological individualism the metaphor of *exchange* was developed against that of organism and function. It was held that individuals employed sophisticated calculations of the costs and benefits of different kinds of 'social exchange'. Such utility-maximising individuals were seen as able, through their individual calculations and behaviours, to produce complex social patterns based on the presumed unintended effects of social exchange processes (see Homans 1961; Blau 1964).

In the case of positivism the metaphor that was counter-posed to the organic metaphor was that of *vision*. Science was seen to develop through the primary human sense of visual observation and anything that interferes with the requirement to establish the brute facts in 'our minds' eye' is presumed to be unscientific and to be rejected. Visual images constitute how science is to be constructed, organised, legitimated and distinguished from non-science (Hempel 1966).

Conflict theory involved replacing the metaphor of society as an organism, with that of society as an increasingly simplified and interest-based social *structure*. Structure was conceived of either as a dichotomy of one part lying over another (see Dahrendorf's conflict theory, 1959), or in terms of a building metaphor of base and superstructure (see Cohen 1978; Keat and Urry 1982: chap. 6).

So in each case, while sociology energetically sought to overthrow metaphorical thinking through its rejection of the organic metaphor, it developed new metaphorical ways of thinking. I will not interrogate all the current brands of social theory to show the general significance of such metaphorical thinking. However, for all the complexity of some theories of society they most depend upon quite simple figurative ideas drawn from other academic fields, especially biology, physics, geography and economics. To amplify this I will consider a recent reworking of Foucault which 'illuminatingly' brings out more general characteristics of especially visual metaphors for thinking about the social 'body'.

Stacey begins with Foucault's analysis of biomedical science and the nature of the clinical gaze (1997: 51–7). She interrogates his analysis of the mechanisms by which 'illness ... came to light ... in the visible ... but accessible space of the human body' (Foucault 1976: 195). She elaborates how modern biomedicine is both highly metaphorical and remarkably adept at covering up its figurative tracks. In the shift from what Foucault terms classificatory medicine to clinico-anatomical medicine, metaphors of space and vision were paramount. Clinico-anatomical medicine involves the reorganisation of the spatial metaphor, from one in which disease and the patient are spatially separate, to one in which the disease is viewed as a spatially integral part of the patient. The disease is taken to be in the body and this presupposes the need for the clinical gaze, in order that the doctor learns to see, to isolate, to recognise, to compare and to intervene. Diseases are no longer classified according to homologous symptoms but to their visible *signs*, 'colours, variations, tiny anomalies, always receptive to the deviant' (Foucault 1976: 89), which designate the truth of the disease.

Such visual metaphors have become central to science. The eye develops as the depository and source of clarity. According to Foucault the clinic is the first effort to order science on the exercise and decisions of the visual gaze of the medical scientist. And clinico-anatomical medicine simultaneously naturalises its dependence upon these visual and spatial metaphors. Such a clinico-anatomical method:

> constitutes the historical condition of a medicine that is given and accepted as positive ... Disease breaks away from the metaphysic of evil ... and finds in the visibility of death the full form in which its content appears in positive terms.
> (Foucault 1976: 196; see also Stacey 1997: 56–7, especially on the non-spatial metaphors employed in acupuncture)

More generally from the seventeenth-century onwards, observation rather than the *a priori* knowledge of medieval cosmology was viewed as the basis of scientific legitimacy; and this subsequently developed into the foundation of the scientific method of the west. Sense-data is principally that produced and guaranteed by the sense of sight, by the 'sanitised methodological form of "observation"' (Jenks 1995a: 3). Foucault shows in *The Order of Things* that natural history thus involves the observable structure of the visible world and not functions and relationships that are invisible to our senses (1970). A number of such sciences of 'visible nature' developed and these were organised around visual taxonomies, beginning with Linnaeus in 1735 (Gregory 1994: 23; Pratt 1992). Such classifications were based upon the modern epistème of the individual subject, of the seeing eye and the distinctions derived from metaphor that it can make. Foucault says that: 'man is an invention of recent date' (1970: 221, 312, 386); and such a 'man' is one who sees, observes and classifies as resemblance gives way to diverse modes of representation.

So what developed was a new visual epistemology which involved the fusing of seeing and believing, and seeing and saying (Stacey 1997: 56). This resulted in contemporary science that appears to be the very antithesis of metaphor, that naturalises its metaphors. But the histories of science and of biomedicine have in fact been based upon mental representations of the external world based on internalised visual images 'in the mind's eye' (Rorty 1980). And science only achieves this through concealing from our gaze just how its positive authority is figuratively constructed. Rorty makes this clear: 'It is pictures rather than propositions, metaphors rather than statements, which determine most of our philosophical convictions ... the story of the domination of the mind of the West by ocular metaphors' (1980: 12–13; see Chapter 4 below).

In the next section I consider an array of metaphors that have recently become socially powerful. They are not ocular metaphors but rather involve the figurative use of exemplars, or icons or characteristics of mobility. I note various metaphors of travel, seeing how widespread they are within contemporary cultural analysis, so much so that various writers have characterised scientific work itself in terms of travel (as in Clifford's 'travelling theory': 1997). Metaphors of home and displacement, borders and crossings, nomads and tourists, have become familiar within public life and academic discourse.

But I go on to consider some other spatial metaphors, of region, network and fluid, developed in relationship to the mobilities of blood and the treatment of anaemia. I argue these provide a fruitful set of metaphors to be employed in the subsequent section concerned with globalisation and how to develop productive metaphors of the global. This is no simple exercise because the globe itself is a metaphor. Indeed there is no single 'globe' but rather different metaphors of the globe and globality. Central to notions of globalisation are various metaphors of the global which embody alternative presumptions of homogenisation/heterogenisation, of simplicity/complexity, of movement/stasis, of inclusion/exclusion and so on. I discuss the distinction between metaphors of scape and flow, and between a globe which includes and a globe which excludes human participants.

Metaphors of mobility

I begin though with Durkheim and his critique of the fluid, unstable, non-authoritative character of 'sensuous representations'. For him the problem is that such sensuous representations: 'are in a perpetual flux; they come after each other likes the waves of a river, and even during the time that they last, they do not remain the same thing' (Durkheim 1968: 433). For science it is necessary to abstract from these flows of time and space in order to arrive at concepts, which are, according to Durkheim, 'collective representations'. Durkheim views concepts as beneath this perpetual, sensuous, surface flux. Concepts are outside of time and change; they do not move by themselves. They are fixed and immutable and it is the task of science to reveal them, and not to be seduced by the endlessly changing 'sensations, perceptions and images' (Durkheim 1968: 432–4).

Game interestingly contrasts Durkheim's elaboration of the authority of the 'concept' and his rejection of the fluidities of sensuousness, with the deployment of metaphors of movement and flow widely found within post-structuralist and feminist analyses of the body, and more generally of writing and sociality (1995). Many writers have developed metaphors of sea, river, flux, waves and liquidity (Bachelard 1983), while others have elaborated notions of the vagabond, the nomad, the pilgrim, the motel (Deleuze and Guattari 1986; Braidotti 1994). Such metaphors of course implicate both the theorist and theory since both are unable to stand, or to be developed, outside of these very movements. Subjects are constituted through the fluidities of especially writing. '*Différance* is incompatible with the static, synchronic, taxonomic, ahistoric motifs in the concept of *structure*' (Derrida 1987: 27).

In the following certain fluid metaphors will be elaborated. Unlike Durkheim I suggest that some such metaphors are in fact scientifically useful and not the product of a mere sensuousness (see Chapter 4 below on the senses). The emergence of such fluid metaphors results from transformations of collective representations in which the 'collective' is no longer purely the societal but extends within and beyond to where metaphors of the global are particularly pertinent.

But also *contra* post-structuralism, I suggest that it is possible to evaluate different metaphors for their scientific productivity. They can be set against each other and many kinds of empirical evidence can be deployed to evaluate their plausibility. We do not simply have to go with the flow, one might say. This ability to assess such images of flow will enable the evaluation of the empirical claims implicit in certain metaphors of flow. One particularly powerful metaphor in popular discourse concerns how the purity of particular national cultures is seen as being 'overrun by hordes of foreigners', moving in and contaminating the essence of each particular culture.

I now turn briefly to some recent metaphors of mobility and travel that have infected contemporary social thought. Probably the most widespread is that of the nomad. Bauman for example talks of 'postmodern nomads' (1993a), while Deleuze and Guattari elaborate on the implications of nomads, external to each state, for what they term the war machine (1986: 49–53). Nomads characterise societies of de-territorialisation, constituted by lines of flight rather than by points or nodes. They maintain that 'the nomad has no points, paths or land ... If the nomad can be called the Deterritorialized *par excellence*, it is precisely because there is no reterritorialization *afterwards* as with the migrant ... ' (1986: 52). Such nomads present particular conflicts for states whose fundamental task is 'to striate the space over which it reigns ... not only to vanquish nomadism, but to control migrations and, more generally, to establish a zone of rights over an entire "exterior", over all the flows traversing the ecumenon' (Deleuze and Guattari 1986: 59). Virilio likewise describes the state as 'police': 'the gates of the city, its levies and duties, are barriers, filters against the fluidity of the masses, against the penetration power of the migratory packs' (quoted Deleuze and Guattari 1986: 60). I return to Deleuze and Guattari in Chapter 8 when I consider how contemporary states are transformed through the proliferation of nomadic flows and smooth spaces that states increasingly struggle to 'police'.

More generally, nomadic deterritorialisation has been articulated as a way of challenging disciplinary limits and hegemonic cultural practices, to 'marginalize the centre' and especially the masculinist, imperial, white and academic cultures of the 'west' (see Kaplan 1996: chap. 2). Nomadism is associated with the notion that academic and political writing can itself be conceived of as a journey. In order to theorise one leaves home and travels. And according to Van den Abbeele there is no 'home' or fixed point from which the theorist departs and then returns (1980). The theorist is seen as travelling hopefully, neither being at home or away (see Cresswell 1997, for a review of such nomadic metaphors, including de Certeau 1984, and Deleuze and Guattari's rhizomatics, 1988).

Braidotti proposes a new 'interconnected nomadism' to develop multiple, transverse ways of thinking through the complex and diverse patterns of especially women's lives (1994). Feminists, she argues, should develop a nomadic consciousness. Nomadic is not used here literally to refer to patterns of world travel but rather to how the nomad as metaphor provides a critical consciousness that resists dominant cultural codes, especially those that are phallocentric.

However, many of Braidotti's examples do in fact rest upon actual mobilities between different places and hence upon diverse geographical dislocations. Indeed she notes that she does 'have special affection for the places of transit that go with travelling: stations and airport lounges, trams, shuttle buses and check-in areas. In between zones where all ties are suspended and time stretched to a sort of continuous present' (Braidotti 1994: 18–19). She does not explain how a nomadic consciousness could develop without a great deal of this corporeal mobility. Chambers refers to such a process as the *flâneur* becoming the *plâneur* (1990; and see Clifford 1997: 30–1, on the extensive mobilities of inter-war intellectuals and artists). Nor can nomadism be envisaged without virtual and object mobilities. Makimoto and Manners argue that we have entered a new nomadic age. Over the next decade, with digitisation, most of the facilities of home and the office will be carried around on the body or at least in a small bag, making those that can afford such objects 'geographically independent' (Makimoto and Manners 1997: 2). Such people will be 'free to live where they want and travel as much as they want' – they will be forced to consider whether they are settlers or really 'global nomads' (Makimoto and Manners 1997: 6). A rather different version of the nomad is to be found in Raymond Williams' 'nomad capitalism', a concept he deployed to analyse the UK coal-miners strike of 1984–5. He argues that this was caused by the 'logic of a new nomad capitalism which exploits actual

places and people and then (as it suits it) moves on ... real men and
women know they are facing an alien order of paper and money, which
seems all-powerful' (1989: 124).

Various commentators have however criticised some of these nomadic
metaphors. Bauman dispenses with the nomadic metaphor on the grounds
that actual nomads in fact move from place to place in a strictly regular
fashion (1993a: 240). By contrast for Bauman, both the vagabond and the
tourist are more plausible metaphors for postmodern times since they do
not involve such regularised mobility. The vagabond, he says, is a pilgrim
without a destination, a nomad without an itinerary; while the tourist
'pay[s] for their freedom; the right to disregard native concerns and feelings, the right to spin their own web of meanings ... The world is the
tourist's oyster ... to be lived pleasurably – and thus given meaning'
(Bauman 1993a: 241). Both vagabonds and tourists move through other
people's spaces, they both involve the separation of physical closeness from
any sense of moral proximity, and both set standards for happiness. For
Bauman the good life has come to be thought of as akin to a 'continuous
holiday' (1993a: 243).

Wolff criticises the masculinist character of many of these nomadic and
travel metaphors since they suggest that there is ungrounded and
unbounded movement; yet clearly different people have very different
access to being 'on the road', either literally or even metaphorically (1993).
As Cresswell notes, the postmodern nomad is 'unmarked by the traces of
class, gender, ethnicity, sexuality and geography' (1997: 377). Clifford
likewise struggles 'to free the related term "travel" from a history of
European, literary, male, bourgeois, scientific, heroic, recreational, meanings and practices' (1997: 33). Jokinen and Veijola have also demonstrated
the 'maleness' of many nomadic metaphors (1997). They show that certain
male metaphors can be rewritten or coded differently. If they are so recon-
ceptualised as paparazzi, homeless drunk, sex-tourist and womaniser, then
they lose the positive valuation that they have typically enjoyed within
mainstream nomadic theory. They also suggest that we should examine a
variety of female metaphors of movement, including the prostitute, the
babysitter and the *au pair*.

I turn finally to a couple of more specific metaphors of travel and travel
encounters. Gilroy elaborates the chronotype of the ship, a living, micro-
cultural, micro-political system in motion (1993: 4). This metaphor
focuses attention in developing the hybrid 'Black Atlantic' culture of the
middle passage of the triangular slaveship journeys; of the importance
generally of circulation; of powerful images of the sea; and of the complex
movement of peoples and artefacts across the Atlantic. Gilroy summarises:

> ships were the living means by which the points within that Atlantic
> world were joined. They were mobile elements that stood for the

shifting spaces in between the fixed spaces that they connected. Accordingly they need to be thought of as cultural and political units … they were … a means to conduct political dissent and possibly a distinct mode of cultural production

(1993: 16–17; see also Chapter 6 below).

Clifford had argued for the chronotype or metaphor of the hotel lobby, a setting of time and space based upon being away from home, movement and unexpected encounter, in preference to those metaphors of home or dwelling which imply stasis and fixture (1997). However, he proceeds to critique the chronotype of the hotel as being nostalgic and masculinist (or rather gentlemanly); he recommends instead the chronotype or metaphor of the motel (see Morris 1988). The motel has no real lobby, it is tied into the network of highways, it functions to relay people rather than to provide settings for coherent human subjects, it is consecrated to circulation and movement, and it demolishes the sense of place and locale. Motels 'memorialize only movement, speed, and perpetual circulation' (Morris 1988: 3); they 'can never be a true *place*' and one is only distinguished from another in 'a high-speed, *empiricist* flash' (1988: 5). The motel, like the airport transit lounge, represents neither arrival nor departure but the 'pause' (Morris 1988: 41).

Having then considered a diverse array of metaphors of movement I want to systematise my argument here by drawing on a rather different resource, Mol and Law's analysis of the intersecting metaphors of regions, networks and flows (1994). These distinctions are developed to deal with a fascinating spatial question relating to contemporary biomedical science. If someone suffers from anaemia where should we think of that anaemia being located? Where in the body is it to be found? The answer is that anaemia is not anywhere in particular but is everywhere that blood travels to. There are blood vessels located throughout the body, forming an immense network enabling blood ultimately to reach every cell, and not just the larger bodily organs. Blood does not stay within the vessels that carry it since some blood cells migrate through the walls of blood vessels. Thus blood is characterised by a strange spatial pattern. It does not fit the structures or regions of conventional anatomy. Blood is a fluid moving through the extraordinarily complex networks of blood vessels in the human body and as a result it gets more or less everywhere in the body. It thus demonstrates a distinct topology that is not that of a definite structure.

Mol and Law employ this discussion of blood to interrogate the diverse spatial forms of social life. What are the equivalent metaphors of the social that their account of blood and anaemia suggest? There are three distinct metaphors of space or social topologies. First, there are *regions* in which objects are clustered together and boundaries are drawn around each particular regional cluster. This topology of territorialisation is old, secure and familiar (see Lefebvre 1991). Second, there are *networks* in which relative distance is a function of the relations between the components comprising the network. The invariant outcome is delivered across the entire network that often crosses regional boundaries. Third, there is the topology or metaphor of the *fluid* as encountered in the case of blood. Mol and Law argue that with regard to these fluids that flow: 'neither boundaries nor relations mark the difference between one place and another. Instead, sometimes boundaries come and go, allow leakage or disappear altogether, while relations transform themselves without fracture. Sometimes, then, social space behaves like a fluid' (Mol and Law 1994: 643).

Mol and Law utilise this conception of a fluid space to describe the way in which anaemia is medically dealt with world-wide and especially the apparent differences between its clinical monitoring and treatment in the Netherlands as compared with various 'African' countries. They argue that there is no simple *regional* difference to be drawn between its monitoring and treatment in the Netherlands compared with Africa. Nor is there a single clinical *network* world-wide with elements that hang together through invariant relations, which have the effect of transporting what would seem to be the same 'anaemia' to both the Netherlands and to Africa. Rather Mol and Law argue that: 'We're looking at *variation without boundaries and transformation without discontinuity*. We're looking at flows. The space with which we are dealing is *fluid*' (1994: 658; original emphasis).

'Anaemia' then, like blood, can be seen as flowing in and out of different regions, across different borders, using diverse networks. It changes as it goes, although this is often in ways which are more or less imperceptible at the time. Anaemia as a illness is like a fluid, like blood, and is subject to transformation. Fluids are subject to mixtures and gradients with no necessarily clear boundaries. The objects generated may not be clearly defined. Normality is a gradient and not a clear absolute. In a fluid space it is not possible to determine identities nice and neatly, once and for all; nor to distinguish inside from outside. Various other fluids may or may not be able to combine together with each other. A 'fluid world is a world of *mixtures*' (Mol and Law 1994: 660). Fluids are not solid or stable or the only spatial types to be analysed here. Moreover, fluids can get around absences such as a laboratory in an African war zone and are contingent. In short, Mol and Law conclude:

> The study of fluids, then, will be a study of the relations, repulsions and attractions which form a flow ... So *how* does anaemia flow? How does it move between the Netherlands and Africa and back again? ... It may flow in people's skills, or as part of the attribute of

devices, or in the form of written words ... And as it moves, it changes its shape and character.

(1994: 664).

I have thus considered various metaphors of mobility, including the nomad, the vagabond, the tourist, the ship, the hotel, the motel and the transit lounge. Many of these are illuminating and I return to a number when considering various intersections of belonging and travelling. However, in order to develop more convincing analyses of the 'global' I have turned to the spatial metaphors of region, network and fluid.

Mol and Law bring out the power of these metaphors in relationship to anaemia, to account for the uneven and heterogeneous skills, technologies, interventions and tacit knowledges of those involved in its monitoring and treatment in clinics across the globe. The extent and power of such networks and fluids stretching across societal borders raise important questions about the power of societies ('regions'), to resist. Especially the fluid of 'anaemia' will take different forms as it gorges within, or trickles through, any particular region. Any such fluid can be distinguished in terms of the *rate* of flow, its *viscosity*, the *depth*, its *consistency*, and its *degree of confinement*. In the following section I shall consider some of the global equivalents of regions, networks and fluids, as I seek to develop some diverse metaphors of the global.

Metaphors of the global

The sociological concept of society is organised around the metaphor of a region, namely that 'objects are clustered together and boundaries are drawn around each particular cluster' (Mol and Law 1994: 643). Thus there appear to be different societies with their clustering of social institutions, and with a clear and policed border surrounding each society as region. In the following I shall examine how globalisation fractures this metaphor of society and hence problematises sociology's dominant discursive framework.

One way to study globalisation is through seeing it involved in inter-regional competition with 'society'. Globalisation could be viewed as replacing one region, the bounded nation-state-society of the 'west', with another, the global economy and culture. And as both economy and culture are increasingly globalised, so the old dominant region of society appears to become relatively less powerful. In the fight between these two regions it looks as though the global region will win out and defeat the societal region (see Robertson 1992). Behaviour and motivation are less societally produced and reproduced but are the effect of a more globally organised culture that increasingly breaks free from each and every society.

But this is only one way of understanding so-called globalisation. In the following I argue that globalisation should not be viewed in this way, as one larger region replacing the smaller region of each society. Rather globalisation involves replacing the metaphor of society as *region* with the metaphor of the global conceived of as *network* and as *fluid*. It is this postulated replacement of one social topology with these others that constitutes the significance of globalisation. I show that the global presupposes the metaphors of network and flow rather than that of region (Brunn and Leinbach 1991; Lash and Urry 1994; Waters 1995; Albrow 1996; Castells 1996, 1997; Eade 1997). There has of course been an astonishing growth in the writings on globalisation from around 1989 (see Busch 1997).

Most obviously, the globalisation literature has described the wide variety of new objects, of new *machines and technologies* which dramatically compress or shrink time–space. Globalisation entails infrastructural developments routed literally or symbolically across societal borders. Such technologies include fibre-optic cables, jet planes, audiovisual transmissions, digital television, computer networks including the Internet, satellites, credit cards, faxes, electronic point-of-sale terminals, portable phones, electronic stock exchanges, high speed trains and virtual reality. There are also large increases in nuclear, chemical and conventional military technologies and weapons, as well as new waste products and health risks that are not simply caused within and treated within societies as 'regions'. These technologies carry people, information, money, images and risks. They flow within and across national societies in increasingly brief moments of time. In what Tom Peters calls the 'nanosecond nineties' a set of technologies has been implemented which generates new fluidities of astonishing speed and scale (1992; see Chapter 5 below on instantaneous time). These technologies do not derive directly and uniquely from human intentions and actions. They are intricately interconnected with machines, texts, objects and other technologies (Michael 1996). As suggested in Chapter 1, there are no purified *social* structures as such, only hybrids (Latour 1993).

Moreover, the appropriate metaphor to capture these intersections of peoples and objects is not that of a vertical structure. The metaphor of structure typically involves a centre, a concentration of power, vertical hierarchy and a formal or informal constitution. Castells argues, by contrast, that we should employ the metaphor of network, 'the unit is the network' (1996: 198). 'Networks constitute the new social morphology of our societies, and the diffusion of networking logic substantially modifies the operation and outcomes in processes of production, experience, power and culture ... the network society, characterised by the pre-eminence of social morphology over social action' (Castells 1996: 469).

Castells defines a network as a set of interconnected nodes, the distance between social positions are shorter where such positions constitute nodes within a network as opposed to those which lie outside the particular network. Networks are to be viewed as dynamic open structures, so long as they are able to effect communication with new nodes and to innovate (Castells 1996: 470–1). Much economic geography has detailed the apparently increased significance of such networks within the contemporary economy, at the intra-firm level, at the inter-firm level and at the firm-community levels (see Amin and Thrift 1992; Cooke and Morgan 1993).

Network does not mean here simply *social* networks. This is because the 'convergence of social evolution and information technologies has created a new material basis for the performance of activities throughout the social structure. This material basis, built in networks, earmarks dominant social processes, thus shaping social structure itself' (Castells 1996: 471). Networks thus produce complex and enduring connections across space and through time between peoples and things (see Murdoch 1995: 745). They spread across time and space which is hugely important, since according to Law, if 'left to their own devices *human actions and words do not spread very far at all*' (1994: 24). Different networks possess different reaches or abilities to bring home distant events, places or people, to overcome the friction of space within appropriate periods of time. This requires mobilising, stabilising and combining peoples, actions or events elsewhere into a stable network (Latour 1987). Accountancy, for example, is particularly effective at reducing the variety of activities in distant regions to a common set of figures, the informational flow, that can be instantaneously translated back to other parts of the network and especially to its control and command headquarters (Murdoch 1995: 749). Networks are thus in and of space, they are temporal and spatial as I discuss in subsequent chapters (on 'actor-networks', see Law and Hassard 1999).

By contrast with the immutable mobiles of accountancy, the networks of measurement of haemoglobin levels is less secure (Mol and Law 1994: 647–50). Mol and Law ask how it is possible to produce regional maps of such comparative haemoglobin levels (which are analogous to accountants producing regional maps of the relative profitability of different plants of a global company). They argue that this requires a network constituted across many different regions, comprising appropriate technologies, measuring machines and people with suitable medical and technical skills.

There are two points to emphasise here. First, such a network is problematic to establish because in parts of the world, such as poor African countries, there are inadequate numbers of machines to undertake the measurement of haemoglobin levels, and even where they do exist they may not be appropriately maintained. Thus Mol and Law say that on occasions there is a 'failing network', that the network does not work. Haemoglobin measurement is not immutable (see Latour 1990, on the power of the immutable mobile). As devices and techniques move from centre to periphery 'their truths become progressively less reliable' (Mol and Law 1994: 652). Second, where a successful network is established across a number of regions, this transforms the configurations of space and time that are no longer regional. In a network established for measuring haemoglobin levels two hospitals can be close together even if they are hundreds of kilometres away from each other. They are nodes within that network, just as two hub airports can be close together in the network of air travel, even if they are apparently located thousands of miles apart. It is necessary to map different networks and to consider areas of dense networks, of sparse networks and of blanks (Brunn and Leinbach 1991; Lash and Urry 1994: 24).

I now return to globalisation and develop the distinction between scapes and flows. *Scapes* are the networks of machines, technologies, organisations, texts and actors that constitute various interconnected nodes along which the flows can be relayed. Such scapes reconfigure the dimensions of time and space. The following are the main scapes:

- transportation of people by air, sea, rail, motorway roads, other roads
- transportation of objects via postal and other systems
- wire and co-axial cables
- microwave channels used by cellular phones
- satellites for radio and television
- fibre-optic cable for telephone, television and computers.

Once particular scapes have been established, then individuals and especially corporations within each society will normally try to become connected to them through being constituted as nodes within that particular network. They will seek to develop their own hub airport or at least have regular flights to such airports; they will wish their local schools to be plugged into the Internet; they will try to attract satellite broadcasting; they may even seek to reprocess nuclear waste products, and so on. Between certain nodes along some scapes extraordinary amounts of information will flow, of financial, economic, scientific and news data and images, into which some groups are extremely well plugged-in while others are effectively excluded. What becomes significant is what Brunn and Leinbach term 'relative' as opposed to 'absolute' location (1991: xvii). This creates novel inequalities of flow which are constituted as 'tunnels', as opposed to the inequalities of stasis. Graham and Marvin maintain that what is involved here is a rewarping of time and space by advanced telecommunication and transportation structures, as scapes pass by some areas and connect other areas along information and transport rich 'tunnels' (1996: 60).

Certain of these scapes are in part organised at the global level. Organisations involved in the globalisation of scapes include the UN, the

World Bank, Microsoft, CNN, Greenpeace, EU, News International, the Oscar ceremony, the World Intellectual Property Organization, UNESCO, IATA, the ILO, the Olympic movement, Friends of the Earth, Nobel Prizes, Bandaid, the Brundtland Report, the Rio Earth Summit, the European Court of Human Rights, British Council and the English language and so on. These 'organisations' themselves employ most of the machines and technologies that facilitate time–space compression.

By contrast with the structured scapes, the *flows* consist of peoples, images, information, money and waste, that move within and especially across national borders and which individual societies are often unable or unwilling to control directly or indirectly. These flows create new inequalities of access/non-access which do not map on to the jurisdictions of particular societies. Such flows generate for late twentieth-century people, new opportunities and *desires*, as well as new *risks*. Such risks include: the spread of AIDS throughout most of the world over the past 15 years; the growth of environmental risks moving across national borders such as the flows of 'nuclear monsters'; the loss of national sovereignty as various global scapes and flows by-pass national governments; a tendency for the homogenisation of the culture of different places; and being exiled from one's country of origin or finding that one is an asylum seeker with very limited rights of residence in the country that one lands up in.

At the same time, however, globalisation allows people new opportunities and new activities to develop. These include: relatively cheap overseas travel; the ability to buy consumer goods and lifestyles from across the world (such as Mexican food, Indian rugs, African jewellery, south American coffee); the opportunities to communicate with people in many countries through the use of the Internet; the ability to form 'new social groups' which are often opposed to, or provide alternatives from, aspects of globalisation; the possibility to participate in global cultural events such as the World Cup or listening to 'world music'; and the reinforcing of certain kinds of local identity, as in the pronounced rediscovery of many ethnic traditions and identities.

These flows thus produce the hollowing out of existing societies, especially as a plethora of 'sociations' have developed, concerned to reflect upon, to argue against, to retreat from, to provide alternatives to, to campaign for, these various flows, often going beyond the limits of the societal 'region'. This generates within any existing 'society', a complex, overlapping, disjunctive order, of off-centredness, as these multiple flows are chronically combined and recombined across times and spaces often unrelated to the regions of existing societies, often following a kind of hypertextual patterning. Such flows across societal borders makes it less easy for states to mobilise clearly separate and coherent *nations* in pursuit of goals based upon society as region. These configurations weaken the power of the societal to draw together its citizens as one, to govern in its unique name, to endow all with national identity and to speak with a single voice of the nation-state. We do not inhabit a risk society with its implied fixities of a 'regional' institution and social structure. Rather we inhabit an indeterminate, ambivalent and semiotic risk culture where the risks are in part generated by the declining powers of societies in the face of multiple 'inhuman' global flows and multiple networks (Lash 1995). With globalisation the flows of information and image are apparently of heightened significance and this produces different kinds of control. As has been said of Japan: 'network-type systems emphasise a type of human control that involves *inducement or persuasion by manipulating informa-tion* rather than a method of control that depends upon power-based or contractual political action' (cited in Dale 1997: 33).

I have so far talked rather generally of global networks and flows which criss-cross the regional borders of society, thus bringing out some aspects of the 'de-territorialisation' of contemporary social life (see Lefebvre 1991: 346–8, on the 'de-territorialised' banking system). I will now make these notions rather more precise, bearing in mind the discussion of blood and anaemia above. I distinguish between *global networks* and *global fluids*.

Numerous 'global' enterprises, such as American Express, McDonalds, Coca-Cola, Disney, Sony, BA and so on, are organised on the basis of a global network (see Ritzer 1992; 1995; 1997). Such a network of tech-nologies, skills, texts and brands ensures that more or less the same product is delivered in more or less the same way in every country in which the enterprise operates (if not exactly the same product; no pig products being served in McDonalds in Muslim countries). Such products are produced in predictable, calculable, routinised and standardised envi-ronments, even where there is franchising. These companies have produced enormously effective networks with few 'failings' (unlike some African testing of haemoglobin levels). An African McDonalds will be every bit as 'good' as an American McDonalds! Such networks depend upon allocating a very large proportion of resources to branding, advertising, quality control, staff training and the internalisation of the corporate image, all of which cross societal boundaries in standardised patterns so sustaining the network. Distance is measured in terms of the time taken to get to the next McDonalds, the next Disney park, the next BA hub airport and so on, that is, from one node in a global network to the next.

McDonaldisation thus involves new ways of organising companies on a global scale with a minimum of central organisation (American Express or Disney Parks are similar examples). McDonaldisation produces new kinds of low-skilled standardised jobs for especially young people (McJobs), new products such as Big Macs or the simulated Chicken McNuggets which radically alter people's eating habits, and new social habits world-wide such as eating standardised fast food from take-out restaurants ('grazing').

These global networks produce not only predictable material goods and services, but also calculable and controllable simulations of experiences apparently 'more real than the original' (Ritzer 1997; Eco 1986; Baudrillard 1983). Such simulations of historical sites, underwater swimming, ancient tribes, 'traditional dances', Indian reservations and so on, are produced through global networks. Much tourism involves an ecstatic spiralling search for further and ever more bizarre inauthentic simulations produced by, and within, the safe modern environments of global networks (Ritzer 1997: 108–9). Ritzer argues that people increasingly want their tourist and leisure experiences to be as 'McDonaldized as their day-to-day lives' (1997: 99). This McDisneyisation of the tourist industry on a global scale involves the power of non-human mechanical, audio, electronic technologies to be able to produce homogeneous, calculable and safe experiences wherever they are to be consumed.

Interestingly, these attempts to create such a global network can also be found within oppositional organisations such as Greenpeace. Like other global players it devotes much attention to developing and sustaining its brand identity throughout the world. Greenpeace's brand identity has 'such an iconic status that it is a worldwide symbol of ecological virtue quite above and beyond the actual practical successes of the organisation' within particular societies (Szerszynski 1997: 46).

In some of the earlier globalisation literature attention was principally directed to such global networks and to the ways in which they appeared to generate cultural homogenisation. This was also associated with what has been called the 'American century', where globalisation and homogenisation were to be viewed as its final triumphant expression (Taylor 1997).

However, recent attention has been directed instead to global fluids, to the remarkably uneven and fragmented flows of people, information, objects, money, images and risks across regions in strikingly faster and unpredictable shapes. The emphasis of a sociology of fluids (as opposed to networks) would be upon heterogeneous, uneven and unpredictable mobilities. The following are the main characteristics of such global fluids (see Deleuze and Guattari 1986, 1988; Lefebvre 1991; Mol and Law 1994; MacCannell 1992; Augé 1995; Kaplan 1996; Shields 1997b). They:

- demonstrate no clear point of departure or arrival, just de-territorialised movement or mobility (rhizomatic rather than arboreal)
- are channelled along particular territorial scapes or routeways which can wall them in
- are relational in that they productively effect relations between the spatially varying features of a scape which would otherwise remain functionless
- move in particular directions at certain speeds but with no necessary end-state or purpose

- possess different properties of viscosity and, as with blood, can be thicker or thinner and hence move in different shapes at different speeds
- move according to certain temporalities, over each minute, day, week, year and so on
- do not always keep within the walls – they may move outside or escape like white blood corpuscles through the 'wall' of the scape into tinier and tinier capillaries
- power is diffused through these various fluids into very many often minute capillary-like relations of domination/subordination
- power is exercised through the intersection of various fluids working on diverse senses
- different fluids spatially intersect in the 'empty meeting grounds' of the non-places of modernity, such as motels, airports, service stations, the Internet, international hotels, cable television, expense account restaurants and so on

I shall now illustrate the importance of such fluids through three brief case-studies, of computer systems in France and the US; 'western' goods in the former 'Eastern Europe'; and the diverse forms of opposition to the very processes of globalisation. Each example shows the power of these diverse social fluids of peoples and objects criss-crossing national borders and resulting in heterogeneous, overlapping and unintended effects within across various national societies.

The first example concerns the French Minitel computer system (see Castells 1996: chap. 5 on the following). The videotext Minitel system has been based within the borders of France and resulted from initiatives by the French national state to develop its domestic electronic industries. It was started in the mid-1980s and by the mid-1990s was used by one-third of the French population. Each French household was offered a free Minitel terminal (based on limited video and transmission technology) instead of the usual telephone book. Many businesses and other services became available on the Minitel, including sex chat lines. Minitel was thus established as a national system organised by the French nation-state, and based on the ordered character of the telephone book and homogeneous tariffs wherever one lived in France. The French system was thus based upon a national network in which the same service was delivered to all subscribing households in the same form whatever one's address. The national or societal network eroded differences of space and linked all subscribers in the same national pattern.

However, Minitel's technology was proving out-of-date by the mid-1990s. Its terminals were not those of the normal computer systems. Also the system's architecture was based upon a hierarchy of server networks and this meant that it possessed little capacity for horizontal communication and for generating flows across national borders. In the end it became necessary to provide a way of linking these Minitel terminals (at a price) to the international Internet, and this has now been provided. Minitel has thus become yet another network plugged into the ungoverned, anarchic and generalised system of the Internet which links at least 44,000 networks with 100 million or so users worldwide. The Internet demonstrates the social topology not of a network, but of a fluid.

The Arpanet or Internet system was developed by the US military and designed to enable military communications to continue in the event of a nuclear attack. This security from attack was achieved through developing a computer network independent of the various military command and control centres. The crucial innovation was that of 'packet-switching', that messages should be broken down into equal sized units, these packets would make their own way to their destination, and then be combined when they had arrived (Rheingold 1994: 74). Different parts of the same message could flow along different routeways and then be recombined. Message units were able to find their own routes, flowing as sub-divided packages and hence if any part of the system were eliminated through enemy attack, the messages would still arrive. There is no vertical hierarchy and if any particular node is inoperative the network routes around it. Rheingold summarises: 'If you build a message-passing network on this scheme, and use computers to do the routing, you can build a network that will survive as node after node is blasted away' (1994: 74).

The transformation of this military-based system into the hugely fluid potentially global Internet also resulted from initiatives by American scientific and research networks (especially at UCLA, MIT, Harvard), and by more countercultural efforts to produce a computer network with universal (horizontal) public access (see Rushkoff 1994). For example, students were responsible for 'inventing' the modem in 1978 and the Web browser Mosaic in 1992. These were key moments in the development of a personal computing counterculture. As Castells notes: 'the openness of the system also results from the constant process of innovation and free accessibility enacted by early computer hackers and the network hobbyists who still populate the net by the thousands' (1996: 356). The Internet has developed into a system enabling horizontal communication which cannot be controlled or effectively censored by national societies. It is one of the clearest examples of how a technology invented for one purpose, military communication within the US in the event of a nuclear attack, chaotically evolves into purposes wholly unintended by those inventing and developing it.

Thus by the end of the twentieth century the Internet is a metaphor for the social life as fluid. It involves thousands of networks, of people, machines, programmes, texts and images in which quasi-subjects and quasi-objects are mixed together in new hybrid forms. Ever-new computer networks and links proliferate in unplanned and mixed patterns. In such a fluid space it is not possible to determine identities once and for all, since a fluid world is a world of *mixtures*. Messages 'find their way', rather like blood does through multiple capillaries. Fluids can get around absences. Such computer networks are not solid or stable and are hugely contingent. Plant describes hypertext programmes and the Net as 'webs of footnotes without central points, organizing principles, hierarchies' (1997: 10; see Chapter 3 below).

The second case-study concerns the significance of various flows connected with the collapse of communist state regimes in 'Eastern Europe' (see Braun *et al.* 1996). Following the Second World War, the individual societies of central and eastern Europe constructed exceptionally strong frontiers both from the 'West' and, most strikingly, from each other. Cultural communication into and out of such societies was exceptionally difficult. The Cold War chilled culture as well as politics. So although such societies were internationally linked via the hegemony of the USSR (economically via COMECON and politically and militarily via the Warsaw Pact), there was a parallel emphasis upon cultural involution and the reinforcement of strongly reinforced national networks that sought to produce uniform patterns of especially consumption. It constituted an interesting social laboratory based upon the 'society'.

But what happened was that regional frontiers of each society were transgressed, to be got around through various fluid-like movements. The attempt to maintain or perhaps to freeze the peoples and cultures of 'Eastern Europe' could not be sustained. The Berlin Wall was of course the most dramatic example of this attempted preservation of the peoples of a society. But through the 1960s, forms of communication and later of leisure travel did in fact increase. Both peoples and especially objects began to flow across the carefully constructed borders, often involving what has been termed the 'invisible hand of the smuggler' (Braun *et al.* 1996: 1).

Objects of the 'West' became used and talked about in multiple informal ways, helping the citizens of such societies to form new bases of personal identity, new ways of collectively remembering and new images of self and society. Many citizens went to inordinate lengths to learn about and to acquire objects that seemingly represented western taste, objects that were immutable in their westernness. Because there was little chance to develop identity within work or politics so it has been argued many people poured their energies into both high (books) and low (pop memorabilia) culture and especially the material objects which symbolised or captured new cultural identities. Braun *et al.* argue that these 'socially constructed desires did, in fact, play a larger role in the implosion of state socialist systems of Europe than any political ideology' (1996: 2).

In particular these central and east European economies had been organised around the primacy of industrial production and the restriction of consumer demand, somewhat akin to the relative short-term wartime austerity in the 'west'. But such restrictions upon the scale and variety of consumption were not freely assented to; indeed the more restricted the choices, especially by comparison with what appeared to be happening in the 'west', the greater the importance consumer goods or their substitutes acquired for individuals and for various social groups. Waters summarises: 'perhaps a majority[,] of the populations embraced consumer culture on the basis of glimpses of life in the West ... The "velvet revolutions" of the late 1980s can be viewed as a mass assertion of the right to unlimited privatized consumption' (1995: 143).

'Shopping tourism' to the 'west' developed on a large scale in the 1970s and 1980s. This involved diverse, overlapping and intersecting flows, resulting in the arrival of objects in these countries often then sold on through local social networks. These further raised people's expectations of the wealth and consumer riches of the 'west'. Such objects constituted significant cultural markers. Braun *et al.* argue that the multiple flows of people in search of various material objects flowing from other cultures were a key feature of societies in which barriers to consumption were constituted as official state policy (1996: 6). The objects sought for could often be relatively valueless in the west (beer mats), but if that was all that was available then that is what people creatively endeavoured to obtain.

There are a number of ways in which flowing objects thus functioned within the history of the present of eastern Europe. There was simply a fascination with consumer goods, with distinctions of style and taste and more broadly with shopping as an intensely pleasurable activity – to be able to shop was a powerful desire. There was a process of generating 'cult' products such as American jogging shoes or western books, as well as a more general belief that the 'west' set the standard for what was appropriately 'classy'. Travel to other countries and especially to the 'west' always involved extensive purchases of consumer goods, both for family-members but especially to sell on to others. There was also extensive smuggling of goods by tourists, lorry drivers and others who used social networks on their return to sell their goods which marked out the sophistication of the 'west' and the presumed failure of the 'east'. The flows of shoppers, tourists, travellers, black marketers, smugglers and so on, combined with particular consumer objects and modes of transportation, undermined these severely bounded 'societies'. These societies did not possess the social power to stem the inevitable march of goods, services, signs, images and people across some of the most powerfully policed of national borders.

This account also shows the way in which apparently the same object can possess quite different cultural biographies in different contexts. This is shown in Kopytoff's description of the biography of a car in Africa, as opposed to that of apparently the same physical object in France. Its biography reveals how it was acquired, from whom money was obtained to pay for it, the relationship of seller to buyer, the uses of the car, the identity of its frequent passengers, the garages where it may be repaired, the movement of car from owner to owner and the final disposition of its remains (Kopytoff 1986: 67).

The third example concerns the paradoxical way that global flows engender multiple forms of opposition to their various effects. Many groups and associations are energised by passionate opposition to the institutions and flows of the new global order. Globalisation generates its opposition, although there is little agreement on the causes and consequences of global disorder. Such a resistant order to global institutions is fragmented and disparate. It includes the Zapatistas in Mexico, the American Militia and the Patriots more generally, Aum Shinrikyo in Japan, many environmental NGOs, the women's movement concerned with the impacts of the global marketplace upon women and children in developing countries, New Age-ists, religious fundamentalisms and so on. All oppose aspects of the new global order and are organised around what Castells terms 'resistance identities' (1997: 356). They are virtual communities which 'exist only to the extent that their constituents are linked together through identifications constructed in the non-geographic spaces of activist discourses, cultural products and media images' (Rose 1996: 333). And partly through their practices of resistance to the flows they themselves serve to 'de-totalise' each national society. Castells argues that: 'civil societies shrink and disarticulate because there is no longer continuity between the logic of power-making in the global network [global fluids in my terminology here] and the logic of association and representation in specific societies and cultures' (1997: 11).

Moreover, such groups routinely employ the machines and technologies of globalisation in order to construct and reproduce appropriate flows. Castells terms the Zapatistas the 'first informational guerrillas' since they particularly deploy computer mediated communication and the establishment of a global electronic network of solidarity groups (1997: chap. 3). Similar widespread use of the Internet is to be found amongst the American Patriots who believe that the Federal state is turning the US into a part of the global economy and destroying American sovereignty and local customs and culture.

Thus there are very varied flows of peoples and objects. These identities of resistance, as with the East European example, are often mediated through consumer purchases. Burgess describes new forms of global cultural politics which focus upon the Amazonian rainforest: 'the alliance between actors, musicians, Brazilian Indians, population music promoters, conservation organisations, the media industry and mainly young consumers who buy records to support the campaign against the destruction of the Amazonian rainforest' (1990: 144; Elton John's *Candle in the*

Wind would be another example of resistant identities resulting from consumer purchase).

These flows of consumer goods relate more generally to changes taking place in what it is to be a 'member' of organisations in the emergent global age. Membership has typically been thought of in terms of joining organisations that then provide various rights and duties to their members. Such organisations were structured through vertical hierarchies. Trade unions were the classic model of this pattern based upon a vertical social structure.

But what is now happening is that new 'organisations' have developed which are much more *media*-ted through various global fluids. People can imagine ourselves as members (or supporters) of such organisations through purchases, wearing the T-shirt, hearing the CD, surfing to the organisation's page on the web, buying the video of iconic figures and so on. Objects can provide for that sense of vicarious or fluid 'network-membership'. This may connect to the development of what elsewhere I have described as a polling culture where people are interpellated as consumer-citizens through being polled about pertinent issues. They do not need to be members for the views of people to be surveyed, measured, reported in the media and consumed (see Macnaghten and Urry 1998: chap. 3). Indeed at least some of the time people can think of themselves as 'members' of organisations which they do not join (such as the world community, Friends of the Earth), or where they merely identify with a global brand that flows in and across national borders, such as Greenpeace (Szerszynski 1997; see Chapter 7 below).

So what seems to be developing are various fluids, with no clear points of arrival or departure. They can involve resistance, opposing states and corporations and their attempts to manage, regulate and order protest. They appear to be producing something of a cosmopolitan civil society with no originating subject, no agreed on objects which are to be contested and no necessarily progressive utopias of the future (see Held 1995: chap. 10, on the notion of democracy as 'transnational'). Such a cosmopolitan civil society begins to free itself from the overarching societies of the contemporary world. It ushers in an immensely heterogeneous civil society, a civil society which is as much materially constituted as it is social, and which may be able to act at very considerable distances through deploying unexpected and unpredictable global scapes and flows. However, for all the power of global fluids, 'members' of organisations will intermittently come together to 'be with' others in the present, in moments of intense fellow-feeling. These moments will include festivals, business conferences, holidays, camps, seminars or sites of protest (Szerszynski 1997; Boden and Molotch 1994, on the compulsion to proximity).

Castells generalises how: 'subjects ... are not built any longer of the basis of civil societies, that are in the process of disintegration, but as prolongation of communal resistance' particularly to various global processes (1997: 11; all emphasised in original). However, I have so far used the terms globe, global or globalisation without much further reflection. Global has been employed as an unproblematic adjective, normally in front of region, network or flow. I have not yet interrogated just what kind of metaphor is involved in the noun from which the terms, global and globalisation, derive, namely the globe itself.

Globes and spheres

I turn to Ingold's examination of 'globes' and 'spheres' in the context of contemporary environmentalism (1993a). He points out that there is something paradoxical about the phrase which has come to be enormously widely used in scientific, political and policy debates, namely, *global environmental change*. Environment typically means something that surrounds and always involves a relationship with that which is surrounded. One cannot exist without the other. However, in relationship to the globe it is unclear what is meant by such an 'environment'. Of course there is the biosphere which surrounds the globe and which is partly the focus of contemporary environmental concern, as in Lovelock's Gaia hypothesis (1988). However, as Ingold argues, also implicit in global environmental change is a notion of our globe that is under environmental threat. But if so how, or in what senses, can humans be surrounded by the globe? The globe does not surround us. Indeed to think of the earth as a global environment signals the culmination of a process of separating humans from the earth (Ingold 1993a: 31).

Ingold proceeds to discuss the distinction between globes and spheres, to consider different metaphors of the earth and hence of those processes which increasingly criss-cross localities and societies. He points out how familiar the image of the globe is to us, from models, photographs taken from spaceships and satellites and moving images employed on television, film and so on. But in fact since almost no-one has seen, let alone touched, heard or smelt the globe, this is obviously not based on direct human sensing of the 'globe'. Life is lived at very close proximity to the earth's surface and hence there is no direct global perception or experience with which to connect. Ingold summarises: 'the world imaged as a globe, far from coming into being in and through a life process, it figures as an entity that is, as it were, presented to or confronted by life. The global environment is not a lifeworld, it is a world apart from life' (1993a: 32).

Cosgrove has shown how contemporary conceptions of the globe have particularly drawn upon the Apollo 17 photograph of the 'whole-earth' taken in 1972 (1994). He explores how this picture of the earth has become an ideological and marketing icon of immense power. It has been used *inter alia* by computer companies and airlines who emphasise the global reach of their activities; by environmentalists who emphasise the loneliness and fragility of the earth in the blackness of space and hence the need for planetary stewardship; and by the American government who saw the American Apollo mission as the crowning achievement of mankind's [sic] universal destiny. This photograph of the globe demonstrates the incredible power of visual representations that are reproduced and circulated on a vast scale, turning up in multiple and directly competing discourses (see Chapter 7 below).

This notion of the world as a solid and opaque globe, a world that at best is only seen, can be compared with that of the world as a series of concentric spheres. A sphere is hollow and transparent and can be experienced from within. The spherical view is inward-looking, centrifugal and experienced through listening rather than only through sight. The medieval world, as well as various tribal societies, conceived of the world as a series of inclusive spheres. Ingold suggests that the movement from spherical to global metaphors is one in which the world is increasingly distant from the matrix of lived experiences based upon the diversity of the senses (1993a; see Chapter 4 below). The persuasive power of the global metaphor stems from a dominant visualism. This has constructed and reproduced the alleged dichotomy between what is global and what is local. The presumed power and significance of the former stems from how visual images dominate other kinds of sensory mediation.

In particular the environment came to be understood as global and hence opposed to the environment as local. Ingold argues that the difference between the global and local is not one of degree or scale but of kind. The local is not more limited or narrowly focused than the global. Rather it rests upon a different mode of apprehension: 'one based on an active, perceptual engagement with components of the dwelt-in world, in the practical business of life, rather than on the detached, disinterested observation of a world apart' (Ingold 1993a: 40). To see the environment as global is to collude in a privileging of the global ontology of detachment over the local ontology of engagement – it is to celebrate technology, intervention, expert management and the relative disempowerment of the local people.

A good example of the limitation of global thinking is the analysis of 'local knowledges and practices' which can challenge the explanatory power of the global technical and natural sciences. Such sciences often rest upon social assumptions that mean that the predictions of the theory derived from the laboratory do not work out in particular 'real world' circumstances. The laboratory is itself a very particular social and natural setting and the lay public may be better informed about the scientific understandings that will apply within their places of work or residence. They may be in that sense better 'scientists'. In the case of the effects of the fallout from Chernobyl upon sheep farming in the English Lake District, Wynne summarises:

Although the farmers accepted the need for restrictions, they could not accept the experts' apparent ignorance of their approach on the normally flexible and informal system of hill farm management. The experts assumed that scientific knowledge could be applied to hill farming without adjusting to local circumstances ... Experts were ignorant of the realities of farming and neglected local knowledge.

(Wynne 1991: 45).

What this shows is the importance of identifying and analysing local social practices, often in some sense based on local knowledges, which mediate forms of global scientific knowledge. Implicit in western models of science is a process of global standardisation, which often means that scientists will ignore the particular local conditions and the forms of local knowledge relevant to the appropriate assessments of risk.

There are in conclusion two further points to add to this analysis of the power of, and the deficiencies of, the metaphor of the globe. First, the development of global thinking itself involves a process of cultural inter-pretation, partly because, as we have seen, the globe itself is not straightforwardly experienced by any of our senses. This process of construction can be seen in relationship to *global* environmental change. Elsewhere it has been shown that there is not an already formed and causally powerful environment that in and of itself can generate global environmental change (Macnaghten and Urry 1998). The development of a global environmental crisis is not simply the product of the globalisation of risks.

Rather a range of diverse environmental 'bads' came to be viewed as operating on a global scale that presumes that many people living in diverse societies could imagine themselves as inhabiting one earth and subject to risks shared by everyone (partly as a result of the Apollo photo-graph). This global imagined community thus stems from a variety of economic and cultural processes (see Wynne 1994). By 1970 in the US and some parts of Europe, attention began to be drawn to a much wider range of problems that were apparently threatening the environment, including nuclear radiation, pesticide use, vehicle emissions, and other systemic forms of air and water pollution. These events began to generate a sense of a more general crisis of environmental bads, bads moving across national borders and potentially invading everyone's body, rather than more sporadic and geographically isolated excesses. Various organisations and governments began to refer to the global character of these risks, to suggest that they were threatening the entire 'spaceship earth' which now could be visualised (see Cosgrove 1994). It was argued that such risks were interconnected elements of a general global crisis rather than having sepa-rate causes and geographically specific consequences.

Second, in his analysis of the global and the local Ingold seems to presume that there is something about the concept of the local that is non-metaphorical. He presumes that the local really exists and is characterised by geographical propinquity, a set of overlapping work and residential patterns, clear boundaries that mark off each local and a profound sense of embedded dwellingness (1993a). But what Ingold does here is to set up a reformulated *gemeinschaft*, only this time it is to be contrasted with a kind of global *gesellschaft*. The deployment of the term local is in part metaphorical – its use invokes the notion of clearly bounded communities within which intense social relationships are characterised by belonging-ness and warmth. Such local relationships are taken by Ingold to be embedded and involving all the senses, by contrast with the visually-dependent conception of the separate 'globe'. This 'globe' is taken to be waiting out there to be acted upon and in which, as Cosgrove argues about the Apollo photograph, 'it is hard to keep faith with the local because [of] the photograph's erasure of human signs' (1994: 290; Ingold 1993a: 41).

Conclusion

I have thus shown just how widespread metaphorical thinking is within the social sciences. Further metaphors to be encountered in subsequent chapters include global village, glacial time, relays of power, diasporas, strangers, mapping, exploration, gardening, gamekeeping and so on. A key point about many of these metaphors in sociology is that they are spatial. They confer upon social phenomena, through analogy or metonymy, the presumed characteristics of various spatial entities (the globe) or of mobili-ties through space (see Gibson-Graham 1997, on the consequences for 'geography' of the recent popularity of spatial metaphors).

I have particularly considered metaphors of movement and suggested that notions of network and fluids can illuminate the 'global'. One further issue that this raises concerns what we might call the nature of social edges, of how to think through what happens when social processes meet, and with how they are traversed. To use the terminology of 'society' criti-cised in the last chapter, how should we conceptualise through metaphor where it is that one society stops, how do we know that it has stopped, what is over the edge, what is the nature of non-society and what is society's 'other'?

In the next chapter I consider the diverse kinds of travel alluded to in this chapter, of corporeal travel, the mobility of objects, virtual travel and imaginative travel, mobilities that pass over the edges of society, through and into the 'other'.

Chapter 3

Travellings

[The train] is something through which one goes, it is also something by
means of which one can go from one point to another, and then it is
something that goes by.

(Michel Foucault 1986: 24)

Introduction

I have already indicated that mobilities, as both metaphor and as process,
are at the heart of social life and thus should be central to sociological
analysis. In this chapter I examine some of the socio-spatial practices
involved in such mobility and analyse some consequences for social life
more generally. I show how significant these mobilities are, as peoples,
objects, images and information travel and hence produce and reproduce
social life and cultural forms. Cultures are themselves mobile as a result of
the mobilities that sustain diverse patterns of sociality.

In the next section I consider some of the main socio-spatial practices
involved in corporeal travel; in the following sections I outline object,
imaginative and virtual travels. I try to bring out some of the intersections
between these different mobilities rather than treating each as
autonomous. Overall I see such travellings as constitutive of the structures
of social life – it is in these mobilities that social life and cultural identity
are recursively formed and reformed. I have also emphasised that sociologists think through metaphors. In Chapter 2 I briefly discussed many such
metaphors of movement, including nomad and vagabond, hotel and motel,
pilgrim and tourist, and stranger and adventurer. Some of these re-emerge
in this chapter as aids in developing a sociology of personal mobility. As a
metaphor of this chapter it is hard to improve upon du Gay *et al.*'s account
of the significance of the Sony Walkman:

> it is virtually an extension of the skin. It is fitted, moulded, like so
> much else in modern consumer culture, to the body itself ... It is
> designed for movement – for mobility, for people who are always out

and about, for travelling light. It is part of the required equipment of the modern 'nomad' … it is testimony to the high value which the culture of late-modernity places on mobility.

(1997: 23–4)

I do not here develop a full-blown sociology of travel and tourism, nor do I say much about various kinds of disabling processes which limit or constrain the mobilities of many. I also do not specifically analyse the various kinds of forced migration which have resulted in at least 140m migrants and refugees currently worldwide.

Corporeal travel

I begin here with the introduction to Kaplan's *Questions of Travel* (1996). Because of the location of Kaplan's extended 'family' across various continents, as well as some of it being scattered across the USA, travel was for her 'unavoidable, indisputable, and always necessary for family, love and friendship as well as work' (1996: ix). She was 'born into a culture that took the national benefits of travel for granted' as well as presuming that 'US citizens [could] travel anywhere they pleased' (Kaplan 1996: ix). Elsewhere Prato and Trivero describe 'transport' becoming the primary activity of existence; it is no longer a metaphor of progress when it characterises how households generally are organised (1985; see Morris 1988: 43). If households are forever on the move, then the distinction of home and away loses its organisational and ideological power and the home loses its ability to sediment women's work. In Chapter 7 I examine further the idea that one is entitled to travel; that it should be an essential part of one's life. I consider whether contemporary citizens (not just Americans!) do possess the rights to pass over and into other places and other cultures; and whether such mobile citizens have also corresponding responsibilities to those places and cultures.

For the present I consider some of the socio-spatial practices involved in travelling, especially as in many cultures travelling appears to be 'always necessary' for family life, leisure and friendship, as well as for work and security. The scale of such travelling is awesome. There are over 600 million international passenger arrivals each year (compared with 25m in 1950); at any one time 300,000 passengers are in flight above the US; a half million new hotel rooms are being built each year worldwide; and there is one car for every 8.6 people worldwide (Kaplan 1996: 101; Makimoto and Manners 1997: chap. 1). International travel now accounts for over one-twelfth of world trade. It constitutes by far the largest movement of people across boundaries that has occurred in the history of the world. International *and* domestic tourism together accounts for 10 per cent of global employment and global GDP. And this affects everywhere;

the World Tourism Organisation publishes tourism statistics for 200 countries. Almost no country now is not a sender and receiver of significant numbers of visitors. However, the flows of visitors are not even. Most travel occurs between advanced industrial societies and especially within western and southern Europe and within north America. These flows still account for about 80 per cent of international travel; 25 years ago they accounted for 90 per cent (see WTO 1997).

The following discussion focuses upon certain socio-spatial practices involved in such travel, namely, walking, travelling by rail, driving and air travel (see Macnaghten and Urry 1998: chap. 6, for an earlier version). I begin with the modest practices of walking.

Before the late eighteenth century in Europe, walkers were generally considered to be the dangerous 'other'. Hewison notes that: 'when Shakespeare's King Lear leaves court to wander on the heath, he does not meet bobble-hatted hikers in sensible boots enjoying a refreshing tramp across the moors. He is among the naked, the starving and the mad, the excluded of society in this hostile wilderness' (1993). Walkers were regarded as necessarily poor, mad or criminal (hence the term 'footpad'; Jarvis 1997: 22–4). But during the course of the nineteenth century walking came to be viewed much more positively across Europe.

Since ordinary people increasingly did not have to walk because of the availability of new forms of transport, so walkers were no longer regarded as necessarily poor or disreputable (Wallace 1993; Bunce 1994: chap. 4; Tester 1995; Jarvis 1997). Transport changes from the late eighteenth century onwards, especially the turnpikes and then the railway, gradually removed the association of walking with necessity, poverty and vagrancy. Indeed the railway was particularly instrumental in allowing the development of 'rambling' and of popular campaigns for access to open land. Further, the diversity of modes of transport increasingly enabled people to compare and contrast different forms of mobility and on occasions to see the virtues of slower ways of overcoming the 'friction of distance'. Jarvis emphasises the 'freedom' of the road and the development of leisurely walking as indicating a modest act of rebellion against social hierarchy (1997: chapters 1 and 2 on 'radical walking'). Agricultural changes threatened the existing rights of way which walkers then struggled to keep open through regular usage and later through collective campaigning. A new discourse, the 'peripatetic', developed and this represented excursive walking as a cultivating experience that refreshed both the individual and the society.

Wallace argues that such a practice of walking: 'preserves some portion of local topographies against widespread, nationalising physical changes and, by extension, partially preserves the sites in which the ideal values of agrarian England were supposed to have flourished' (1993: 12). It became clear that aesthetic choice was one of the main reasons why people came to be voluntarily walking. Excursive walking, disciplined and organised, grew greatly (see Wallace 1993: chap. 3).

Wordsworth refers to this as the walking tour. The walker does not wander aimlessly or in a socially disruptive fashion. The wanderer returns along paths that have already been walked. This ensures connection and stability with the clear intention to return and not to wander aimlessly. The conspicuous example set especially by Wordsworth and Coleridge in the Lake District stimulated pedestrian activity by their contemporaries and then by many other relatively affluent men. By the middle of the nineteenth century 'the very highest echelon of English society regarded pedestrian touring as a valuable educational experience' and developed a 'peripatetic theory' based upon how the mostly male walker comes to be re-created with nature (Wallace 1993: 168).

In the twentieth century leisurely walking has become intertwined with various products, including boots, maps, socks, anoraks, shorts, hats and so on. Together they serve to constitute the hybrid, 'the [leisurely] walker'. Samuel describes how rambling in 1930s and 1940s Britain 'required stamina and strength, "practical" clothing and "sensible" shoes' (1998: 133). Such a uniform obliterated many gender differences. Both men and women were ramblers or hikers and they were constituted through these uniform products. According to Samuel rambling 'encouraged women to dress like men, to look like men, and to act like men' when faced by the need to rough it in all weathers (1998: 133). For his mother walking was a kind of religion, 'in which "fresh air", "exercise" and "scenery" took the place of the Holy Trinity' (1998: 139).

The mass enthusiasm of inter-war hiking revolved around the open air that was thought to make people better, as they experienced open, panoramic, uninhibited scenery. Walking holidays were not so much relaxation but a way of strengthening body and soul, even or perhaps especially, when the weather was hostile. For Samuel's mother's the importance of walking stemmed from the degree of hardship and sacrifice involved. She preferred walking the bleak hilly terrain of the Celtic periphery to the soft sleek undulations of an English landscape (see Urry 1995: chap. 13).

More generally, for the young ramblers of the north: 'the countryside was seen as an energizer: their intention was not so much to see the landscape as to experience it physically, to walk it, climb it or to cycle through it', to touch it with all the senses (Samuel 1998: 146; see Chapter 4 below). These new multisensuous spatial practices ignored the existing farming activities of the countryside. Rather than being regarded as visual enticements, villages in the inter-war period were 'rural slums, with rising damp, leaky roofs, tiny windows, and squalid interiors' (Samuel 1998: 146). The spatial practices of rambling (and climbing, cycling, camping and so on) mostly ignored the lives and habitats of those dwelling in that countryside.

Chapman likewise describes how the hybrid of the 'rambler' has come to fit certain landscapes, certain places of dwelling, such as the English Lake District (1993). However, just a few miles 'outside' that area are various former industrial towns where leisurely 'walking' is an inappropriate spatial practice. Chapman describes walking into one of these towns, Cleator Moor, wearing the clothing appropriate for walking in the Lake District, that is, breeches, boots, brightly coloured socks, orange waterproofs and a rucksack. Instead of feeling intrepid, as one is permitted to do on descending a modest Lakeland mountain into the nearby Lake District towns of Ambleside or Keswick, he felt acutely out of place. He was wearing fancy-dress in Cleator Moor. He had literally walked out of the Lake District with its appropriate spatial practices of leisurely walking and the appropriate hybrid of 'the walker'. It should also be noted that other technologies and objects, such as the Sony Walkman, have produced a new kind of solitary 'cool walker' who is especially tuned into the soundscapes of city-life (see du Gay *et al.* 1997: 33–5).

More generally de Certeau regards walking as constitutive of the city in the way that speech acts constitute language (1984). He contrasts the strategies with the tactics of walking. The former involves the victory of space over time. Strategies involve disciplining and regimentation, based upon notions of what are proper activities and ways of walking within and through particular spaces. Tactics by contrast consist of the seizing of opportunities that arise through time within the city. They serve to constitute lived space and are improvisational and unpredictable. Diken shows in the case of Turkish migrants living in Aarhus in Denmark how 'in a way [they] subvert, or make holes in existing urban plans'; 'they develop their own 'tactical' ways of walking and conversing within those plans and creating their own pathways by, so to say, manipulating the plan' (1998: 83). Walking is privileged, stimulated by a plethora of desires and goals stemming from the interrelations between bodily movement, fantasy, memory and the texture of urban life.

Walkers and walking thus give shape to how places are dwelt in and used. For de Certeau, while a place, such as a street, is ordered and stable, spaces only exist through movements, velocities. They are activated by the ensemble of movements occurring within it. Space is thus a performed place (Morris 1988: 36–7; Edensor 1999). Such performances generally involve conflictual tactics and uses of space by various social groups (see Massey forthcoming, on the daily battles over the physical appropriation of contemporary British streets).

Also some places particularly invite strolling around and possessing the place. One feels invited into its nooks and crannies, or one's eye is drawn along its grand vistas. Places can provide different affordances. Nineteenth-century Paris was the first city of the modern period which provide astonishing new affordances to the peripatetic visitor. It came to be possessed by those who were able to consume, as they walked along the new boulevards and passed by, and often into, the brightly lit shops and cafes, a 'kaleidoscope which changes, stirs, bemuses' (contemporary commentator cited in Green 1990: 75). Such flâneurs were able to give themselves ecstatically to the crowd, as Baudelaire poignantly describes. Strolling in some places 'out of time' is almost itself subversive. The *flâneur* both seeks the essence of a place while at the same time consuming it – there is both consumption and subversion (Game 1991: 150). This way of walking, as though one had 'all the time in the world', 'is oppositional to the counting of time, Taylorism, the production process ... scrutinising, detective work, and dreaming set the *flâneur* apart from the rush-hour crowd' (Game 1991: 150). There can be tactile pleasures from walking in a crowd, from an embodied participation as one co-ordinates one's body with that of the moving mass of other bodies (Shields 1997a: 25).

But of course walking is very different for diverse social groups. For working-class women in the late-nineteenth-century space of Paris the crowd was full of risks. Such women lived almost literally on the streets and would have been generally presumed to be sexually available as prostitutes. Paris was overwhelming in its size and grandeur for those who were only able to travel on foot (see Edholm 1993; although see Massey 1994, on women and the city). More generally, movement around the city is mediated by power relations that determine where, and when, different social groups are able to walk.

Research at the Taj Mahal shows that there are very different walking practices that occur within the same 'place' (Edensor 1998). In 'enclavic tourist spaces' around the Taj, walking is relatively smooth and ordered. There is rapid movement and the clear functions of the different zones eradicate confusion. Various personnel are responsible for regulating the walking practices of visitors, who have often internalised how to effect appropriate walking in such areas. Space dominates time and, *contra* de Certeau, there is little opportunity for fantasy, memory and desire to effect tactical subversion (see Macnaghten and Urry 1998: chap. 6, on similarly regulated walking in the English countryside). There can be a remarkable choreography of walking with tutored bodies held in a particular mannered fashion (Edensor 1998).

By contrast in 'disorganised tourist spaces' backpacker progress is less programmed. Walking may be more improvisational and entails vivid encounters with diverse and disruptive elements. Local people will often seek to interrupt movement through particular spaces and it will be difficult to avoid touching the 'other'. Contact with vehicles and with animals is also unavoidable. The trajectories of visitors will co-exist with, and criss-cross, local pathways. Edensor argues that this engenders less rigid bodily postures and a more casual wandering and lounging, even the deliberate seeking out of risky environments that enhance the possibilities of getting lost.

Muslim visitors stay longer in the Taj than other domestic Indians and linger a long time in the grounds, particularly reading the Quranic script on the building. As they slowly circumambulate around the mausoleum or sit on the marble terrace in silent contemplation, Muslim visitors exhibit a 'reverential gaze'. The movement of Muslim visitors follows a purposive and predictable spatial pattern but one which differs from the directed routes of Western package tourists or the meanderings of western back-packers.

For many the spatial practice of walking (as well as of climbing, cycling and so on) has involved the idea of effort. It is maintained that only if some natural feature involves real exertion to get to it or to climb it can it be properly appreciated (the term travel comes from *travail*, to work; see Buzard 1993). This emphasis upon effort is elaborated in Barthes' analysis of the *Guide Bleu* which combines together three characteristics: the cult of nature, puritanism and an individualistic ideology (1972). Morality is associated with effort and solitude. Certain social practices are only deemed appropriate within nature or to know nature if they entail a more or less solitary achievement, particularly to overcome uneven ground, mountains, gorges, torrents and so on. Barthes talks of how the *Guide* emphasises 'regeneration through clean air, moral ideas at the sight of mountain tops, summit climbing as civic virtue, etc.' (1972: 74). Such practices cannot therefore overcome the friction of distance effortlessly. The individual must travel in order to appreciate nature and so these various spatial practices entail lengthy and often very slow movement (see, for example, Spufford's 1996 cultural analysis of Scott's expedition to the Antarctic). Slowness can be a highly valued way of moving across an envi-ronment and exerting the minimum of impact, a notion seen in much of the talk and writing about adventure climbing (see Lewis 2000).

This contrasts with the speed and rush of much modern life, as the strolling *flâneur* of the nineteenth century has given way to a variety of transient and fleeting forms in the twentieth (see Tester 1995). According to Buck-Morss, these twentieth-century forms of *flânerie* are found in the department store and generally in consuming practices; in magazines with photographs which imply 'look, but don't touch'; in radio which Adorno described as 'aural Flâneurie'; in the optical *flâneurie* of television; and 'with world travel, the mass tourist industry now sells Flâneurie in two- and four-week packets' (1989: 366). Sontag sees the urban photographer as the twentieth-century version of the solitary walker (1979: 79). Central of course to all these forms are modes of travel that are far from slow. The stagecoach, the railway, the bike, the motor coach, the motorcycle, the plane and especially the car have generated newly fast mobilities that have mostly reduce the pleasures and usefulness of walking and strolling.

I begin briefly with the railway that has been exceptionally important in the structuring of modern mobility (Schivelbusch 1986; Thrift 1996). It brought machinery into the foreground of people's everyday experience outside the workplace. An incredibly powerful, moving mechanical apparatus became a relatively familiar feature of everyday life. The age of the train generated one of the most distinctive experiences of the modern world, restructuring the existing relations between nature, time and space. The very building of railways flattened and subdued the existing countryside. The train was a projectile slicing through the landscape on level, straight tracks, with countless bridges, cuttings, embankments and tunnels. The landscape came to be viewed as a swiftly passing series of framed panorama, a 'panoramic perception', rather than something which was to be lingered over, sketched or painted (Kern 1983; Schivelbusch 1986). As Nietzsche notes about the late nineteenth century: 'everyone is like the traveller who gets to know a land and its people from a railway carriage' (quoted Thrift 1996: 286).

Railways democratised longer-range travel. Passengers were thrown together with very large numbers of strangers within an enclosed space. Soon there developed new ways of maintaining social distance. Raymond Williams writes of how on a station platform there was 'this moving away [from other passengers], a habit no less his own because it was the habit of this crowded society' (1988: 315).

As I discuss in Chapter 5, the increased pace of rail traffic meant that the existing patchwork of local times came to be replaced with a standardised time based upon Greenwich. And the exceptional mechanical power of the railway appeared to create its own space linking many different places into ever more complex and extended systems of speeded-up circulation. Railway travel thus became a 'value in and for itself as speeds increased, another country with its own distinctive practices and culture' (Thrift 1996: 267). Particular places became known as being on the way to, or on the way from, somewhere else. Thus 'localities were no longer spatially individual or autonomous: they were points in the circulation of traffic that made them accessible' (Schivelbusch 1986: 197).

Moreover, people's subjectivities came to be constituted through their connections with elsewhere. Even Henry Thoreau in his return to 'nature' on the banks of Walden Pond in the mid-nineteenth century did not complain about the sound of the railway. Rather he considered that he was

> refreshed and expanded when the freight train rattles past me, and I smell the stores which go dispensing their odours all the way from Long Wharf to Lake Champlain, reminding me of foreign parts ... and the extent of the globe. I feel more like a citizen of the world.
> (1927: 103; see also Chapter 6, on the dialectics of belonging and travelling in Raymond Williams' novels)

This is somewhat akin to Thomas Cook's belief in the railway as a democratic and progressive force. He argues that: 'Railway travelling is travelling for the Million; the humble may travel, the rich may travel ... To travel by train is to enjoy republican liberty and monarchical security' (quoted Brendon 1991: 16). At first, however, the railway companies did not realise the economic potential of the mass, low-income passenger market. It required a specialist in the *social* organisation of rail travel. Cook simplified, popularised and cheapened travel, turning the technological innovation of the railway into a social innovation. He initiated the provision of tickets in advance for different lines, the negotiation of block bookings so as to obtain favourable rates, the development of the railway coupon, the sending of luggage in advance, and hotel coupons and circular notes (Lash and Urry 1994: 263–4). Cook, the 'Emperor of Tourists', maintained that travel 'provides food for the mind; ... it promotes universal brotherhood' (quoted Brendon 1991: 31–2). 'To remain stationary in these times of change, when all the world is on the move, would be a crime. Hurrah for the Trip – the cheap, cheap Trip!' (quoted Brendon 1991: 65).

Finally, the effect of the railway was that passengers were propelled through space as though they were mere parcels. The body is akin to an anonymised parcel of flesh, shunted from place to place, just like other goods (Thrift 1996: 266). Such power-based technology of the railway is not in control of human beings. Rather, according to Heidegger, such machinery 'unfolds a specific character of domination ... a specific kind of discipline and a unique kind of consciousness of conquest' over humans (quoted Zimmerman 1990: 214).

In the twentieth century, this disciplining and domination through technology was most dramatic with the system of production, consumption, circulation, location and sociality engendered by the 'motor car'. There are now 500 million cars world-wide and the figure is expected to double by 2015 (Shove 1998). The hybrid social and technical system of the car should be examined through a number of interlocking dimensions:

- as the quintessential *manufactured object* produced by the leading industrial sectors and the iconic firms within twentieth-century capitalism (Ford, GM, Rolls-Royce, Mercedes, Toyota, VW and so on)
- as the industry which has generated key *concepts*, Fordism and Post-Fordism, employed in understanding the development of, and changes within, the trajectory of contemporary capitalism
- as the major item of *individual consumption* which provides status to its owner/user through the sign-values with which it is associated (speed, home, safety, sexual desire, career success, freedom, family, masculinity), as well as being easily anthropomorphised (given names, having rebellious features, seen to age and so on)

- as a *machinic complex* constituted through the car's technical and social inter-linkages with other industries, including car parts and accessories; petrol refining and distribution; road-building and mainte-nance; hotels, roadside service areas and motels; car sales and repair workshops; suburban house building; new retailing and leisure complexes; advertising and marketing, and so on
- as the single most important *environmental* issue resulting from the exceptional range and scale of resources used in the manufacture of cars, roads and car-only environments, and in coping with the mate-rial, air quality, medical, social, ozone, visual, noise and other consequences of automobility
- as the predominant form of 'quasi-private' *mobility* which subordi-nates other 'public' mobilities of walking, cycling, travelling by rail and so on, and reorganises how people negotiate the opportunities for, and constraints upon, work, family life, leisure and pleasure
- as the dominant *culture* that organises and legitimates socialities across different genders, classes, ages and so on. It sustains major discourses of what constitutes the good life and it provides potent literary and artistic images and symbols. Literary contributions include Forster's evocation in *Howard's End* of how cars generate a 'sense of flux' (1931: 191), and Ballard's *Crash* which uses the car 'as a total metaphor for man's life in modern society' (1995: 6). According to Barthes the car is 'consumed in image if not in usage by the whole population ... [it is] the exact equivalent of the great Gothic cathe-drals' (1972: 88; see Graves-Brown 1997).

Sociology however has barely noticed these interlocking dimensions of automobility. Three sub-disciplines that should have examined the car and its social impacts are industrial sociology, the sociology of consumption and urban sociology. However, each has failed to deliver pertinent anal-yses. Within industrial sociology there has been little examination of how the mass production of cars has transformed social life. It failed to analyse how the huge number of cars being produced through 'Fordist' methods, especially within the US, were impacting upon the patterns of social life as car ownership became 'democratised'. Within the sociology of consump-tion there has not been much examination of the use-value of cars in permitting extraordinary modes of mobility, new ways of dwelling in movement and the car culture to develop. The main question for the soci-ology of consumption has concerned sign-values, with the ways that car ownership in general or the ownership of particular models does or does not enhance people's status position. The car as the locus of consumption remains on the drive of the house. Urban sociology has concentrated on the socio-spatial practice of walking and especially upon *flânerie* or 'strolling' around the city. It has been presumed that the movement, noise,

smell, visual intrusion and environmental hazards of the car are irrelevant
to strolling the city and more generally to deciphering the nature of
contemporary city-life. Much urban sociology has been remarkably static
and has concerned itself little with any of the forms of mobility into and
across the city. One exception is Shields' account of Rodeo Street in Seoul
that brings out the tactile interchanges between walking and driving
(1997a). The cars involved in symbolic display are bumped up against as
young men and women walk the street and take every opportunity to meet
each other in spaces in part structured by the flashy parked cars.

In general, however, sociology has regarded cars as a neutral technology, permitting social patterns of life that would have more or less
occurred anyway. Sociology has ignored the key significance of *automobility* which is not simply a system of production or of consumption,
although it is of course both of these. The car's significance is that it reconfigures civil society involving distinct ways of dwelling, travelling and
socialising in, and through, an automobilised time–space. Civil societies of
the west are societies of automobility. I examine this further in Chapter 8
when I consider the more general implications of mobility for the nature of
the social world, something discussed in Raymond Williams' novels which
bring out how social life exists through interconnecting routeways (see
Chapter 6 below). The socialities of civil society are sustained through
technologies of movement which, both literally and imaginatively, connect
peoples together over significant, complexly structured, heterogeneous
distances. Those multiple socialities, of family life, community, leisure, the
pleasures of movement and so on, are interwoven through complex
jugglings of time and space which car journeys both allow, but also necessitate.

These complex jugglings are the consequence of two interdependent
features of automobility: that the car is immensely flexible *and* wholly
coercive. Automobility is a source of freedom, the 'freedom of the road',
because of its flexibility which enables the car driver to travel at speed, at
any time in any direction, along the complex road systems of western societies which link together almost all houses, workplaces and leisure sites.
Cars therefore extend where people can go to and hence what they as
humans are able to do. Much social life could not be undertaken without
the flexibilities of the car.

But at the same time such a flexibility is coerced, it is necessitated by
automobility because the moving car forces people to orchestrate in
complex and heterogeneous ways their mobilities and socialities across
very significant distances. Automobility necessarily divides workplaces
from the home producing lengthy commutes; it splits home and shopping
and destroys local retailing outlets; it separates home and various kinds of
leisure site; it splits up families which live in distant places; it necessitates
leisure visits to sites lying on the road network; it entraps people in

congestion, jams and temporal uncertainties; and it encapsulates people in a privatised, cocooned, moving environment (Graves-Brown 1997). Automobility coerces – it might be thought to be as powerful a structure as any that confronts people and yet it is rarely analysed within sociological debates. It is perhaps the best example of how systematic unintended consequences get produced as a result of individual or household desires for flexibility and freedom. As Shove writes: 'more freedom means less choice, for it seems that cars simultaneously create precisely the sorts of problems which they also promise to overcome' (1998: 7).

How then did this monster of automobility come to emerge? John Ruskin perceptively maintained that: '... all travelling becomes dull in exact proportion to its rapidity' (quoted Liniado 1996: 6; see Thrift 1996: 264–7). Speed and its effects were the key issue when the earliest cars came on to the scene in the late nineteenth century, soon after Ruskin's death (Liniado 1996; Kern 1983). In Britain there was a preoccupation with the breaking of speed records, especially as these were recorded by increasingly precise watches. Life appeared to be accelerating as humans and machines combined in new and intricate 'machinic complexes', following the development of railway which had so perturbed Ruskin. The shock of seeing cars racing through the English countryside provoked intensely heightened opposition between rustic images of a defenceless countryside already ravaged by the Great Depression, as against images of technological progress and the dominance of a machine culture (Liniado 1996: 7).

Thus at first the car was constituted as a speed machine, to propel humans ever-faster (in fact rich humans). There was an obsession with the setting of new speed records although controversy raged over the costs and benefits of such speed. Many motorists described their experience of speed in mystical terms, as though this were an experience not so much opposed to the natural world but one which expressed the inner forces of the universe. The author Filson Young wrote of the sensuous experience of riding in a racing car as 'the exultation of the dreamer, the drunkard, a thousand times purified and magnified' (quoted Liniado 1996: 7). He also captures the cyborgised character of such a machinic complex. 'It is, I think, a combination of intense speed with the sensation of smallness, the lightness, the responsiveness of the thing that carries you, with the rushing of the atmosphere upon your body and the earth upon your vision' (quoted Liniado 1996: 7). Elsewhere he writes of the racing driver having to wrestle with the speed, power and dynamism of the car and the need to tame it rather like a Nietzschean *Übermensch* struggling with the intense natural forces of life and power.

In Edwardian and later in inter-war England an alternative machinic complex developed. This was based around the concept of the 'open road' and the slow meandering motor tour that became a highly favoured middle-class pursuit. This complex developed after some of the exceptional uncertainties of car travel had been overcome (Bunce 1994; Thrift 1996; Liniado 1996). Motor touring was thought of as 'a voyage through the life and history of the land'. There was an increasing emphasis upon slower means of finding such pleasures. To tour, to stop, to drive slowly, to take the longer route, to emphasise process rather than destination, all became part of the performed art of motor touring as ownership of cars became far more widespread. Filson Young wrote of how 'the road sets us free ... it allows us to follow our own choice as to how fast and how far we shall go, to tarry where and when we will' (quoted Liniado 1996: 10).

Such a complex became possible partly because of the democratisation of car ownership, especially within the US where even the dispossessed of the Great Depression travelled by car (Graves-Brown 1997: 68). But it was also made possible by various organisational innovations partly taken over from the early cycling clubs. These innovations and objects included a road map industry, motoring organisations, hotel rating systems, road signs, village signposts, a national road building programme and many guidebooks (J. Taylor 1994: 129). Collectively they served to generate a new machinic complex organised around a certain cosiness of inter-war family life (see J. Taylor 1994: chap. 4). And they paved the way for the inter-war transformation of the motor car, from alien threat to a 'natural' part of the rural scene. Light notes how 'the futurist symbol of speed and erotic dynamism – the motor car – [was turned] into the Morris Minor' in the inter-war years (1991: 214). The increasingly domesticated middle classes, comfortably and safely located in their Morris Minors: 'began to tour England and take photographs in greater numbers than ever before' (J. Taylor 1994: 122, and see 136–45, on the 'Kodakisation' of the English landscape).

An additional feature found in north America was the way in which the car was enthusiastically adopted by the wilderness camping and touring fraternity (see Bunce 1994: chap. 4). Even by the 1920s motor camps were springing up to cater for the touring motorist. The enabled huge increases in the use of national parks, transforming so-called 'wilderness' from an élite space approached by rail, to a mass space visited and partially lived in by the mass motorist (Bunce 1994: 119).

Indeed in the development of automobility, north America has been seminally important in providing experiences, scenes and literature that have become icons of the car (see Eyerman and Löfgren 1995, on American road movies). Particularly important in the development of American automobility was the Interstate Highway System that began construction in 1956 funded by a specific gasoline tax (Wilson 1992: 30). This building of 41,000 miles of freeway involved a huge federal subsidy to automobility and to the various social practices with which it became entwined, such as camping, leisure and tourism. Wilson summarises how the speeding car along the open road has become a metaphor for progress in the US and for the cultural taming of the American wilderness:

> The new highways were thus not only a measure of the culture's technological prowess but they were also fully integrated into the cultural economy. They were talked about as though they had an important democratizing role: the idea was that modern highways allowed more people to appreciate the wonders of nature.
>
> (1992: 30)

American culture is in some ways inconceivable without the culture of the car. Some obvious examples include Kerouac's *On the Road*, and the films *Easy Rider, Rolling Stone, Alice Doesn't Live Here Anymore, Bonnie and Clyde, Vanishing Point, Badlands, Thelma and Louise, Paris, Texas* and so on (Eyerman and Löfgren 1995). More generally, Baudrillard writes of the post-war American landscape as the 'empty, absolute freedom of the freeways ... the America of desert speed, of motels and mineral surfaces' (1988: 5). American post-war landscapes are empty and stand for modernity and the rejection of the complex histories of European societies. This emptiness is a metaphor of the American dream. Mostly this movement of 'hitting the road, Jack' has been highly gendered, the unending movement of men in their cars conspicuously consuming the planet's carbon resources. Whitelegg emphasises the resulting invisibility of the 'other' to this all-conquering car, of women, children, the elderly, pedestrians, cyclists and so on, indeed anyone who steps outside the car (1997: 46).

Baudrillard suggests that 'America' undertook to make utopia real, to realise everything through the strange destiny of simulation. Culture then in America is 'space, speed, cinema, technology' (Baudrillard 1988: 100). These empty landscapes of the desert are experienced through driving huge distances across them; travel involves a 'line of flight'. Deserts constitute a metaphor of endless futurity, a primitive society of the future, combined with the obliteration of the past and the triumph of time as instantaneous rather than time as depth (Baudrillard 1988: 6). Driving across the desert involves leaving one's past behind, driving on and on, seeing the ever-disappearing emptiness framed through the windscreen (see Kaplan 1996: 68–85).

Wilson also emphasises the horizontal quality of the landscape seen through the car windscreen: 'the faster we drive, the flatter the earth looks' (1992: 33). He describes how in the post-war period certain landscapes in the US were substantially altered so as to improve the view that they afforded from the newly constructed roads. In the case of the Blue Ridge Parkway in the southern Appalachians, 'hillbilly' shacks and derelict farmhouses, as well as any signs of commercial development, were removed from sight. What was generated was a landscape of leisure 'pleasing to the motorist ... using the land in a way that would "make an attractive picture from the Parkway", (Wilson 1992: 35). The Federal and then the local states turned nature into something 'to be appreciated by the eyes alone', looking out and over the scene laid out before the invincible car driver (Wilson 1992: 37).

In each car the driver is strapped into a comfortable armchair and surrounded by micro-electronic informational sources, controls and sources of pleasure, what Williams calls the 'mobile privatisation' of the car (see Pinkney 1991: 55). Many aspects involved in directing the machine have been digitised, at the same time that car drivers are located within a place of dwelling that insulates them from the environment that they pass through. The sights, sounds, tastes, temperatures and smells of the city and countryside are reduced to the two-dimensional view through the car windscreen, something prefigured by railway journeys of the nineteenth century. The environment beyond the windscreen is an alien other, to be kept at bay through the diverse privatising technologies which have been incorporated within the contemporary car. These technologies ensure a consistent temperature, large supplies of information, a relatively protected environment, high quality sounds and sophisticated systems of monitoring which enable the hybrid of the car driver to negotiate conditions of intense riskiness on especially high-speed roads.

I noted in Chapter 2 the plausibility of the metaphor of the 'motel' which is one of the quintessential non-places of super-modernity (Augé 1995). Such non-places are neither urban nor rural, local nor cosmopolitan, sites of pure mobility. Airports exhibit parallel characteristics, as peoples and cultures are linked together through the intersection of enormously elaborate relays. These relays come together within the departure lounge of any airport. Such lounges are places of intense sameness produced by the global networks and immutable mobiles of the aviation industry *and* of intense hybridity as mobile peoples and cultures unpredictably intersect as they 'dwell-in-transit'. Air travel is of course the quintessential mode of dwelling within the contemporary globalising world resulting from what Makimoto and Manners term the 'nomadic urge' (1997: chap. 3). By contrast with roads, the scapes, and hence the flows, of air travel are more spatially delimited and integrally interconnected with limousines, taxis, air-conditioned offices, business class hotels and restaurants, forming a kind of seamless scape along which nomadic executives can effortlessly travel (see Castells 1996: 417).

Crucial to such scapes are hub airports. Not to have access to such an airport is to be seriously excluded from the scapes of the airlines that, with partners, cover most of the globe. Such increasingly global scapes have dramatic effects upon those places that are unconnected, as well as on the previous form of slower international mobility, namely shipping. A commentator notes that:

Jumbos have enabled Korean computer consultants to fly to Silicon Valley as if popping next door, and Singapore entrepreneurs to reach Seattle in a day. The borders of the world's greatest ocean have been joined as never before. And Boeing has brought these people together. But what about those they fly over, on their islands five miles below? ... Air travel might enable businessmen to buzz across the ocean, but the concurrent decline in shipping has only increased the isolation of many island communities.

(cited in Massey 1994: 148)

The mobilities of objects

So far I have considered corporeal mobility. I turn now rather more briefly to the mobility of objects, to examine how 'it is things-in-motion that illumine their human and social context' (Appadurai 1986: 5). In Chapter 2 I showed how in eastern Europe there had been a fascination with consumer goods from the 'west', with distinctions of style and taste, with shopping as an intensely pleasurable activity and with 'cult' products such as American jogging shoes or western books. Travel to other countries and especially to the 'west' involved extensive purchases of consumer goods. The flows of shoppers, tourists, travellers, black marketers, smugglers and so on, combined with particular consumer objects and modes of transportation, undermined these severely bounded 'societies'. Such states were unable to stem the march of goods, services, signs, images and people. What Makimoto and Manners term the 'new nomadic age' was spearheaded in eastern Europe by often cheap and shoddy consumer goods, circling free from the conditions under which they had been produced, and moved and located within new patterns of social life (1997). Objects that in the west would barely have counted as commodities commanded in Eastern Europe a high exchange-value resulting from their sign-value of 'western taste and sophistication'.

These spiralling mobilities of objects demonstrate a number of intersecting processes. First and obviously, objects travel often in conjunction with the movements of people. This implies that in some senses cultures travel and are not simply fixed in terms of sets of objects which are *rooted* in place. Rather objects follow diverse and complex *routes*. The dwelling-ness of objects is not fixed or given – they appear to travel as much as they dwell (see Clifford 1997).

Lury in fact argues that we can distinguish between three kinds of mobile objects whose cultural biographies are elaborately intertwined with diverse modes of corporeal travel (1997b). *Traveller-objects* travel well since they maintain their meaning immanently. These objects sustain an authenticated relation to their original place of dwelling; place and culture are bound together in a smooth movement through space. Examples of traveller-objects include artworks, handicrafts and items of folk or national significance. They maintain their distance from the commodity and hence sustain their aura.

Tripper-objects also travel well since they are not bound by ritual, convention or tie to a particular place of dwelling. Their travelling is teleologically determined by their final resting place, as they are brought home as souvenirs, mementos, found objects, postcards and photographs. The meaning of tripper-objects is arbitrary, determined by the journey home and the final dwelling place (on the mantelpiece, sideboard, photo album and so on). Their meanings are produced through their ultimate resting-places.

Tourist-objects are those objects for whom movement is all – objects that are in, and of, the 'in-between'. Examples include T-shirts, many television programmes, types of food, goods whose meaning is defined through their movement such as a 'Global Collection' of cosmetic products or 'West Coast Surf Bath Bubbles'. In these objects of pure mobility image and object are mutually authenticating as images of exotic other peoples and places are systematically deployed and circulated.

Overall Lury argues that 'objects move in relations of travelling-in-dwelling *and* relations of dwelling-in-travelling in the practices of global cosmopolitanism' (1997b: 83). This argument brings out how objects are not to be viewed as preformed, given and fixed in their unique meaning. What we think of as 'objects' are mostly comprised of a substantial number of material and symbolic components, each being essential to constituting the resulting object. And such an object can then be consumed and used in varieties of ways. There is no finished object as such. This can be seen in the case of Sony Walkman that was originally provided with two headphone sockets so that, as used indoors, two people could listen together. However, it soon became clear that the Walkman was in fact used much more individualistically than this, especially outdoors by individuals:

> The Walkman, then, was not simply presented as a device for individual listening – it became this through a process in which production and consumption were articulated … Consumer activities were crucial to the introduction, modification and subsequent redevelopment and marketing of this product.
>
> (du Gay *et al.* 1997: 59)

Lupton further argues that certain objects lose their exchange-value as they become 'used' and are emotionally charged. Much emotional charging arises through corporeal or imagined mobility. These include the anthropomorphised car that took one (hopefully) to the airport on time, the postcards from others wishing you were with them, the pair of shoes that one wore on the 'romantic' beach and which are not thrown away, the meal that reminds one of the restaurant visited on holiday, the scent from the 'Global Collection' and so on (Lupton 1998: 144–5).

It is also important to note how objects are materially produced and symbolically conceived of, within a number of different societies. Each may 'contribute' materially and/or culturally to the apparent final product. These different material, informational and image components often travel vast distances in order that they can then be combined together within one particular place. Although we can call this the place of assembly, this should be understood as indicating the assemblage of all components and not merely of the physical elements to be combined. When this assemblage is effected, as with a personal computer, a Coke can, a football shirt, a baguette and so on, then that object demonstrate its constitution from a complex combination of local, national and transnational components. Objects thus can be said to demonstrate a cultural biography as they have been assembled from objects, information and images drawn from diverse cultures in a specific temporal and spatial order.

The Sony Walkman again shows this well. It is clearly inflected by aspects of 'Japanese' design, especially its compactness, simplicity and fine detailing (du Gay 1997: 70–3). However, this is a complex process because Japanese design has itself been significantly constituted through extensive contact with the west. Moreover, certain Japanese designers suggest that the Walkman is more the product of a western aesthetics as Japan borrowed from design notions from the west in the 1950s and 1960s. Clearly the Walkman (including its odd ungrammatical international-English name) is a hybrid, stemming from multiple, intersecting flows of technology and image across borders over a number of decades.

Finally, there are complex relationships between objects and places, whereby the consumption of certain objects involves metaphorically the consumption of other places or cultures. This is referred to by bell hooks in relation to food as 'eating the Other' (1992); this can be seen as a more general process of consuming central objects of another's culture. And this can occur through travel to that culture and bringing the traveller-objects back or by being part of a system of production-consumption whereby the objects of the 'other' are made routinely available for consumption.

Imaginative mobilities

I have already mentioned the importance of visual images with regard to the constitution of certain objects. I turn now to such topics directly, beginning with television (and to a lesser extent with radio) and its capacity to generate 'imaginative travel'. There are now over one billion television sets in the world, and the number is growing by 5 per cent per annum (Castells 1996: 339). Television transforms how it is that people dwell within their homes, this transformation resulting from television's threefold functioning as object, as media and as culture (see Silverstone *et al.* 1992, for a related version).

First, television is an *object* to be purchased and, once purchased, dwells in a particular place within the layout of a given room. In its chosen location it serves to constitute what is the home and where and how household members should dwell within it (the television may also constitute other spaces such as bars or cafes). At least within the living room the TV directs the gaze of all those who enter that room, whether or not the set is actually turned on. Conventionally the rest of the furniture is turned towards the TV set, waiting for it to spring into life. It is the focus of the room. The TV set and the rest of the furniture in that room are mutually constituting. They together produce an appropriate room enabling those located within it to dwell through the TV's mediated and cultural interchanges with the world beyond. The television is part of the background of everyday existence; it is 'ready-to-hand', unremarkable and everyone knows what it does and how to use it (see Scannell 1996: chap. 7; Meyrowitz 1985).

Second, a single television set provides an exceptional array of *media*, of many services, sources of information and modes of entertainment. These media flow constantly and indiscriminately, constituting a televisual flow (Allan 1997; Meyrowitz 1985: 81–2; Myers 1999: chap. 7). Such media flows are provided to all the household members and are consumed both individually and co-operatively. Often there is competition over access to the TV or at least the remote controller because of this exceptional flow of media. Domestic routines (including contestations) within households, which occur at particular times of the day, are organised around the consuming of particular media outputs, to intervening in the televisual flows. Such outputs are, we might say, time-of-the-day-coded (and in which there is a different attending to time at different moments).

Scannell convincingly brings out how these different outputs serve to constitute how it is that people dwell through the patterns of everyday life (1996: chap. 7). Viewers are 'thrown' into such media outputs which organise the multiple and overlapping mediations of time. Such outputs constitute a variety of temporalities: programmes which produce a sense of dailiness including the social interactions occurring around certain programmes at particular times of the day (see Scannell 1996: 159, on the gossip-function of soap operas); the patterning of the week and especially the division between the working week and the excited anticipation of the weekend; the quite different schedules marking each of the main seasons of the year; and an annual cycle of sporting, cultural and political programmes with certain schedules signifying particular holidays. Part of this temporal-coding involves disclosing certain events as 'live'. The consuming of a live event enables one to be in a sense in two places at once. We imaginatively travel and are at Princess Diana's funeral, in war-torn Bosnia, seeing the world record being broken, with Mandela being released from jail and so on (Scannell 1996: 172). These events are part of our lives and undermine certain historic senses of place (see Meyrowitz 1995; Allan 1997).

Third, radio and TV generate the dominant communicational interchanges between households and the world beyond. In many ways TV is *culture*. It mediates all other cultural processes including that of the car culture discussed above. And even though there is increased concentration of ownership of the mass media, audiences appear to have become more segmented and diversified. Castells summarises: 'While the media have become indeed globally interconnected, and programmes and messages circulate in the global network, we are not living in a global village, but in customized cottages globally produced and locally distributed' (1996: 341; emphasis removed). The notion of TV as such a powerful yet differentiated culture parallels Heidegger's comment about the radio made in 1919:

> I live in a dull, drab colliery village ... a bus ride from third rate entertainments and a considerable journey from any educational, musical or social advantages of a first class sort. In such an atmosphere life becomes rusty and apathetic. Into this monotony comes a good radio set and my little world is transformed.
>
> (cited in Scannell 1996: 161)

The radio (and later the TV) discloses the public world of events, persons and happenings. The media pitches that public world into one's private world. People are thrown into the public world disclosed on the radio and more powerfully on television. That public world enters one's own 'little world' and brings them together in often bizarre and contradictory ways. This public world which is brought into how one dwells at home is not only a world of impersonal events and happenings but also of people. Scannell describes how the mass media have powerfully 'contributed to repersonalizing the world', especially 'television has personalized politics' (1996: 165). Television personalises discourse, favouring informal and back region styles of address (Meyrowitz 1985: 106). It makes public much of what once had been private, especially people's private lives. Before broadcasting 'public life was not "for me". It was definitionally, beyond the reach of me-or-anyone. As such it showed up then, of necessity, as anonymous, impersonal and distant' (Scannell 1996: 166).

Heidegger describes how the radio 'has so expanded its everyday environment that it has accomplished a de-severance of the "world"' (quoted Scannell 1996: 167). By this he means bringing close, within range, abolishing distance or farness with events and especially people. 'Heidegger interprets the possibility of radio as transforming spatiality; as bringing things close and hence within the reach of concern; as making the ... the great world beyond my reach ... as accessible and available for me or anyone' (Scannell 1996: 167). In particular, public figures are brought into the home and we think that we know them privately as individuals (Princess Diana being of course the paradigm case of someone with whom billions had imaginatively travelled). Television thus produces a global village, blurring what is private and what is public, what is frontstage and what is backstage, what is near and what is far. Little remains hidden from view as television makes almost everything public, on display, available (see Meyrowitz 1985: 119, on 'para-social interaction' with those we feel we know).

In subsequent chapters I consider how this de-severance of the great world and everyone's little worlds transforms what it is to conceive of the public sphere and civil society. I show that the public sphere has been turned into a visible public *stage* transforming the possibilities of social interaction and public dialogue. As Gitlin presciently showed with regard to the mediatisation of the new left in the US, 'the whole world is watching' (1980). And in particular the identification of potentially shameful behaviour can happen to every person and every institution. No-one is exempt. Backstage behaviour can be revealed, put on display, revealed around the globe and re-presented over and over again. Where behaviour transgresses norms, where others express their disapproval through what Thompson terms a opprobrious discourse, and where those involved have a reputation or 'name' to lose, then a scandal will ensue. The person or institution will be nationally or globally shamed (Thompson 1997, especially on how those 'who live by the media are most likely to die by the media').

We may also note the paradox that because media images are so commonplace a feature of all of our little worlds, they often provide more stable forms of meaning and interpretation than do books or radio. In a culture in which 'seeing is believing', especially as those images are seen time and time again, to see in our living rooms on the TV screen is to have had it disclosed to us, that for example a person or corporation really is 'guilty' of what they have been accused (see Meyrowitz 1985: 90–1, on how Watergate only became real when TV stations reported the *Washington Post*). It should of course be noted that virtual travel is beginning to provide a similar placing on display of the 'shameful' (as with the Matt Drudge home page and its Monica Lewinsky revelations)

I have set out some characteristics of imaginative travel, by which distant events, personalities and happenings are mundanely brought into the living room and transform everyday life. As a consequence we imagine ourselves sharing events, experiences and personalities with many others, with whom we constitute certain kinds of community. This is in turn to revisit a somewhat similar argument in Anderson's conception of the nation as an 'imagined community' (1989). I consider in Chapter 7 the concept of the global citizen and the role of television in fostering new modes of citizenship based upon imagined travel and a possible imagined global community. Also of course imaginative travel brings into the home images of other places which provide a kind of imaginative travel which is complexly intertwined with many processes of corporeal travel.

Virtual travel

As with television, computers involve the de-materialisation of the means of communication (Harvey 1996: 245). Mobilities become instantaneous (see Chapter 5 below). It becomes possible to sense the other, almost to dwell with the other, without physically moving either oneself or without moving physical objects. Benedikt talks of 'dematerializing the medium and conquering – as they say – space and time' (1991c: 9). Nodes in the computer systems operating through terminals are able to generate networks and virtual communities relatively free from bodily constraints. Cyberspace, Heim argues, 'feels like transportation through a frictionless, timeless medium. There is no jump because everything exists ... all at once' as we effortlessly leap across hypertext links (1991: 71). This sheer instantaneity and simultaneity is significant even where what is circulated are chunks of writing accessed through e-mail and other text-based systems (it has been calculated that there were 95 billion email messages in 1997). But as all sorts of information becomes digital, so the packets of such information will in the future consist of anything that can be digitised. These will include not only text, but also voice, sound, graphics, computer programmes, video and so on. Most senses can be converted into digitised information, to be sent and received through computer terminals (Rheingold 1994: 75; Pickering 1997; taste and smell pose the greatest problems for digitisation!).

This digital convergence and interactivity of multiple media constitutes an enormously powerful force, the 'social' consequences of which are unpredictable although highly patterned. Electronic-based technologies have historically grown in the post-war period in ways which have not been planned or which could have been predicted. The World Wide Web of course was 'unknown' a decade or so ago. There have been some quite unexpected innovations, such as graphical user interfaces, the modem, web browsers (necessary for the 230 million or so web sites as in 1997) and so on. The original investments were minuscule but the consequences have been chaotically huge. The Internet itself is a curious new kind of social–technical phenomenon that is formless, chaotic, changing and unpredictable.

And with the development of global investment and development there will be massive further technical leaps in both hardware and software as the boundaries between media are crossed and recrossed. But what we cannot easily predict is *what* these innovations will be, only that there will be many such innovations. We cannot be precise because these electronic technologies are embedded in complex sets of socio-spatial practices. Many ways in which technologies come to be used are often inconceivable. How they develop depends upon the ways that they transform the dwelling practices of millions of people in diverse societies engaging in various kinds of social practice. One very striking example which will merge with that of the computer are mobile phones, which now account for one-half of all new phones worldwide. It will be out of the hybrids of computer-user-machines that strange, unpredictable desires and uses emerge. Also as Pickering argues, to interact with artefacts as though they were agents will mean that such artefacts will themselves exhibit some of the characteristics of unpredictable agency (1997: 46).

Such technologies have become elements of how people dwell in their places of work and in their home. Interacting with various signs on a flickering screen is part of the mundane way in which contemporary life is being organised in the societies of the west. Turkle further points out how contemporary computers require no knowledge of anything behind the screen – all is simulation, including especially Mackintosh's famous and now endlessly copied visual 'desktop' (Turkle 1996: 34). What consequences follow from what Turkle calls a 'life on the screen'?

Cyberspace is a globally networked, computer-sustained, computer-accessed and computer-generated, multidimensional set of overlapping virtual 'communities' (see on 'cybersociety': Benedikt 1991a; Jones 1995b; Shields 1996; Sardar and Ravetz 1996; Lyon 1997; Loader 1997). Computers constitute windows into and out of such virtual communities. Objects are made up of data or pure information. Thus 'the amount of (phenomenal) space in cyberspace is … a function of the amount of information in cyberspace' (Benedikt 1991b: 166; and see 122–3). Space should not be conceived of as a container or a parameter. Moreover, it is a kind of space where through multi-tasking it is common to be in two or many places at apparently the same time.

In cyberspace the boundaries of the human body blur as machines and humans interact far more intimately than in the age of the machine and clock-time. The body is being reconfigured as more technosocial rather than as 'naturally' defined by the boundary of the human skin (Lyon 1997: 35). We should think that the 'relation between human and machine is based on internal, mutual communication and not on the usage or action' *of* the new machines (Deleuze and Guattari 1988: 3). The allure of the computer is more than utilitarian or aesthetic. Heim suggests that it is erotic since it involves a 'mental marriage to technology', a symbiosis between humans and machines which 'captures our hearts … Our hearts beat in the machines. This is Eros' (1991: 61).

Writing as early as 1967, Heidegger presents a dystopic vision of the 'cybernetic world project' in which the difference between automatic machines and living things disappears. Information about humans becomes part of the gigantic feedback circuit characterised by 'self-ordering, the automation of a system of movement' (quoted Zimmerman 1990: 200). Heidegger would not have been surprised how, at the extreme, the discourses of virtual systems are rife with 'images of imaginal bodies, freed from the constraints that flesh imposes. Cyberspace developers foresee a time when they will be able to forget about the body' (Stone 1991: 113).

There are some further points to make about this marriage of machines and human bodies (Haraway 1991; Harvey 1996: 279–81; Thrift 1996: chap. 7). First and most obviously, there are individual physical bodies involved here which, if they do sit for hours at a time in front of screen, can, as in William Gibson's iconic *Neuromancer*, be turned into a 'white-faced, wasted figure, afloat in a loose fetal crouch ... [with] closed, shadowed eyes' (Gibson 1984: 256; academics should beware!).

Second, in developing cyberspace worlds that are inhabited by communities made of bodies, so computer engineers have to model what those bodies will in fact be like. These mainly young male engineers 'are articulating their own assumptions about bodies and sociality and projecting them onto the codes that define cyberspace systems' (Stone 1991: 103). Almost certainly this will mean that conceptions of humans and their bodies will be similar to the conceptions that we attribute to machines, rather than conceiving of humans as autonomous beings who are well able to choose whether or not to use any particular machine (Thrift 1996: 283–4). The young male computer engineers are likely to produce bodies hooked into the technology, and into speed, power and sexual aggression (see Sardar 1996: 24–5, for some demographic profiling).

Third, exactly how human bodies are transformed will depend upon the particular social–spatial practices that create and recreate new virtual environments and their relationships with existing practices. The most successful virtual environments will be those that best reproduce the kinds of dwellingness in the pre-virtual environment, especially where there is already a strong sense of localness or communion. O'Brien *et al* argue that collaborative virtual environments should be designed which are 'consistent with the social nature of work in a specific environment'; that is, 'how the use of information in practice within the real world may be mapped to the virtual' (1997: 3).

This has also been shown in relationship to the home. Although in one sense the home is now a 'terminal', there are complex ways in which electronic technologies are concretely domesticated within the ways of dwelling occurring within the home (Silverstone and Hirsch 1992). Baym effectively argues against the claim that the computer is the sole determinant of communicative outcomes. She suggest various other determinants such as external context, temporal structure, the system's infrastructure, the purposes of the communications such as work or sociality and the group's more general social characteristics (1995; generally see Castells 1996: chap. 5, on the complex uses of new technology).

Fourth, I argue in Chapter 4 that instantaneous time may be generating new cognitive and interpretative faculties. The fifth generation of computer-youth are apparently able to see on video screens several programmes at the same time and to grasp the simultaneous narrative structures. They are able to develop their own games combining various media, speed and simultaneity. The development of such post-literate 'multi-media' skills will be centrally important in the future. It suggests that humans may develop multi-sensuous sets of skills combined with emerging new virtual objects.

Some argue that this will enable the recuperation of all sorts of objects and images in a transformed 'oral–visual culture' that in turn facilitates new learnings and socialities. Stafford describes how through new digitised technologies a much more interactive and sociable universe may develop, a universe which is endlessly criss-crossed by 'extra-linguistic messages, interactive speech acts, gestured conversations, and vivid pantomimes' (1994: 3). Such a positive view of new diverse socialities contrasts sharply with the dystopic metaphysics that have been drawn from Leibniz's monadology (see Harvey 1996). In many ways the first computer scientist, Leibniz saw the world as comprised of many monads, where each being pursues its desires in isolation from all other beings. They produce space through their own activities – there is no external outer world to access. And what monads see are the projections of their own individual appetites and ideas.

What are some of the likely ways in which virtual interactivity may be thought to generate new forms of dwellingness? In Chapter 6 I distinguish between three notions of community: propinquity, localness and communion. One obvious consequence of new electronic places is that communion may result even where there is no geographical propinquity. People can imagine themselves part of community even where they do not regularly see each other, where their bodies do not inhabit the same space and where they only know each other through some electronic name which may be invented (and reinvented; see Jones 1995b and Turkle 1996 on MUDs). Rheingold's *The Virtual Community* apocalyptically elaborates on how social life, once organised within national societies, is now moving to virtual communities that transcend each society and their characteristic communities, solidarities and identities (1994: 63). As people become inhabitants of new virtual communities this may usher in something of a new 'global civil society' where most of the major communities are no longer organised in and through nation-states (Rheingold 1994: 265). Such a civil society could involve new forms of learning, the establishment of alternative counter-cultures, transformations in what is meant by copyright and privacy and the creation of major new opportunities for participatory democracy (Jones 1995a: 26; see Chapter 7 below).

How is this notion of a cyberspatial civil society to be regarded? First, computers involved in cyberspace do not only overcome space at the speed of nanoseconds. Indeed Benedikt argues that desire partially stems from the very time taken to travel and that if virtual travel were instantaneous then this would constitute a major reduction in the phenomenological experience of travel (1991b: 170). Thus some argue that computer technology is much more important in terms of social ritual, for the various kinds of 'connection, linkage' that it may facilitate and permit, for the diverse hybrid person-machine entities that emerge (Jones 1995a: 32). Studies of virtual communities show the complex ways in which normative conventions develop and are reinforced, so-called netiquette, including temporal norms of relevance (Baym 1995: 159). Also important are the ways in which physical environments can be created which are laden with cultural, communicative and emotional significances (see Reid 1995: 167, on MUD environments).

Moreover, computer mediated communities are 'incontrovertibly social spaces in which people still meet face-to-face, but under new conditions of both "meet" and "face"' (Stone 1991: 85). In cyberspace, people do not dwell within a particular place, although of course there are some markers of where users should gather, such as sites, nodes, home pages and so on. People dwell in the scapes of movement (here today and gone a nanosecond later!). People 'belong' in the conduits of 'travel'. Cyberspace is thus a space only of movement (Benedikt 1991b: 126–7). Such computer-mediated communication in effect dissolves the distinction between belonging and travelling.

Hence, in many virtual communities, identities themselves can be mobile, people can flow in and out of fixed identities, becoming 'digital nomads' (Makimoto and Manners 1997). People can develop playful, transient and contingent relationships to mobile communities, as alternative and multiple identities are adopted, often ironically (Plant 1997). Turkle argues that the Internet: 'has become a significant social laboratory for experimenting with the constructions and reconstructions of self that characterize postmodern life' (1996: 180). It also seems that much computer-mediated communication, although normatively sanctioned, is relatively less inhibited and more intimate (Reid 1995: 173). Email – which is neither writing nor speech – is highly informal and often involves a curiously confessional style. More generally, we can suggest that virtual communities, in exchanging vast amounts of information, come to constitute the world rather than simply reporting it. Aycock and Buchignani describe, in the context of email discussion of various murders, that there was the 'nearly instantaneous interpenetration of ethnographic text and referential context ... in computer-mediated communication' (1995: 191).

A further major theme in cyberspatial debates is the claim that 'virtual communities' are not 'real communities' (see Jones 1995a: 24; Sardar 1996). Virtual communities have been viewed as involving more and more connections, as occur between Leibniz's monads, but where these connections 'grow more fragile, airy, and ephemeral' as cyberspace supplants the rich complex diversity of pre-existing social physical space (Heim 1991: 74). Virtual communities have been viewed as lacking the substance of 'real communities' partly because the majority of members of virtual communities appear only to lurk in cyberspace, reading messages and not posting any.

However, Rheingold for one suggests that broader changes are occurring in what we anyway mean by the idea of community, so that much of the time people interact and form 'communities' with those who are geographically distant (and hence the importance of various mobilities). I examine this further in Chapter 6. Moreover, Rheingold emphasises the importance of *intermittent* 'presence-availability' even within virtual communities. He shows the importance of this in the case of virtual communities that are apparently characterised by intense virtual communion (see 1994: 235–40; and see Baym 1995: 157). Such virtual communities do in fact meet up from time to time, they dwell together in a shared place for periods. This 'compulsion to proximity' (Boden and Molotch 1994) has the effect of reinforcing the 'magical, intensely personal, deeply emotional bonds that the medium had enabled them to forge among themselves' (Rheingold 1994: 237). Thus virtual travel has to be understood in relationship with corporeal travel and the ways in which face-to-face conversation is crucial for the development of trustful relationships within cyberspace.

There are thus complex interrelations between the flows of electronic messages and of people. Indeed new virtual communities may well presuppose an enhanced corporeal mobility of people rather than the elimination of such flows (as well as the use of phone conversations). Or to put the argument the other way round: an IT executive argues that the 'daily information and entertainment needs of a traveller are typically multitudes greater than those of the average residential customer' (quoted Graham and Marvin 1996: 199). The more people travel corporeally, the more that they are likely to travel in cyberspace.

However, in one of the few studies on the content of such virtual communications, Aycock and Buchignani found relatively little evidence of the decentring, liberating and cosmopolitan discourses that are supposedly encouraged through virtual and corporeal travel (1995: 225–6). It was found that people displayed disappointingly conventional views about authority, science, authorship, guns, foreigners and madness!

Moreover, not all virtual communities are consensual, in that both parties are knowledgeable about, and accept, the information-mediated relationship. What have been called quaternary relationships occur where new electronic media facilitate the obtaining of information about others, without those people knowing in general about the information flow or about the specific details (Lyon 1994, 1997: 26–7). Examples include the use of databases to generate details of creditworthiness, surveillance cameras and satellites, computer hacking, the targeting of potential customers using information acquired from other sources, illegal tapping of phone calls, the use of GIS software to produce highly differentiated insurance rates and so on. These all reconfigure humans as bits of information which are subject to computerised monitoring and control through various 'systems'.

Such forms of monitoring and control within consumption practices, within workplaces and within urban areas all generate new inequalities of access and power. This is taken to its dystopic extreme within many north American cities which are characterised by exceptional levels of physical and electronic 'fortressing', channelling the mobilities of the secure along safe and electronically monitored routeways while surveilling and marginalising the mobilities of the insecure (see Graham and Marvin 1996: 213–28). Davis talks of how such inequalities produce an electronic ghetto within the emerging information city (1990; Graham and Marvin 1996: 229). More generally, Virilio describes the development of 'vision machines' which involve sightless vision, the automation of perception, the industrialisation of vision and the fusion of the factual and the virtual (1994: 59–61). Such developments have even led to the proliferation of manifestos or constitutions for cyborgs (see Gray 1997).

Conclusion

I have finished this review of various modes of travelling by considering some sources of inequality with regard to virtual travel. More generally, the development of these travel scapes create new spatial inequalities, since they both enhance the powers of those organisations who can deploy them, and weaken the powers of those who are excluded from them. What is involved here are new spatialisations of social inequality, new configurations of power/knowledge.

I have so far talked of these four modes of travel in a somewhat disembodied fashion. In the next chapter I try to correct this by elaborating on some of the ways that these travellings are sensed, both in terms of the objects involved and in terms of the 'places' that get to be visited. Overall I seek to show that the sensing of objects and places should constitute a central concern of a sociology of mobility.

Chapter 4

Senses

London was a foretaste of this nomadic civilization which is altering human nature so profoundly ... Under cosmopolitanism ... we shall receive no help from the earth. Trees and meadows and mountains will only be a spectacle ...

(E.M. Forster 1931: 243)

Introduction

In much current literature there is said to be a death of the *human* subject. A wide variety of discourses and disciplines have problematised the role of human subjects and their apparently unique powers to create and sustain distinctive patterns of human life. Discourses which have made the future of the human questionable include post-structuralist analyses of the death of the author/subject (Derrida 1991); anthropology's interrogation of 'cyborg cultures' (Haraway 1991); analyses of the implications for the human of prosthetic technologies (Lury 1997a); the development of a sociology and anthropology of material objects (Miller 1998); actor-network theory from the sociology of science (Latour 1993); the social science interest in the growing riskiness of waste and the physical environment and its threats for the future of the human species (Beck 1992b); analyses of the partially independent effects of time and space (Adam 1998); sociobiological attacks on dualistic notions of mind and body (Wilson 1980); the post-modern critique of metanarratives of human redemption (Lyotard 1984); and the implications for the human-social world of recent chaos and complexity theories (Casti 1994).

In various ways these question whether humans retain powers to realise outcomes which are species-specific. I have in particular mentioned various ways in which objects are not mere receptacles of the human subject but can function as 'actants', defining the roles played by humans within networks, such as in the testing of haemoglobin levels, serving fast food, travelling by car and so on. Phenomena thought of historically as separate human and physical entities appear to combine into various inhuman networks (Law and Hassard 1999). Machines, objects and technologies are neither dominant of, nor subordinate to, human practice, but are jointly constituted with and alongside humans. Many developments massively significant for humans with regard to technology, science, the body, nature and the environment do not result from purely human intentions and actions.

Objects thus appear to be crucially part of how humans effect agency. Agency is to be seen as an accomplishment and this is brought about through various objects, such as desks, papers, computer systems, aircraft seats and so on. This agency is achieved in the forming and reforming of chains or networks of humans and non-humans. The human and the material intersect in various combinations and networks, which in turn vary greatly in their degree of stabilisation over time and across space. These networks contingently produce, not so much social order, but an ordering (Law 1994). In such an account the human is highly decentred and is not to be seen as separate from the non-human (Latour 1993: 137). Latour advocates a new constitution that recognises hybrid or variable geometries and redefines the human as more of a mediator or translator. Non-humans can often replace potentially unreliable humans – disciplining the latter to behave appropriately would involve a considerable expenditure of effort that can be avoided through replacing it with a delegated non-human.

One example of a hybrid is that of the 'citizen-gun' (Michael 1997). As one enters into association with a gun both that person and the gun are transformed. We should avoid positing an essence to humans or the gun. What acts in the firing is the gun-citizen. It is an agency effected by and through the network or relationship between the gun and the person. Often of course stories are told which suggest that it was the gun or the person who was responsible for the gun going off. But we should develop accounts that recognise the co-agency of the network of the gun-citizen. There are very many hybrids at all sorts of different levels, involving both relationships with objects (the car driver) and with non-human nature (the dog on a lead; see Michael 1997). I consider in this chapter the hybrids of the photographer, the map-maker, the viewer of landscapes, the car driver, the TV-viewer and so on.

In particular I consider the role of the 'human' senses in relationship to such objects and machines, as well as to 'nature'. My claim here is that for all the general emphasis upon dissolving the boundaries of subject and object this aim remains somewhat vacuous. In order to concretise the role of the body, it is essential to develop a more detailed examination of the sensuous constitution of these various hybrids. I therefore try to develop Marx's critique in the first *Theses on Feuerbach*: 'the thing, reality, sensuousness, is conceived only in the form of the *object* ... but not as *human sensuous activity, practice*, not subjectively ... idealism does not know real, sensuous activity as such' (Marx and Engels 1955: 403).

And this exploration of human sensuous practices involves interrogating the hierarchies of the bodily senses that in combination produce these hybrids. In this chapter I therefore generalise an issue noted in Popper when he characterises 'closed societies' as a 'concrete group of individuals, related to one another ... by concrete physical relationships such as touch, smell, and sight' (1962: 173). I try to analyse not so much the senses powerful within such closed societies but how various senses operate in mobile 'open societies'. Which sense dominates and what role does it play in constituting the often mobile hybrid entities? What happens when one or more of such senses are rendered inoperative (as with the flows of nuclear radiation)? How do senses operate not just in relationship to man-made objects but also to the physical world? How have the senses been embodied within material objects and what role do the senses play in facilitating new mobilities?

To illustrate these issues I briefly consider Beck's argument that we have moved towards a new kind of society, risk society as opposed to industrial society (1992). Risk societies are those organised around the dangerous flows of wastes produced by diverse social practices and of their frequently unknowable consequences. Risks are incalculable, uncompensatable, unlimited, unaccountable and, most importantly here, invisible to the human senses. The paradigm case is that of nuclear radiation, which involve risks that cannot be directly touched, tasted, heard, smelt and especially seen. Beck argues about Chernobyl:

> We look, we listen further, but the normality of our sensual perception deceives. In the face of this danger, our senses fail us. All of us ... were blinded even when we saw. We experienced a world, unchanged for our senses, behind which a hidden contamination and danger occurred that was closed to our view.
> (cited in Adam 1995a: 11; see also Stacey 1997: 138, for photographs of 'cancer' also possessing an awesome power to deceive the eye)

Beck proceeds to argue that particular kinds of society develop on the basis of this disempowerment of the senses and of the catastrophic effects of the globalisation of such risks upon human life. Many of the differences between supposedly different societies are eroded because risks have developed that know no national borders and which subject everyone to their insensible power. This power stems from novel machinic complexes which have treated the globe as a laboratory and produced the Frankenstein-generated monster of mobile nuclear waste stretching into an unimaginable future (Macnaghten and Urry 1998, chap. 8; Sullivan 1999).

As well as the social character of the senses that is emphasised by Simmel (Frisby and Featherstone 1997), Rodaway shows that senses are also geographical. Each sense he says contributes to people's orientation in space; to their awareness of spatial relationships; and to the appreciation of the qualities of particular micro and macro environments. Moreover, each sense gives rise to metaphors that show the relative importance of each within everyday life. With regard to touch, examples include 'keeping in touch', 'rubbing someone up the wrong way', someone being a 'soft touch', the avoidance of 'touchy subjects', something being a 'touching' gesture, someone being 'skinned alive', 'hard cases' and so on (Rodaway 1994: 41). With regard to the enormously powerful sense of sight, it is claimed that 'we see' something when we understand it; someone who does not understand a topic is said to be 'blind'; far-sighted leaders are said to be 'visionary'; while intellectuals may be able to 'illuminate' or 'shed light' on a particular topic. By contrast those who cannot understand some issue remain 'in the dark' (Hibbitts 1994: 240–1). This chapter incidentally does not examine the more general issues of the 'disabling society' and the senses.

There are five distinct ways in which different senses are interconnected with each other to produce a sensed environment of objects: *co-operation* between the senses; a *hierarchy* between different senses, as with visuality during much of western culture; a *sequencing* of one sense which has to follow another sense; a *threshold* of effect of a particular sense which has to be met before another sense is operative; and *reciprocal* relations of a certain sense with the object which appears to 'afford' it an appropriate response (see Rodaway 1994: 36–7). In the following discussion of vision, examples of each of these relationships with the other senses will be encountered.

Visuality

A 'hegemony of vision' has characterised western social thought and culture over the past few centuries (Rorty 1980). This was the outcome of a number of developments across Europe. These included new ecclesiastical styles of architecture of the medieval period which allowed increasingly large amounts of light to filter through brightly coloured stain-glassed windows. The medieval fascination with light and colour was also seen in the growth of heraldry as a complex visual code denoting chivalric identification and allegiance (Hibbitts 1994: 251). In the fifteenth century the development of linear perspectivism enabled three-dimensional space to be represented on a two-dimensional plane. The science of optics also developed, as well as the fascination with the mirror as both object and as metaphor (lawyers being characterised as 'mirrors' reflecting what was good or bad for the community; see Hibbitts 1994: 252). An increasingly 'spectacular' legal system was characterised by colourful robes and courtrooms. Most significant of all was the invention of the printing press that enormously reduced the relative power of the oral/aural sense and enhanced the significance of seeing the written word, as well as seeing pictures and maps (Hibbitts 1994: 255).

Sight moreover has been regarded as the noblest of the senses and as the basis of modern epistemology. Arendt summarises: 'from the very outset, in formal philosophy, thinking has been thought of in terms of *seeing*' (1978: 110–11; Jay 1993; Levin 1993b). Rorty has famously demonstrated that post-Cartesian thought has generally privileged mental representations 'in the mind's eye', as mirror reflections of the external world (1980). The dominant conception of philosophy has thus been that of the mind as a great mirror, which to varying degrees and in terms of different epistemological foundations permit us to 'see' the physical world.

Vision has also played a crucial role in the imaginative history of western culture. Jay points out the clusters of images which surround the sun, moon, the stars, mirrors, night and day and so on; and how the basic visual experience has helped to construct efforts to make sense of both the sacred and the profane (1986; 1993). He summarises the significance of this visual sense within the broad sweep of western thought: 'with the rise of modern science, the Gutenberg revolution in printing and the Albertian emphasis on perspective in painting, vision was given an especially powerful role in the modern era' (Jay 1986: 179). Fabian characterises this dictatorship of the eye as that of 'visualism' (1992). While Marshall McLuhan argued that: 'as our age slips back into the oral and auditory modes ... we become sharply aware of the uncritical acceptance of visual metaphors and models by many past centuries'; to be real a thing must, he says, be visible (1962: 238; Hibbitts 1994: 238–9). Nietzsche emphasised the visual aspects which are inherent within the very notions of abstract thought (such as clarity, enlightenment, veil, perspective), as well as how the visual sense has increasingly taken precedence over each of the other senses (see Lefebvre 1991: 138–9; Haraway 1989, on the gendering of vision).

Three general points need to be made here about vision, partly building on Simmel's sociology of the senses. First, according to Simmel, the eye is a unique 'sociological achievement' (Frisby and Featherstone 1997: 111). Looking at one another is what effects the connections and interactions of individuals. Simmel terms this the most direct and 'purest' interaction. It is the look between people (what we now call 'eye-contact') which produces extraordinary moments of intimacy. This is because '[o]ne cannot take through the eye without at the same time giving'; this produces the 'most complete reciprocity' of person to person, face to face (Frisby and Featherstone 1997: 112). The look is returned, and this results from the expressive meaning of the face. What we see in the person is the lasting part of them, 'the history of their life and ... the timeless dowry of nature' (Frisby and Featherstone 1997: 115). By contrast the ear does not reciprocate – it takes but does not give.

Second, Simmel also notes that only the visual sense enables possession and property; while that which we hear is already past and provides no property which can be possessed (Frisby and Featherstone 1997: 116). More generally the visual is the crucial sense enabling people to take possession, not only of other people, but also of diverse objects and environments often at a distance. The visual sense enables the world of both people and objects to be controlled from afar, combining detachment and mastery (see Robins 1996: 20). It is by seeking distance that a proper 'view' is gained, abstracted from the hustle and bustle of everyday experience (see Hibbitts 1994: 293). I return to this distancing and objectifying role of visuality when I consider the materialisation of the visual sense in photographs, landscapes and maps of places both near and far.

Third, there is an increased mediatisation of the visual sense, especially involving the move from the printing press to electronic modes of representation, and from the camera, where people have to be present, to the circulation of digital images from around and beyond the earth. The visual sense has then been enormously extended since Simmel's examination of the senses. Such elaboration of the visual sense has also been associated with some transformations of other senses, especially of hearing through records, tapes, CDs, the Walkman, and of touch through virtual reality (see Robins 1996). So three points I consider below are the degree to which the look is returned, the complicity of the visual in effecting possession, and the degree to which visual sense is 'materialised'.

Thus far I have treated visuality and visual metaphors as simply dominant within western Europe (other cultures have of course followed different sensuous trajectories). However, this is misleading since there was in fact a centuries-long struggle for visuality to break free from the other senses with which it was elaborately entangled (involving *co-operation* and *reciprocation*). Writing about the sixteenth century, Febvre argues that: 'Like their acute hearing and sharp sense of smell, the men of that time doubtless had keen sight. But that was just it. They had not yet set it apart from the other senses' (1982: 437; Cooper 1997). As a result people at the time were said to live in a fluid world where entities rapidly changed shape and size, boundaries rapidly altered and where there was little systematic stabilisation of the social or physical worlds. According to Cooper 'interaction' describes the fluid, changing forms of perception that characterised the sixteenth century:

> The conversion of this state of perpetual ambiguity into a more determinate structure necessitated the hierarchical step of raising the status of sight over the 'primitive' senses of touch, taste and smell in favour of the *visualization* of perception ... [this] enables greater control over the physical and material world through enhanced clarity, transparency and visual certainty *at a distance*.
>
> (1997: 33)

From the late sixteenth century onwards there was an increasing concern with the arts of government and of political economy. There was a growing management of 'society', that was enhanced by the harnessing of a separate visual sense, *le regard*, within the specialised institutions of hospitals and medical practice, in schools, in the treatment of the mad, in prisons, and in the appreciation of the physical world (see Foucault 1970, 1976; Cooper 1997; Adler 1989). Visuality then becomes increasingly central to the very constitution of a visible 'society' that can be examined and monitored; what Bentham termed in relationship to the panoptic metaphor, a 'transparent society, visible and legible in each of its parts' (cited in Cooper 1997: 34; see Chapter 1 above).

There are two key power/knowledge processes which are linked together here: the detailed visual examination developing within each domain of social activity; and the notion that it is 'society' as a whole that is being made transparent and controllable at a distance. By the nineteenth-century in western Europe we reach one of the most visual of historical periods, with asylums, hospitals, schools and prisons designed so that the authorities could visually survey their inmates through variants of the panoptic view (Hibbitts 1994: 258). More generally, the most significant commentator writing in English, John Ruskin, claimed that the 'greatest thing a human soul ever does in this world is to see something ... To see clearly is poetry, prophecy, and religion' (quoted Hibbitts 1994: 257). Areas of wild, barren nature, which had been sources of terror and fear, were transformed into what Raymond Williams terms 'scenery, landscape, image, fresh air', places waiting for visual consumption by those visiting from places of industrial civilisation (1972: 160). These different kinds of place engender very different emotional responses (see Lupton 1998: 153–4).

A clear 'separation of the senses' develops the course of the nineteenth century, especially of the visual sense from those of touch, smell and hearing. The autonomisation of sight through new constituting objects enables the quantification and homogenisation of visual experience. Many new objects of the visual began to circulate, including commodities, mirrors, plate-glass windows, postcards and especially photographs. These objects displayed a visual enchantment in which magic and spirituality are displaced by visual appearances and surface features, reflecting in the newly emergent cities, for example, the mass of consumers routinely passing by and narcissistically seeing themselves reflected or captured in the new visual technologies.

And beyond the cities, the physical environment came to be understood as scenery, views, perceptual sensation and romanticised. Partly because of the writings of the romantics: 'Nature has largely to do with leisure and pleasure – tourism, spectacular entertainment, visual refreshment' (Green 1990: 6). Green demonstrates the effects of this spectacle-isation in the region surrounding Paris in the mid-nineteenth century. There was a prolonged 'invasion of surrounding regions by and for the Parisian spectator' (Green 1990: 76). This invasion was facilitated by the short trip out of the city and the increased ownership of country houses. These combined to generate around Paris a 'metropolitan nature', safe sites for leisure and recreation for the city dweller to visit from time to time. Much advertising for houses in this period brings out the importance of the visual spectacle for visitors: 'The language of views and panoramas prescribed a certain visual structure of the experience. The healthiness of the site was condensed with the actual process of looking at it, of absorbing it and *moving round it with your eyes*' (1990: 88; emphasis added). Rather similarly a house constructed in the English Lake District in the mid-nineteenth century was used 'as it were, as *a camera* to take and present the views' (cited in Abercrombie and Longhurst 1998: 79; emphasis added).

Societies themselves become transparent, as symbolised in the British case with the Great Exhibition of 1851 (see Chapter 6 below). The modalities of power/knowledge of 'society' are transformed, as the visual is separated off from the other senses, as vision comes to occupy a primary position in a sensuous *hierarchy*, and as it is crucial in the very structuring of each society seen and controlled as at a distance. Diken points out implicit in the notion of 'theory' is that of the outside observer (of society, economy, politics) who looks at the object from a distance and thereby produces a detached 'theory' (1998: 248–50). He summarises: 'Much theoretical re-presentation is visual in its essence, and this visuality is more based on an objectifying gaze than on a mutual glance; the 'master' point of view of analytical gazing is de-contextualized, a-temporal and de-corporealized' (Diken 1998: 259). In Chapter 7 I consider whether the visual construction of the 'globe' is generating a new kind of global society which is also to be seen as a de-contextualised object viewed from afar and controllable as at a distance (as in the conceptualisation of 'global environmental change').

For the present however I turn to the connections between the senses and some of the modes of travelling discussed in the previous chapter. I suggest in the modern period that 'society' comes to be known through various mobilities and not just through the static gazes located within the institutions of incarceration described by Foucault. And these mobilities presume new technologies and modes of visual appreciation. Especially important is the hybrid of 'the photographer' which I discuss at length; following that I discuss the map-reader, the viewer of landscapes and the screen viewer.

In 1839 in France Louis Daguerre announced the production of the daguerreotype, and in 1840 in England Fox Talbot publicised the discovery of the photographic process involving the negative and a paper-based image (Batchen 1991: 14; Crary 1990; see Crawshaw and Urry

1997, on the following). Nevertheless, however impressive these 'discoveries' were, Gernsheim argues that 'the circumstances that photography was not invented earlier remains the greatest mystery in its history' (1982: 6). Much of the scientific basis of photography was known in the second quarter of the eighteenth century and yet none of the artists who employed the 'camera obscura' in its various forms sought to fix images permanently. Why was there so little desire to produce permanent photographs until well into the nineteenth century?

There had been three tributaries of such a desire. First, there were the 'photo-photographers', authors and experimenters who in the late eighteenth and early nineteenth centuries expressed a desire to 'photograph'. This list of notable inventors included Morse, Wedgwood, Davy and the younger Daguerre who all expressed frustration of not being able to fix permanently their impressions and experiences (Batchen 1991: 16).

Second, there was the striking shift in the nature of landscape appreciation. Over the course of the eighteenth century travellers could no longer expect that their scholastic observations would become part of scientific understanding (Adler 1989; J. Taylor 1994: 12–17). Corporeal travel came to be justified not scientifically, but through connoisseurship, first of buildings and works of art and later of landscapes. Adler summarises: 'Experiences of beauty and sublimity, sought through the sense of sight, were valued for their spiritual significance to the individuals who cultivated them … In its aesthetic transformation, sightseeing became simultaneously a more effusive passionate activity and a more private one' (1989: 22). Such connoisseurship came to involve new ways of seeing, new kinds of observations. Bryson describes such a gaze as involving a 'prolonged, contemplative [look] regarding the field of vision with a certain aloofness and disengagement, across a tranquil interval' (1983: 94; see J. Taylor 1994: 13).

Third, from the end of the eighteenth century onwards, influential writers and artists articulated a desire for fixing their sensations of landscape. In 1782, the famous proponent of the picturesque, the Reverend William Gilpin, expressed certain annoyance at not being able to contain and capture the fleeting visual sensations that he experienced on a journey down the river Wye. On a later excursion, he wrote of the frustration at being unable to 'fix and appropriate the scene' viewed through his Claude Glass (Batchen 1991: 17). William Cowper expressed similar sentiments in 1785, a desire:

> To arrest the fleeting images that fill
> The mirror of the mind, and hold them fast
> (cited in Batchen 1991: 17)

Samuel Taylor Coleridge, Thomas Gray, John Clare and John Constable all expressed similar frustrations at not being able to capture and to fix such fleeting images that they encountered on their corporeal travels.

These three tributaries coalesced from the 1790s onwards. Prior to then there is relatively little talk which expresses the photographic desire. But from then on such talk becomes a torrent. The discourse of photographic desire was established from the 1790s; and by the 1830s this discourse was well-developed amongst the intelligentsia in both Europe and parts of north America. Thus photography is not to be viewed as part of the gradually unfolding and continuous history of visual representation. Rather it is a crucial element in a 'new and homogeneous terrain of consumption and circulation in which an observer becomes lodged', involving the 'industrialization of image making' (Crary 1990: 13). It is the most significant component of a new cultural economy of value and exchange in which visual images are given extraordinary mobility and exchangeability. Photography is ineluctably bound up with the modern world and with the subjectivity of the observer and the proliferation of increasingly mobile signs and images (see Crary 1990: 149). Adam summarises the way in which the hybrid 'photographer' functions: 'The eye of the camera can be seen as the ultimate realisation of that vision: monocular, neutral, detached and disembodied, it views the world at a distance, fixes it with its nature, and separates observer from observed in an absolute way' (1995b: 8).

Such a hybrid has been enormously significant in democratising various kinds of human experience, particularly involving the mobilities of peoples and objects. As Barthes says, photography makes notable whatever is photographed (1981: 34). It also gives shape to the processes of corporeal travel so that one's journey consists of being taken from one 'good view' to capture on film, to a series of others (Urry 1990: 137–40). The objects then of cameras and films serve to constitute the nature of corporeal travel, as sites turn into sights, and have also helped to construct a twentieth century sense of what is worth going to 'sightsee' (see Crawshaw and Urry 1997). Gregory describes the 'kodakisation' of Egypt in the late nineteenth century (1999). Egypt became scripted as a place of constructed visibility, with multiple, enframed theatrical scenes set up for the edification, entertainment and visual consumption of 'European' visitors. This produced the 'new Egypt', of the Suez Canal, of 'Paris-on-the-Nile', of Thomas Cook and Sons, of a cleaned-up 'ancient Egypt', of the exotic oriental 'other' and of convenient vantage-points and viewing platforms.

The hybrid photographer deploys particular aesthetics that excludes as much as it includes. It is, for example, very unusual to see postcards or tourist photographs of 'landscapes' of waste, disease, poverty, sewage and despoilation (see Crawshaw and Urry 1997; J. Taylor 1994; Parr 1995). The photographer is a powerful hybrid whose outputs can produce a dominant set of visual images (of say the 'orient') while concealing the way that its character is indeed constructed (Sontag 1979).

Taylor particularly brings out the way in which our conception of landscape typically involves the notion of 'mastery' (J. Taylor 1994: 38–9). The photographer, and then the viewer, are seen to be above, and dominant over, a static and subordinate landscape, which lies out beyond us inert and inviting our inspection. Such photographic practices thus demonstrate how the environment is to be viewed, as dominated by humans and subject to their mastery. The hybrid of the landscape-photographer thus entails a dominant visual gaze, including that of the male over the landscape/bodyscape of the female. Irigaray argues: 'More than other senses, the eye objectifies and masters. It sets at a distance, and maintains a distance' (1978: 50).

Wilson summarises the photographer's further impact upon nature, which is turned into a set of graspable objects (just as photography turns women into materialised objects on a page or video): 'the snapshot transforms the resistant aspect of nature into something familiar and intimate, something we can hold in our hands and memories. In this way, the camera allows us some control over the visual environments of our culture' (A. Wilson 1992: 122). Nature, other environments and humans are transformed into objects that travel from person to person. Such objects are put on walls to become part of the decoration of a house, they can structure reminiscences and they create images of place (Spence and Holland 1991; Pinkney 1991: 39, on photos in Raymond Williams' novels). Photographs are thus both subjective and objective, both personal and apparently accounting for how things really were.

The photograph emphasises instantaneous results rather than process. There is minimisation of performance, compared with other ways in which the environment can be hybridised (such as through music, sketching, painting, singing, sculpting and so on). Ruskin for example considered that the proper seeing of landscape could only come about through sketching or painting and not through anything as brief as composing a photograph (Smith 1992: 77). More generally photography produces the array of mobile signs and images which constitutes the visual culture of the late twentieth century. Heidegger argues that the 'fundamental event of the modern age is the conquest of the world as picture', that is, as though it were a picture or form of human representation (1977: 134; Zimmerman 1990: 86–7).

Two further objects of visual framing hugely intertwined with various corporeal mobilities have been the landscape and the map (see Macnaghten and Urry 1998: chap. 4). Such technologies of enframing serve to constitute not only the object that is framed but also the observers who are involved in that very framing (see Gregory 1994: 37). Hybrids of the walker-in-the-landscape and the map-user are thereby generated.

With regard to landscape, this is a particular way of seeing, in which artists have been able to reduce the three-dimensional visual experience of scenery to two-dimensional images. Such images appear to be mimetic of the scene as viewed from a given point of view. The eye, indeed the single eye, is regarded as the centre of the visual world. Cosgrove says that 'Visual space is rendered the property of the individual, detached observer' as a result of such a conception (1985: 49; and see 1884; Barrell 1972; Bryson 1983). In the nineteenth century this conception of landscape as linear perspective was augmented by romantic conceptions, of sublime and barren landscapes in which a more multi-sensuous relationship of the individual to the physical world was experienced and represented (see Macnaghten and Urry 1999: chap. 6, on the sublime).

In both cases there is a presumed power relation between viewer/artist and the viewed/observed. It is the former that possesses the privileged viewpoint and power to compose the view and to see the painting. Landscape implies mastery of the scene and of its representation (see Gregory 1994, on the varied conceptions of landscape, of the world as picture, within the 'science' of geography). Landscapes then involve quite distinct social practices; in English there is, for example, no word which denotes a tract of land which is not appreciated in some sense visually. Landscape is something to be attended to; it involves a relationship of pictorial or visual consumption and it may have been travelled to over a very considerable distance (Barrell 1972: 65; Bell 1993; Abercrombie and Longhurst 1998: chap. 3).

Maps are a related means of visual representation and are especially connected to the increased observation and surveillance of diverse landscapes (Harley 1992; Rodaway 1994: 133–42). They are a different form of representation from that of paintings/pictures. Maps involve taking an imaginary bird's eye view of the world rather than that of an actual or imagined human subject. They involve a scale drawing and do not realise an exact or realist reproduction of the landscape. Maps like photographs involve the deliberate exclusion of many aspects of the landscape. They are intensely symbolic, with the use of all sorts of apparently arbitrary signifiers, of figures, lines, shapes, shadings and so on. Mostly maps were developed as practical tools for merchants, government officials and especially armies. Their emergence in the 'west' was only possible with the development of printing and they represent a peculiarly modernistic process of visual abstraction (Rodaway 1994: 133–4). Ong summarises the consequences of the emergence of such printed maps: 'Only after print and the extensive experience of maps that print implemented would human beings, when they thought about the cosmos ... [would] think primarily of something laid out before their eyes, as in a modern printed atlas' (1982: 73).

Both landscapes and maps are culturally specific visual technologies produced by modes of corporeal mobility that reinforce a particular

'western' view of the world. Both reduce the complex multi-sensuous experience to visually encoded features and then organise and synthesise these
into a meaningful whole. They both capture aspects of nature and society
through visual abstraction and representation; both express distance and
objectivity from what is being sensed. They usher in new ways in which
visuality is complicitous in the operation of power, and organise and articulate control or mastery over what is being viewed. Landscapes and maps
deploy the visual sense as a means of control and surveillance (although
maps can be used more democratically as described in Raymond Williams'
novels; Pinkney 1991: 43–5). There are some parallels with the inscription
or visual display devices characteristic of spatially dispersed scientific
communities. These means of visual representation are mobile across space
and able to convince others working 'at a distance' of the accuracy of their
research findings (Latour 1987; see Chapter 2 above).

Obviously within the visual culture of the late twentieth century the
television screen is of exceptional significance. In describing some of the
main characteristics of such 'imaginative travel' in Chapter 3 I showed that
television is important as object, as media and as culture. I will make two
further points here: that with television visual perception occurs at a
distance; and that sound is also important for the relationships that people
have with 'their' TV.

First, the TV has become incorporated into normal domestic space and
domestic routines, part of the dwelling-place of at least a billion households (Morley 1995; Silverstone and Hirsch 1992). Such dwelling-places
are organised on the basis of telesthesia or perception at a distance,
through a transformed 'virtual geography' based upon diverse, intersecting
and unpredictable vectors (Wark 1994). Wark rhetorically notes, 'We no
longer have roots, we have aerials' (1994: xiv). These aerials and the
omnipresent TV screens reflect an extraordinary visual world lying beyond
that of the domestic regime, an instantaneous mirror reflecting the rest of
the world which is then mirrored into people's homes. In an Indian context
Arundhati Roy writes of an elderly female character whose life has been
transformed by instantaneous and often 'live' visual perception of the
world at a distance:

> She presided over the World in her drawing room on satellite TV … It
> happened overnight. Blondes, wars, famines, football, sex, music,
> coups d'état – they all arrived on the same train. They unpacked
> together. They stayed at the same hotel. And in Ayemenem, where
> once the loudest sound had been a musical bus horn, now whole wars,
> famines, picturesque massacres and Bill Clinton could be summoned
> up like servants.
>
> (1997: 27)

Vectors of fixed length and direction provide trajectories along which images and information pass. Such vectors can link almost any two points in the world together. 'The technical properties are hard and fast and fixed, but it can connect enormously vast and vaguely defined spaces together and move images, and sounds, words and furies, between them' (Wark 1994: 11–12).

Second, Morley argues that the predominant sense involved in relationship to TV is not watching but listening. He points out that a wide array of other activities are engaged in while the TV set is on; activities which are mainly carried on with the comforting sound which remains available in the background. So although obviously TV is a component of a visual culture, it is also an important part of certain 'soundscapes'. Its sounds are part of the domestic life of most households, and increasingly of various 'private' public spaces, such as bars, clubs and cafés. Sound here might be said to organise sight. With regard to the sense of sight the dominant visual mode of viewing TV is through the glance, or sometimes an oscillation between the glance and the gaze, as people skilfully move in and out of different regimes of watching. Morley contrasts these visual patterns with the more sustained gaze that characterises how people visually attend to the cinema screen (1995; Sharratt 1989; Urry 1995, on the glance and the gaze).

Screens are of course part of other hybrid entities that transform vision within contemporary societies. There has been an 'automation of perception', involving digital cameras, X-rays, night vision, thermal and other sensing equipment, remote-controlled sensors and satellites (Thrift 1996: 280–1). Most systems of incarceration in the twentieth century involve the autonomised sight in their routine operations of power. Deutsche writes: 'Distancing, mastering, objectifying – the voyeuristic look exercises control through a visualization which merges with a victimization of its object' (1991: 11). In such a 'surveillance society', people are automatically recorded even when apparently roaming free through a shopping centre or even the countryside (see Lyon 1994). There is a kind of 'sightless' vision created by the machine for the machine in which visual images are neither visible nor viewed (see Thrift 1996: 281).

Virilio has particularly emphasised the importance that surveillance techniques have in changing the morphology of the contemporary city and hence of the forms of trust that people have to invest in such institutions of surveillance (1988). It has been calculated that one is 'captured' twenty times during a walk through a major shopping centre. What is striking about such CCTV techniques is their ordinariness, much akin to the child playing video games in an arcade or on a home computer (Robins 1996: 20–1). Other spaces of visualisation include the extraordinarily advanced scale of surveillance through 'outer space'. It is estimated that the US now monitors 42,000 separate targets across the globe, mostly involving the 'automation of [visual] perception' (Robins 1996: 55).

So far then I have elaborated various hybrids of the visual sense, the photographer, the viewer of landscapes, the map-reader, the screen-gazer, systems of surveillance and so on. The visual sense has through materialisation spun off a set of hybrids that exert awesome dominance over the other senses as I detail in the next section. In the rest of this section I outline some critiques of the power of the visual, critiques that reveal the dark side of sight (see Jay 1993; Levin 1993a, 1993b, on Derrida's examination of the 'metaphysics of presence', Heidegger on 'what-is in representation' and Foucault's 'disciplinary power').

The denigration of the visual is especially prevalent within discourses surrounding travel. In one sense we do live in a society of spectacle – there are many ways in which most environments have been transformed into diverse and collectable spectacles (see Debord 1994). But simultaneously there is denigration of the mere sightseer or tourist to these often contrived environments (see Buzard 1993, on the history of those discourses organised around this tourist/traveller distinction). The person who only lets the sense of sight have free rein is ridiculed. Such sightseers are taken to be superficial in their appreciation of environments, peoples and places. Many people are often embarrassed about mere sightseeing. Sight is not seen as the noblest of the senses but as the most superficial, as getting in the way of real experiences that should involve other senses and necessitate longer periods of time in order to be immersed in the site/sight. Wordsworth argued that the Lake District demands a different eye, one that is not threatened or frightened by the relatively wild and untamed nature. It requires 'a slow and gradual process of culture' (Wordsworth [1844] 1984: 193).

Rather similarly Ruskin argued how the new sensibilities of the city undermine certain features of the imagination of artists and of their ability to wander over the mass of treasure stored in their memories (see Wheeler 1995). Particularly striking is the contrast between the painting and the photograph. The latter lacks the infinite richness and complexity of the painting. And more generally life in the nineteenth century city trained the eye to anticipate shock and hence destroyed the ability 'to attend to the infinite richness offered by art and nature alike' (cited in Mallett 1995: 54; note incidentally similarities with Simmel's analysis of the blasé attitude). The city bombards the eye with advertisements and yet offers nothing to be really looked at. There is a poverty of the imagination of the city; and the starkest of contrasts between most urban buildings and the 'grace of nature'. Modern London according to Ruskin teaches the 'adoration of chaos', compared with how in the natural world the eye is in perfect repose in the midst of profusion (cited in Mallett 1995: 57).

The critique of the sightseeing tourist is taken to the extreme in analysis of the 'hyper-real', those simulated experiences which have the appearance of being more 'real' than the original (Baudrillard 1981; Eco 1986). The sense of vision is reduced to a limited array of features, it is then exaggerated and it comes to dominate the other senses. Hyper-real places are characterised by surface which in no way responds to or welcomes the viewer. The sense of sight is seduced by the most immediate and visible aspects of the scene, such as the façades of Main Street in Disneyland (incidentally hyper-real experiences can also be organised around other senses, such as smell at the Fishing Heritage Centre in Grimsby in north-east England). What is not encountered in hyper-real places is the baroque (Jay 1992; Buci-Glucksmann 1984). Jay seeks to celebrate:

> the dazzling, disorientating, ecstatic surplus of images in baroque visual experience ... [the] rejection of the monocular geometricalization of the Cartesian tradition ... the baroque self-consciously revels in the contradictions between surface and depth, disparaging as a result any attempt to reduce the multiplicity of visual spaces into any one coherent essence.
>
> (1992: 187)

Jay talks of baroque planning being addressed not to reason but to the engagement and indulgence of all the senses as is found in some carnivals and festivals. He objects to the dominance of any single sense, or to the separation and hyper-real exaggeration of one (Jay 1992: 192). The baroque can be seen as the unexpected, the surprising, the unplanned, the incongruous. This critique partly parallels Sennett's examination of the blandness of the 'neutralised city' based upon fear of social contact with the stranger involving diverse senses and not just vision (1991). Sennett advocates the positive uses of disorder, contradiction and ambiguity in the development of contemporary cities.

Likewise feminists have argued that the concentration upon the visual sense, particularly developed through the male invention of objects that reduce the world to two-dimensional visual texts, over-emphasises appearance, image and surface. Irigaray argues that in western cultures: 'the preponderance of the look over the smell, taste, touch and hearing has brought about an impoverishment of bodily relations. The moment the look dominates, the body loses its materiality' (1978: 123; Mulvey 1989). The emphasis upon the visual reduces the body to surface, marginalises the multiple sensuousness of the body and impoverishes the relationship of the body to its environment. And at the same time the visual over-emphasises masculinist efforts to exert mastery over the female body, particularly through the voyeurism effected via the pornographic picture (Griffin 1981), and over nature or landscape which are commonly conceived to be a metaphor of the body of a passive woman lying out for male inspection (Plumwood 1993; Taylor J. 1994: 268). By contrast a feminist consciousness seeks to integrate all of the senses in a more rounded way which does not seek to exert mastery over the 'other' (Rodaway 1994: 123). Especially significant is the sense of touch to female sexuality. Irigaray argues that: 'Woman takes pleasure more from touching than from looking, and her entry into a dominant scopic regime signifies, again, her consignment to passivity: she is to be the beautiful object of contemplation' (cited in Jay 1993: 531). Other writers have particularly emphasised the significance of aural traditions in women's lives – to talking and listening, telling stories, to engaging in intimate detailed dialogue or gossip and to the use of the metaphor of 'giving voice' (Hibbitts 1994: 271–3).

The critique of the visual can also be seen in the literature on the gendering of empire. McClintock for example demonstrates how in the history of Empire there is an intertwining of male power over both colonised nature and the female body (1995). The male look over both is to seen as endlessly voyeuristic. She describes the tradition of male travel as an erotics of ravishment, as the western traveller conquered or fantasised the conquering of both nature and the native woman. McClintock characterises the tradition of converting non-European nature, often called virgin territory, into a feminised landscape, as that of the 'porno-tropics' (1995: chap. 1).

Finally, objects and technologies that extend the visual sense do not return the look to the viewer. Simmel argued that one cannot take through the eye without at the same time giving back through the eye. This he says produces the most complete reciprocity of person to person, face to face (Frisby and Featherstone 1997: 112). The look is returned when we momentarily see the other. However, the materialisation of the visual sense means that the look is not returned, the visual sense in relationship to objects is one-dimensional. This is what for Benjamin, Proust and Ruskin distinguishes the flat unresponsive photograph from the aura, plenitude and responsiveness of a painting (Mallett 1995: 52–4). Some objects can give back something to the viewer, such as the 'affordances of nature' (see Chapter 8 below). This is also why Levinas argues for an 'ethics of blindness' since sight distances subject and object. Touch re-establishes proximity. It is the face that speaks and establishes authentic discourse of face-to-face, as opposed to the instrumental manipulation of the visual (Levinas 1985).

I have therefore described the impact of particular objects and hybrids of visual representation, especially photographs, maps, landscapes and screens. I have shown how the visual sense has generated an array of intersecting hybrids that have come to overwhelm the other senses. And I have considered some of the main critiques mounted to the dominance of the visual, implicit in which are claims for the superiority of the other senses to which I now turn more briefly.

Smelling, listening, touching

I return to nineteenth-century England. The House of Commons Select Committee of 1838 argued that because there were whole areas of London through which no thoroughfares passed the lowest class of person was therefore secluded from the observation and influence of 'better educated neighbours' (Stallybrass and White 1986: 134). Engels likewise noted how the social ecology of the industrial city had the effect of 'hiding from the eyes of wealthy gentlemen and ladies ... the misery and squalor that ... complement ... their riches and luxury' (cited in Marcus 1973: 259). And it was claimed that such 'lower' classes would be transformed and improved once they did become visible to the middle and upper classes, both through surveillance of their behaviour and through the inculcation of politeness. There are of course parallels with the rebuilding of Paris and the hugely enhanced visibility, to see and be seen, which resulted from the replacement of the street layout of medieval Paris by the grand boulevards of the Second Empire (Berman 1983).

These references in mid-nineteenth-century British Parliament demonstrate how visibility was central to the regulation of the lower classes within urban areas. However, this is not all that was involved here. As the 'other' class was now seen moving through the massive cities of nineteenth-century Britain, the upper class sought also not to touch them (unless of course they were prostitutes or domestic servants who could be touched by upper class men). Notions of 'contagion' and 'contamination' were the tropes through which nineteenth-century city life was apprehended by that upper class (Stallybrass and White 1986). As the 'promiscuity' of the public space became increasingly unavoidable so the upper and middle classes sought to avoid touching the potentially contaminating 'other', the 'dangerous classes'.

This was even reflected in the development of Victorian domestic architecture designed to regulate the flows of bodies, keeping servants apart from the family 'below stairs', adults apart from children who were in the nursery, and male children apart from female children. There were:

> two currents of 'circulation' in a family dwelling ... There is the activity of the master and his friends, which occurs on the most visible, genteel and accessible routes, and there is the 'circulation' of the servants, tradesmen and everyone else who provides the home with services, and this should take place in the least conspicuous and most discreet way possible.
>
> (contemporary commentator quoted in Roderick 1997: 116)

Thus the upper class mainly sort to gaze upon the other, while for example standing visibly on their balconies and overlooking the 'other'.

The balcony took on special significance in nineteenth-century life and literature as the place from which one could gaze but not be touched, could participate in the crowd yet be separate from it. It was one of the earliest examples of how the city of touch is turned into the city of visibility (see Robins 1996: 20). According to Benjamin the balcony demonstrates superiority over the crowd, as the observer 'scrutinizes the throng' (1969: 173).

The later development of the skyscraper, beginning in 1880s Chicago, with their panoramic windows also enabled those inside to gaze down and across the crowd, while being insulated from the smells and the potential touch of those below. In Chicago the avoidance of the smells of the meat processing industry was a particularly important spur to building skyscrapers up into the light. And there are parallels with the way in which the contemporary tourist bus gives a bird's eye view, in but not of the crowd, gazing down upon the crowd in safety, without the heat, the smells and the touch. It is as though the scene is being viewed on a screen, and sounds, noises and the contaminating touch are all precluded because of the empire of the gaze effected through the windows of the bus. Thus the dominance of sight over the dangerous sense of smell has been effected through a number of physical objects and technologies, such as the balcony, the skyscraper and the air-conditioned bus (see Edensor 1999).

Smell was particularly significant in the cultural construction of the nineteenth-century western city. It demarcated the unnaturalness of the city. Stallybrass and White argue that in the mid-nineteenth century: 'the city ... still continued to invade the privatised body and household of the bourgeoisie as smell. It was, primarily, the sense of smell which enraged social reformers, since smell, whilst, like touch, encoding revulsion, had a pervasive and invisible presence difficult to regulate' (1986: 139). Smells played key roles in the nineteenth-century construction of class relations within the large cities. Cobbett described such towns as 'unnatural embossments; these white swellings, these odious wens, produced by corruption and engendering crime, misery and slavery' (cited in Bunce 1994: 14). Likewise Birmingham was seen by Robert Southey as involving: 'noise ... beyond description ... The filth is sickening ... active and moving ... which fills the whole atmosphere and penetrates everywhere' (cited in Bunce 1994: 15). The upper class in nineteenth-century British cities experienced a particular 'way of sensing'. George Orwell noted similarly powerful odours along the road to Wigan Pier in the 1930s (1937: 159).

The romantic construction of nature was powerfully forged through the odours of death, madness and decay that were thought to be particularly present in the industrial city (Tuan 1993: 61–2; Classen *et al.* 1994: 165–9; Corbin 1986: chap. 9, on the 'stench of the poor' in Paris). There was a pronounced rhetoric of the delights of the 'open air' (that is air that did not smell) for those apparently confined to living within the nineteenth-century city. While the countryside came increasingly to be desired because of its visual qualities mediated through the representation of space via the notion of landscape, the industrial town was seen as thoroughly polluted, as unnaturally invading all the human orifices. In *Hard Times* Dickens described the river in Coketown that 'ran purple with ill-smelling dye', while Ruskin described nineteenth-century industrial London as 'that great foul city ... stinking – a ghastly heap of fermenting brickwork, pouring out poison at every pore' (cited in Bunce 1994: 15). It was the smells of the city that became particularly central to the representation of the countryside. However, that was paradoxical since rural England was rich with odours, of farm animals, raw sewage, rotting vegetables, smoke and especially foul-smelling stagnant water (see Giblett 1996: 22–3 on how stagnant water is culturally associated with death, darkness and disease).

It is normally thought that smell is much more developed amongst so-called savages than amongst those who are apparently civilised (Porteous 1985, 1990; Corbin 1986; Classen *et al.* 1994; Tuan 1993: 55–6). Smell is generally denigrated within western culture. Particular venom is directed at those places of ambivalence where land and water meet, which are neither one nor the other. Such wetlands are inimical to the concept of 'landscape' and they and their populations produce simultaneous fascination and horror: 'These sensations are produced more by the immediate and visceral senses of smell, taste and touch than by the distancing and masterful senses of sight and hearing' (Giblett 1996: 13). These are places where the smells of the 'unhomely' seep out of the ground, invading the nostrils of those present. Smells cannot be appreciated in terms of western aesthetic theory. There is a 'lack of an aesthetics appropriate to the smells, textures and tastes of the wetland' (Giblett 1996: 33; and see *passim* on the swamp as 'feminine'). Part of curious ambivalence of the wetland stems from their inaccessibility by normal means of transportation. It is impossible to move across them and hence to see them. As the narrator states in C.S. Forester's *African Queen*, 'no place could be beautiful that presented navigational difficulties' (cited in Giblett 1996: 18).

Lefebvre however strongly argues that the production of different spaces even within modernity is bound up with smell. He says that 'where an intimacy occurs between 'subject' and 'object', it must surely be the world of smell and the places where they reside' (1991: 197). Olfaction seems to provide a more direct and less premeditated encounter with the environment; and one that cannot be turned on and off. It provokes an unmediated sense of the surrounding environment, of proximate objects, townscapes and landscapes. Tuan argues that the directness and immediacy of smell provides a sharp contrast with the abstractive and compositional characteristics of sight (1993: 57; and see 1979). This power of smell can be analysed in terms of the diverse 'smellscapes' that organise and mobilise people's feelings about particular places (including what one might also call 'tastescapes') and about particular peoples. This concept brings out how smells are spatially ordered and place-related (Porteous 1985: 369). In particular, the olfactory sense seems particularly important in evoking memories of very specific places, normally because of certain physical objects and their characteristic smells which are thought to inhabit certain places. Tuan notes that, while sights from his childhood haunts were not powerful enough to invoke childhood memories, the momentary smell of seaweed was sufficient: 'Odo[u]r has this power to restore the past because, unlike the visual image, it is an encapsulated experience that has been left largely uninterpreted and undeveloped' (Tuan 1993: 57).

And even if we cannot name the particular smell it can still help to create and sustain the sense of a particular place or experience that has been visited or lived in previously. It can generate both revulsion and attraction; and can play a major role in constructing and sustaining major distinctions of social taste. Even the smells of the swamp can appeal; Thoreau talks of 'a strong and wholesome fragrance' (cited in Giblett 1996: 232). Rodaway summarises the power of smell in relationship to place: 'the perception of an odour in or across a given space, perhaps with varying intensities, which will linger for a while and then fade, and a differentiation of one smell from another and the association of odours with particular things, organisms, situations and emotions which all contribute to a sense of place and the character to places' (1994: 68). It should also be noted that there have been huge programmes to eliminate the smells of certain places, especially the ambivalent wetlands, to civilise and masculinise huge areas of slimy smelliness and to make them fit for modern farming and visual, aesthetic appreciation (Giblett 1996: 47–50).

Examples within literature of these associations of smell with place include Tolstoy, who described the smells following a spring thunderstorm as 'the odour of the birches, of the violets, the rotting leaves, the mushrooms, and the wild cherry' (quoted Tuan 1993: 62). Similarly G.K. Chesterton wrote of 'the brilliant smell of water, the brave smell of stone, the smell of dew and thunder, the old bones buried under' (quoted Rodaway 1994: 73). While more recently Toni Morrison writes in the *Song of Soloman* of how:

> On autumn nights, in some parts of the city, the wind from the lake [Superior] brings a sweetish smell to shore. An odor like crystallized ginger, or sweet iced tea with a dark clove floating in it ... there was this heavy spice-sweet smell that made you think of the East and striped tents ... The two men ... could smell the air, but they didn't think of ginger. Each thought it was the way freedom smelled, or justice, or luxury, or vengeance.
>
> (1989: 184–5; see also Rushdie 1995: 307; Roy 1997)

McClintock provides a related examination of the role of a particular object, soap, in relationship to the British empire, as the British travelled out and lived abroad. Her book is entitled *Imperial Leather* and quotes a Unilever Company Slogan from the period: 'Soap is Civilization' (1995: 207). Soap advertising had two main effects. First, it reinforced the British cult of domesticity and made this definitive of national identity, through what McClintock terms 'domesticating Empire'. And second, the advertising generated notions of cleanliness and hygiene which would civilise the unwashed natives who had still to learn that smelling of Imperial Leather was the mark of the civilised world. Pears advertising in particular was characterised by ideas of hygiene and purification (in which white is presumed to be hygienic). So the politics of smell did not only enable the production of new commodities for the mass market. It also helped to construct the nature of the colonial encounter between the colonists and those colonised, to domesticate and purify it, and to invest the complex relations with intimate distinctions of bodily smell. New notions of the natural hygienic body came to be imposed by colonial visitors, especially though the real and metaphorical significance of soap and related products which supposedly purify bodily odours. But Ruark captures the paradoxical smellscape of this colonial power when he describes: 'the smell of white man, the white man's food and drink and clothing, the greasy stink of the white man's petrol fumes and belching diesel exhausts' (cited in Rodaway 1994: 72).

Simmel indeed argues that the sense of smell is a particularly 'dissociating sense', transmitting more repulsions than attractions (Frisby and Featherstone 1997: 119). He talks of 'olfactory intolerance', suggesting for example that hostility between Germans and Jews has been particularly generated by distinctions of smell (see Guérer 1993: 27). More generally he thought that the 'effluvia' of the working class posed a threat to social solidarity (Frisby and Featherstone 1997: 118). This became even more pronounced as during the twentieth century domestic hygiene has been very unevenly introduced, reinforcing class attitudes of social and moral superiority. The stigma of odour has provided a constant basis of stratification, resulting from what Simmel terms the 'invincible disgust inspired by the sense of smell' (cited in Guérer 1993: 34).

Modern societies have apparently reduced the sense of smell by comparison with the other senses (as argued by Lefebvre and others, 1991). Pre-modern societies had been very much characterised by distinctions of smell (see Classen *et al.* 1994, on the significance of aroma within the classical world). In modern societies there is an apparent dislike of strong odours and the emergence of various technologies, objects and manuals which seek to purify smells out of everyday life. These include the development of public health systems which separate water from sewerage and which involve channelling sewerage underground away from both the nose and the eye. The development of this in-human complex resulted from the nineteenth-century sanitary reform movement and the structure of 'differentiation-circulation' (see Roderick 1997). Corporeal functions and processes came to occupy a 'proper place' within the home; they were increasingly spatially differentiated from each other based on the control and regulation of the various bodily and piped fluids. In particular as water came to be piped separately from sewerage so it was possible to wash the whole body much more frequently; bath and shower technology were developed and also came to be given a 'proper place' within the home. A lack of smell was taken to indicate personal and public cleanliness, while perfumes become more confined in use to adult women who tend to prefer simpler rather than complex body perfumes. Domestic arrangements are developed so that animal and other smells are excluded. The air is kept 'fresh'. Modern societies are sensitive to smell and institutions organise to prevent those smells which are deemed to be 'unnatural' (these may of course include many smells such as rotting vegetables which are quite 'natural').

Bauman indeed argues that: 'Modernity declared war on smells. Scents had no room in the shiny temple of perfect order modernity set out to erect' (1993b: 24). Modernity sought to neutralise smells by creating zones of control in which the senses would not be offended. Zoning became an element of public policy in which planners accepted that repugnant smells are in fact an inevitable by-product of urban-industrial society. Refuse dumps, sewage plants, meat processing factories, industrial plants and so on are all spaces in which bad smells are concentrated, and are typically screened-off from everyday life by being situated on the periphery of cities. Domestic architecture developed which confined smells to particular areas of the home, to the backyard, the water-closet and the toilet. This war of smell within modernity was carried to the extreme in the Nazi period, where the Jews were routinely referred to as 'stinking' and that their supposed smell was associated with physical and moral corruption (Classen *et al.* 1994: 170–5).

But smell is a subversive sense since it cannot be wholly banished (Bauman 1993b). Smell reveals the artificiality of modernity; it shows following Latour that we have never been really modern (1993). The modern project to create a pure, rational order of things is undermined by the sweet smell of decomposition that continuously escapes control and regulation. Thus the 'stench of Auschwitz' could not be eliminated even when at the end of the war the Nazis desperately tried to tried to conceal what had happened through ridding the camps of the stench of death (Classen *et al.* 1994: 175). Even more poignantly, Barham discusses how the survivors of Auschwitz sought to recapture forgotten habits such as using a toothbrush or toilet paper, as well as recapturing 'forgotten tastes and smells – blossom, the sweet smell of rain in spring'. This was by contrast with Auschwitz 'where the rain smells of diarrhoea and the winds carry the odour of burning flesh' (Barham 1992: 40; Clarke *et al*. 1996).

The way in which smells emanate from diverse objects, including especially the human body, results in the social significance and power of diverse hybrids such as sewerage systems, notions of hygiene and new discourses and technologies of domestic architecture. More generally Roderick argues that, although there are all sorts of *smelly* substances within houses and apartments (such as sewerage, dirty water and gas, as well as the *dangerous* flows of electricity and boiling water), modernity has sought to confine their flows within various channels. But of course these flowing substances are always threatening to seep through the walls of these channels and to enter the 'home', analogous to the way that blood does not stay within its own vessels (Roderick 1997: 128). Much women's work within the home has been based upon taking a special responsibility for these dirty fluids, somewhat paralleling Grosz's notion of the female body as 'a leaking, uncontrollable, seeping liquid; as formless flow; as viscosity, entrapping, secreting' (1994: 203; Shildrick 1997). Men only enter the scene when the seepage gets out of hand and it is they who have the responsibility for climbing along the vessels of the house, to clean and repair the pipes that flow above the ceilings and behind the walls, which confine the dirty and the dangerous.

So smells are 'dangerous'. Modern societies had attempted to channel them but without complete success. And more recently, attempts to regulate smells and to keep them flowing in their 'proper place' along the right channels have been partially reversed with the cultural turn to 'nature' (Strathern 1992). Recent smelly trends include the increased attraction of spicy 'oriental' foods and the increased use of natural, often eastern, perfumes for the bodies of both sexes and for the home. There are now even perfumes of leather, dirt, cappuccino and so on. There is a reduced emphasis upon antiseptic cleanliness and a greater use of materials and smells that are deemed to be 'natural' (such as lemon). Also there seems to be a much greater knowledge of and sensitivity to the smells of nature, especially flowers, plants and various environments. There is more use of smells in shops, offices and hotels, as well as a greater awareness of the malodorous smells of the motor car and of the many chemicals in rivers and seas that are metonymic of long-term global risks. Smell has returned, although of course it never went away. Somewhat analogously Giblett suggests that the ecological interest in saving the smelly wetlands stems from their postmodern ambivalence, a 'place of moving values, its meanings circulating and swirling around, like the waters sometimes do, never settling on one definition, never flowing to an end point' (1996: 229).

As with smell the acoustic sense of sound cannot be turned on and off. Both can be contrasted with the visual sense which can be controlled, by switching off a TV set, closing a photo album, or looking away from a landscape whose beauty is too painful to the eye. By contrast, ears cannot be closed and according to Simmel 'the ear is the egoistic organ pure and simple, which only takes but does not give' (Frisby and Featherstone 1997: 115). Ihde argues that, while we are at the edge of the visual sense that in a way always remains partially distant from us, we cannot avoid being at the very centre of the acoustic sense (1976). Its physicality and sociality are simply all around us, connecting us with others even though we do not necessarily reciprocate. Also sound is the result of activity – we hear activities which are often of considerable duration. Hearing takes time – it involves quite long-term sense. Hibbitts argues that 'a hearing-oriented world is a world necessarily focused on the ideas of "duration" and "becoming" (1994: 346).

The power of the acoustic sense is present even where there is an ominous silence. Examples of the 'sound of silence' can include the silence when an engine cuts out, or that experienced when camping in the middle of the arctic, or that which will last into the unimaginable future when an ecosystem dies. With regard to the last of these it is noteworthy that Rachel Carson's classic environmentalist analysis is called *Silent Spring* (1962; and see Tuan 1993: 75; Hibbitts 1994: 273). Tuan notes that before people began to live in large cities, noise was nature's prerogative. While people could shout and scream and play musical instruments, these noises could never match those of nature, of the roar of thunder, of a galeforce wind, of a river in full flood or the sound of a herd of elephants. These constituted overwhelming sensuous mediators between human society and the physical world.

In general it is argued that there has been a historical shift from predominantly oral/acoustic cultures to predominantly visual cultures. For example, aboriginal space is often interpreted as principally acoustic, resulting from the Songlines that meander over Australia and which provide an acoustic sense of place through movement (see Chatwin's *The Songlines*, 1988). Contemporary western space is, as we have seen, more obviously visual. In the US oral traditions have been particularly significant within Afro-American culture. Examples of such forms include storytelling, preaching, toasts, jazz, rap, as well as a suspicion of silence (see Hibbitts 1994: 276–9). Exclusively visual expression and experience have often been denigrated by Afro-American intellectuals. They have pointed out the superior integration of sound, touch, sight and movement within the African societies that provide the 'roots' of Afro-American culture.

More recently, just as with smell, there appears to be something of a reinvigorated oral culture within western societies. This is reflected in the ubiquity of musak, loudspeakers, ghetto-blasters, telephone bells, traffic, phonehold music, mobile phones, motor boats, walkmans, sex chat lines and so on (see Hibbitts 1994: 302–3). I also noted above how the ubiquitous TV is partly a technology of sound. The TV is endlessly on in the background in both homes and public spaces providing (supposedly) comforting sounds. Also there has been a revolution in sound that partly matches that of vision. This was given a tremendous spur with the 'invention' of pop music in the 1950s and 1960s, as well as technical changes which have produced astonishing improvements in the sound quality of classical music.

The Sony Walkman is iconic of this new post-modern soundscape. In this scape personally selected and listened into sounds are carried around with one as part of the extremely mobile human body that is able to construct a private space of sound in public (du Gay *et al.* 1997: 23). The 1990s sound icon is the mobile phone. This increasing need for 'aural distraction' also stems from the post-modern appeal of those repressed cultures which have more obviously emphasised sound, such as jazz and rap from within Afro-American culture. And even in places of silence such as libraries and galleries various objects now provide aural distraction, including cassette tapes, voice-based exhibits, interactive displays and simply background music.

At the same time it appears that much of this oral culture has come to be viewed as itself unnatural and environmentally polluting. It is common to designate certain sounds as against nature, as involving 'sound pollution'. This designation often involves employing a distinction of taste against those producing particularly polluting soundscapes (see Macnaghten and Urry 1998: chaps 4 and 6). Soundscapes are thus huge sites of contestation.

Finally, I have already touched on touch throughout this chapter. In particular I noted the efforts to transform cities so as to avoid what Canetti terms 'the touch of the unknown' (1973), to replace the city of touch which is full of mobile dangerous strangers, with the radiant city avoiding the 'city of touch' (Sennett 1994; Diken 1998: chap. 3). I have also noted the significance of touch within feminist theorising on the senses – with the argument that for women it is touch that is and should be the organising sense. We might also note the significance of human embodiment and how in all social life we necessarily move amongst bodies within cities which we continuously touch and are touched by, in a kind of reciprocity of contact, which is itself highly gendered (Robins 1996: 33; Shields 1997a). Moreover, unlike the see-er who can look without being seen, the touch-er is of course always touched (see Grosz 1993: 45).

Touch is also central to our relationships with objects. It is a delicate instrument for exploring and appreciating the physical world. Even without 'training' we develop considerable skills of touch by which objects give up to us many of their properties, of texture, strength, scale, contrast, material composition, uses and so on (see Tuan 1993). Often it is only because we have touched an object or walked or climbed up a particular place that we consider that we really know what it is and what it might do (Lewis 2000).

Conclusion

An extraordinary power has been historically exerted by the sense of sight: visual observation as the basis of epistemology and western scientific method; the influence of sight over the other senses and the consequences for class, gender and ethnic relations; the role of sight in relationship to corporeal travel and to the aesthetic appreciation of the scenic; the specialisation of the senses and especially sight in the later nineteenth century; the industrialisation of the visual sense and the enormous impact of visual images and later of simulations; the more general importance of visual technologies and objects, especially photographs, maps, landscapes and screens; and the role of vision in the disembodying of people's relationships with space and the proliferation of new hybrids organised around not what people 'possess' but upon their 'appearances' (Abercrombie and Longhurst 1998: 84; Debord 1994).

But vision has not simply got its own way. There has been the twentieth-century critique of the visual and the development of alternative visual paradigms. There are an exceptional array of spaces that characterise the post-modern world which militate against any direct and unmediated connections between a particular visual experience and a particular slice of an environment. Also there is sheer impact of the other senses which in many cases cannot be simply turned on and off and which in part depend upon their own forms of materialisation. Makimoto and Manners argue that all the senses are likely to be embodied in silicon and digitised within the next few decades (1997: chap. 10 on 'silicon senses'). Long-term memories are rarely just visual. Indeed objects and environments are mediated, contested and partially simulated and constituted complex sources of both desire and repulsion. And there are powerful hybrid forms that develop to regulate and to channel different flows of different substances along diverse pathways so as to avoid or to promote one or other sense.

Moreover, these different senses and the related mobilities that are desired and feared, avoided or sought out, beat to different temporal rhythms as they pass in and through people's day-to-day lives. Rodaway argues that sight is more 'temporal' than the other senses (1994: 124–6). Visual objects exist in both space and time; they have location relative to other objects, and they have duration relative to other objects as well. Film provides the closest analogy here. While watching a film we are aware of the movement of subjects and objects, and of time passing. Some details pass us by, while others proceed much more slowly. As the visual experiences appear to go past us, we are sometimes able to catch glimpses of this or that scene or person, we can linger on some events, and we may be able to put together a collection of temporally organised images. Rodaway summarises: 'Vision is time-specific, in the sense of when an object is illuminated in a particular way at a certain moment, and temporal in the sense that visual images persist over time and give continuity to geographical experience' (1994: 125). In the next chapter I suggest that vision has come to be hugely entangled with the development of a new time, instantaneous time. As the visual sense is digitised, so this sense has spun off and become increasingly dissociated from how people dwell in their regular lives. The visual sense has become interlinked with imaginative and virtual travel, with living life on the screen.

In Chapter 6 on dwelling I suggest that because of the extraordinary materialisation and digitisation of the visual sense, so other senses of smell, sound, touch and 'unmediated' sight remain important to people's sense of belonging. These other senses appear to provide a fragmented and longer-term sense of time. They are more immanent and do not enable us to grasp the same sense of instantaneous time. In Chapters 5 and 6 I show the importance of these temporal rhythms and how different senses and different mobilities are organised in, and through, and sometimes against, various times and memories.

Chapter 5

Times

> ... man is nothing; he is, at most, the carcass of time.
> (Karl Marx, in Marx and Engels 1976: 127)

Introduction

The last chapter ended with some brief comments on the temporal implications of the different senses. In this chapter I confront the issue of time directly and seek to shadow that a reconfigured sociology has to place time at its very centre. This is partly because of the way in which time has come on to the academic agenda criss-crossing disciplinary boundaries and offering opportunities for novel intellectual developments. At the same time new technologies appear to be generating new kinds of time which dramatically transform the opportunities for, and constraints upon, the mobilities of peoples, information and images. Mobilities are all about temporality. Also, new metaphors of time have become influential – particularly the notion of 'timeless' or 'virtual' or 'instantaneous' time which I elaborate below.

But time is not a simple topic as will come clear through the array of materials to be confronted in this chapter. Why does it cause such difficulties? First, unlike some aspects of space, time is, as we noted, invisible to the senses (Elias 1992: 1). Thus we always have to view time through various indicators, such as the clock and the calendar. There is then a complexly mediated relationship between these measuring devices and 'time'. Some writers propose that time is in fact merely these methods of measurement; others that these measuring devices are metaphors for time; and others again that it is a kind of category mistake to conflate lived or real time with its forms of measurement. There are of course many such indicators of the passage of time that have imposed very different temporal divisions upon human history. Such divisions – the day, week, year, decade, century and millennium – often engender enormously powerful emotional sentiments (as with the millennium: see Gould 1997).

Second, it has been widely shown that there is no single time but only a variety of times (see Adam 1995b). Hawking states in the most widely bought book on time: 'there is no unique absolute time, but instead each individual has his own personal measure of time that depends on where he [sic] is and how he is moving' (1988: 33; such a personal sense of time is normally known as *Eigenzeit*: see Nowotny 1994). Moreover, the meaning of time is relative to its system of measurement. According to Einstein, we can imagine as many clocks as we want to (cited in Nowotny 1994: 20). I will elaborate below various clocks and various times. Much historical research also shows enormous variation in the meaning of time and in the degree to which words denoting time feature within the languages of different cultures (Gell 1992).

Third, there is a longstanding dispute as to whether time is an absolute entity, possessing its own nature or particularity as Newton maintained; or whether time, as Leibniz argued, is merely 'an *order* of successions' (quoted in Körner 1955: 33). So is time an absolute separate from any objects in nature, or is the universe comprised of various objects which happen to exhibit temporal relationships between each other and where time itself does nothing? A further dispute is whether time possesses directionality. Is there an arrow of time such that irreducible effects result from time's passage; or is time reversible and there is no distinction between what is past and what is future, as Newton and Einstein both presume (see Coveney and Highfield 1990)? I shall not comment on the scientific literature but I argue that, even if time 'on its own' cannot be said to possess powers which are separate from the interrelationships between objects, different times do seem to exert significantly different social and natural powers and directionality. I discuss the powers and directionality of clock-time and instantaneous time (and in Chapter 6 of 'glacial time') (Smart 1963: chap. 7; Coveney and Highfield 1990). So while there is not an absolute time as such, there are different time-regimes which possess varied powers to transform the physical and social worlds. Such times are best viewed as much social as they are natural, or what can be seen as further hybrids.

Fourth, human activities with regard to these various times are extremely diverse. Some social organisations are structured around the saving of time, since 'time is money' or at least something like money, and hence minimising time or maximising activity (especially someone else's activity) within a fixed period of time, is what is sought. But with other social practices it is the slow passing of time that is enjoyable and desired. The pleasures of time are especially intertwined with the embodied (or sensed) nature of our relationships with objects and environments. For example, corporeal travel is normally examined within the academy in terms of the saving of time or the covering of more space. But this ignores one obvious reason for travel, and that is pleasure. Travel is a performance and some categories of aesthetic judgement are pertinent to its understanding (see Adler 1989 on travel as 'performed art'). And such travel may entail new forms of sociability and playfulness as people travel slowly through time, as on a cruise ship, on a leisurely inter-war motor tour or on a meandering stroll though a supposedly unchanged medieval townscape (see Chapter 3 above).

Finally, most social scientists have operated with a conception of 'social time' that is separate from, and opposed to, the sense of time employed by the natural sciences. Social scientists have generally held that natural and social times are quite different from each other. And this has given rise to deep confusion as to what is particular to human times, as well as ignoring the insights that the physical sciences can provide with regard to the remarkable diversity of times. In the following I develop notions of time influenced in part by Whitehead, who provided early reflection upon the significance of twentieth century physics for notions of time and space (see discussion in Harvey 1996: 256–61). Whitehead rejects the idea that time and space are outside the very relations between objects (and subjects). Time and space are not separate from the processes by which the physical and social worlds operate. His adoption of an 'internal relations' conceptualisation leads also to the claim that there are now thought to be multiple times and indeed multiple spaces.

In the next section I set out some of the main themes in the 'social' analysis of time, before turning to the hermeneutic and phenomenological traditions. In relationship to the themes of dwelling and mobility, I argue that this 'other' tradition needs to be incorporated into the analysis. Following this the distinction between natural and social times is repudiated, bringing out the more general need to transcend the duality of nature and society that has exerted such a baleful influence upon western societies and environments. I show that one particular time, clock-time, has played a singularly powerful role within western societies. Following this I turn to the claim that a new time has more recently come powerfully into view – time as instantaneous or virtual. I consider some of the technologies and objects that have ushered in such a new time and consider their interconnections with the various mobilities I outlined in Chapter 3.

Social time and lived time

Most social scientific accounts have presumed that time is in some sense social and hence separate from, and opposed to, the time of nature. Durkheim argued in *Elementary Forms* that only humans have a concept of time, and that time in human societies is abstract and impersonal and not simply individual (1968). Moreover, this impersonality is socially organised; it is what Durkheim refers to as 'social time'. Hence, time is a 'social institution' and the category of time is not natural but social. Time is an objectively given social category of thought produced within societies and which therefore varies as between societies. Social time is different from, and opposed to, the time(s) of nature.

Sorokin and Merton proceed to distinguish between societies as to whether there is a separate category of clock-time, which is over and above this notion of social time (1937). Much anthropological writing has been concerned with this relationship between time that is based upon 'naturally' determined social activities, such as those around birth and death, night and day, planting and harvesting and so on; and that time which in some way is 'unnaturally' imposed by the clock (Gell 1992).

Sorokin also notes that while most societies have some form of 'week', this can consist of anything from three to sixteen days (1937; Colson 1926; Coveney and Highfield 1990: 43–4; Hassard 1990). No other animal appears to have adopted the week as a temporal unit; or to have developed a unit so independent of astronomic divisions. The seven day week derives from the Babylonians who in turn influenced the Judaic conception of the week consisting of six days plus the sabbath. There have been various unsuccessful attempts to change the length of the week – such as in post-revolutionary France after 1789 with a decimal ten day week and in the Soviet Union with a five day week (see Gould 1997).

Overall clock-time has been presumed to be central to the organisation of modern societies and thus to their constitutive social (and scientific) practices. Such societies are centred around the emptying out of time (and space) and the development of an abstract, divisible and universally measurable calculation of time. The first characteristic of modern machine civilisation is temporal regularity organised via the clock, an invention in many ways more important than even the steam engine. Thompson famously argues that an orientation to time, rather than to task or social activities, becomes the crucial characteristic of industrial capitalist societies based upon the maximal subjection of nature (1967).

This argument depends upon the classical writings of Marx and Weber. Marx shows that the regulation and exploitation of labour time is the central characteristic of capitalism. The exchange of commodities is in effect the exchange of labour times. Capitalism entails the attempts by the bourgeoisie, either to extend the working day, or to work labour more intensively. If the working class is not able to resist such pressures, competition will compel capitalists to extend the work period beyond its social and physical limits. There will be 'over-consumption' of labour-power and it will be in the interests of the bourgeois class as a whole to introduce limits on continuous extensions of the working day. However, this functional need not ensure that reductions on the length of the working day did occur. Capitalist competition has to be constrained in the interests of capital (as well as those of the workforce; see Chapter 8 below).

Later writers have demonstrated just how much conflict in industrial capitalism is focused around time, around capital's right to organise and extend the hours of work and labour's attempt to limit those hours. All these disputes focus around the standardised units of clock time which separate work from its social and physical context. Time is commodified. It comes to constitute the measure of work and structures the division of labour and the ways in which humans relate to their physical environment (see Dickens 1996).

Marx does not though develop just how time comes to be internalised and constitutes people as temporal subjects, having both an orientation to clock-time as well as being disciplined by such a time. Weber, Foucault and Mumford all argue that the origins of such a subjectivity lay in the systems of time orchestrated within Benedictine monasteries. At one point there were 40,000 spread across Europe (Adam 1995b: 64–5). In such monasteries the system of time-keeping synchronised social activities, with annual, weekly and daily routines, a system which was revolutionary when originally introduced in the sixth century. Idleness was not permitted. And according to Weber, the Protestant Ethic had a similar effect in freeing people from their dependence upon 'natural impulses' and developing themselves as subjects oriented to the saving of time and the maximising of activity:

> Waste of time is thus the first and in principle the deadliest of sins. The span of human life is infinitely short and precious to make sure of one's own election. Loss of time through sociability, idle talk, luxury, even more sleep than is necessary to health ... is worthy of absolute moral condemnation.
>
> (1930: 158)

The spirit of capitalism adds a further twist to this emerging subjectivity. Benjamin Franklin maintained 'time is money' – to waste time is, he says, to waste money (Weber 1930: 48). People therefore have taken on the duty to be frugal with time, not to waste it, to use it to the full and to manage the time of oneself and that of others with utmost diligence.

However, time is not literally quite like money. Time can be stored up and exchanged (in time-share holiday accommodation, for example), it can be shared to a limited degree (in a baby-sitting circle, for example), and people vary enormously in their capacity to use time effectively (hence 'time-management'). But these are very limited compared with the ways that the circulation of money has grown and infiltrated itself into almost every corner of the globe (see Leyshon and Thrift 1997). But clock-time constrains human activity more firmly than does money since it methodically passes and subjects everyone and much of nature to its passage and to the resulting minute units and disciplines that it engenders. 'Time is money' is thus at best a useful metaphor.

Indeed rather than time being like money, money is time (Adam 1990:

114). In many cases having a lot of time is of little value to people without money, such as the poor, the unemployed and inmates of total institutions (see Goffman 1968). What is important is access to money which enables time to be put to good use (even if it still passes) and to organise and structure the time of others. Time therefore varies as to the differential possession of money, as well as to differentials of status and power. Important social inequalities arise through the unequal social relations surrounding time (and space).

Although the power of clock-time is well-established, the story of its emergence is more complex than Thompson suggests (1967; Glennie and Thrift 1994). Up to the sixteenth century daily life in England was task-oriented (except in monasteries), the week was not a very important unit of time, and the seasons and related fairs and markets and the church calendar were the bases for temporal organisation. This began to change between the sixteenth and eighteenth centuries when there was some growth in the ownership of domestic clocks; the increasing use of public clocks and bells; the growth of schooling for the upper and middle classes where activities began to be timetabled; the efforts by Puritans to organise work on a weekly basis; the increasing development of a cash economy which implied the need to calculate days of work and rates of pay; and the introduction of the term 'punctuality' into popular vocabulary.

By the eighteenth century time had thus become more clearly 'disembedded' from social activities (see Giddens 1984, on such disembedding). Partly this was due to innovations within the world of work concerned to instil a new time discipline for the emerging industrial work force. Innovations included the use of the hooter and the clock, the regularisation of the week into 'work' and 'leisure' and the curtailment of feasts and wakes holidays. But it was also to do with changes within the leisured English upper class that developed visiting patterns of Byzantine temporal complexity. Indicators of such changes included the use of gongs and house bells, dressing for formal dinner, the leaving of cards and an increasingly elaborate social timetable based on particular calls being permitted at specific times (Davidoff 1973).

The increasing desire for, and means of, corporeal travel were key elements in the development of clock-time. Simmel noted that great planning and precision are necessary within the 'metropolis' in order that social and business life can take place. The relationships and affairs of metropolitan life are so complex that 'without the strictest punctuality in promises and services the whole structure would break down' (Frisby and Featherstone 1997: 177). Metropolitan life would be inconceivable without the punctual integration of social activities into a stable and impersonal time schedule. The extensive use of clocks and watches are necessary in order that people's travel arrangements and appointments occur efficiently, so that there is not 'an ill-afforded waste of time' (Frisby and Featherstone 1997: 177). Clock-time is functionally necessary for the complex social patterns and relatively long distances that had to be travelled within the rapidly growing late nineteenth- and early twentieth-century metropolises.

And even greater distances came to be travelled, not within, but *between* the towns and cities of the rapidly industrialising societies of western Europe and north America. Such longer range mass mobility was crucially significant in enhancing the power of clock-time. Gamst brings out the importance of railway journeys, and of related work practices on the railway, in generating the standardisation of clock-time during the course of the nineteenth century (1993). The timetabling of appointments for those travelling between towns and cities came to necessitate a further need for punctuality, precision and calculability in social life occurring across an extended spatial scale.

In late eighteenth-century England there was a substantial increase in long-range mobility with the establishment of regular coach services. By 1830 for example there were 48 coaches a day travelling between London and Brighton and the journey time had been cut to 4.5 hours (Walvin 1978: 34). But it was only from the 1830s onwards that a national system of turnpike trusts was created and journey times throughout the country fell dramatically. Coach travel though was still expensive and inconvenient. Most towns kept their own time zones and the coach guard had to adjust his timepiece to cope with these different times as the coach passed through each town.

This problem of temporal co-ordination grew even more acute with the development of the railways during the 1840s. Following Gladstone's 1844 Railway Act large numbers of the 'labouring classes', as well as those more affluent, began to travel very significant distances, both on business and increasingly for leisure (Urry 1990: 21; see Chapter 3 above). And yet different times were kept in the different towns through which the railway passed. The Great Western Railway timetable of 1841 contained the following useful information: 'London time is kept at all the stations on the railway, which is about 4 minutes earlier than Reading time; 5 minutes before Cirencester time; 8 minutes before Chippenham time; and 14 minutes before Bridgewater time' (quoted in Thrift 1990: 122). But this lack of national time-keeping could not survive and by around 1847 the railway companies, the Post Office and many towns and cities adopted Greenwich Mean Time (GMT). A standardised national clock-time thus was established in order that mass mobility could develop during the Victorian period.

One commentator writing in 1839 suggested that railways 'compressed' time and space. If they were established all over England, then the whole population would: 'sit nearer to one another by two-thirds of the time which now respectively alienates them ... As distances were thus annihilated, the surface of the country would, as it were, shrivel in size until it became not much larger than one immense city' (quoted Schivelbusch 1986: 34; Harvey 1996: 242–2). Likewise the poet Heine talked of the tremendous foreboding that he felt with the opening of the rail link between Paris and Rouen. He said that 'the elementary concepts of time and space have begun to vacillate. Space is killed by the railways' (quoted Schivelbusch 1986: 34).

The second half of the nineteenth century saw increasing co-ordination of times between European countries and between Europe and north America. Some key developments in mobility included cross-Channel and then cross-Atlantic steamship travel; international telegraph services; the establishment of a system of national time to co-ordinate the services covering the enormous distances travelled by American railways; and the international conference held in 1884 which adopted GMT as the basis for calculating time throughout the world. These intersecting developments resulted from the desire for new kinds of social practice, for mass travel and new modes of communicating between people located both within countries and then between countries. Nguyen summarises the profound consequences of GMT and of the synchronisation of the time zones of the rest of the world:

> gradually all other countries began to adopt the time zone system based on the prime meridian of Greenwich, the specifically western temporal regime which had emerged with the invention of the clock in medieval Europe became the universal standard of time measurement. Indeed its hegemonic development signified the irreversible destruction of all other temporal regimes in the world, the last vestiges of which remain only in the form of historical and anthropological curiosities.
> (1992: 33; see also Zerubavel 1988; the Netherlands only synchronised itself with the rest of the world in 1940)

Greenwich time is a mathematical fiction that both effected and symbolised the emasculation of how humans actually appear to experience time (and space). World time was established in 1913 with the first signal from the Eiffel Tower sent across the globe.

The spread of clock-time into almost all aspects of social life has been extraordinary. It has meant the general replacement of kairological time, which is the sense of time when it is said that *now* is the time to do something irrespective of what any clock indicates (Gault 1995: 155). Kairological time is based upon using the experience of the past in order to develop the sense of when a particular event should take place in the future, of just when it is the right time for something to occur. Education is a particular context where this kairological time has been almost entirely replaced by clock-time. Thus lessons change, people move from room to room, French is spoken instead of German, maps are replaced with computers and so on, because the minute hand has moved from what is signified as 9.59 a.m. to 10 a.m. Adam summarises the awesome power of clock-time within western education:

> The activities and interactions of all its participants are orchestrated to a symphony of buzzers, bells, timetables, schedules and deadlines. These time markers bind pupils and staff into a common schedule within which their respective activities are structured, paced, timed, sequenced and prioritized. They separate and section one activity from another and secure conformity to a regular, collective beat.
>
> (1995b: 61)

I draw this discussion to a close by outlining the main characteristics of clock-time.

Clock-time

- the breaking down of time into a very large number of small precisely measured and invariant units
- the disembedding of time from meaningful social practices and from the apparently natural divisions of night and day, the seasons and movements of life towards death
- the widespread use of various means of measuring and indicating the passage of time: clocks, watches, timetables, calendars, hooters, schedules, clocking-on devices, bells, deadlines, diaries, alarm-clocks, and so on
- the precise timetabling of most work and leisure activities
- the widespread use of time as an independent resource which can be saved and consumed, deployed and exhausted
- the orientation to time as a resource to be managed rather than to time as activity or meaning
- the scientific transformation of time into mathematically precise and quantifiable measures in which time is reversible and possesses no direction
- the synchronised time-disciplining of schoolchildren, travellers, employees, inmates, holiday-makers and so on
- the synchronised measure of life across national territories and across the globe
- the permeation of a discourse around the need for time to be saved, organised, monitored, regulated and timetabled

---

These characteristics are not only produced by the widespread use of clocks and watches; indeed clocks of some sort had been in existence for some millennia. Rather clock-time is an appropriate metaphor for 'modern times'. During the latter half of the nineteenth and for most of the twentieth century these characteristics appear more or less simultaneously and transform the natural and social worlds (Adam 1990, 1995b, 1998; Nowotny 1994; Luhmann 1982; Rifkin 1987; Lash and Urry 1994: chap. 9). Adam notes that: 'neither the reckoning of time nor its measurement ... constitutes the specific nature of industrial [or modern] time. Rather industrial time is a time that is abstracted from its natural source; an independent, decontextualized, rationalized time. It is a time that is almost infinitely divisible into equal spatial units ... and related to as time *per se*' (1995b: 27).

Lefebvre summarises this march of clock-time through society and nature (1991: 95–6). He argues that the lived time experienced in and through nature has gradually disappeared. Time is no longer something that is visible and inscribed within space. It has been replaced by measuring instruments, clocks, which are separate from natural and social space. Time becomes a resource, differentiated off from social space. It is consumed, deployed and exhausted. There is the expulsion of lived (and kairological) time as 'clock-time' dominates. Lefebvre describes this changing nature of time in terms of metaphor. In pre-modern societies lived time is encrypted into space as in a tree-trunk, and like a tree-trunk shows the mark of those years that it has taken to grow. While in modern societies time is absorbed into the city such that lived time is invisible or reduced to its methods of measurement. Lived time 'has been murdered by society' (Lefebvre 1991: 96).

However, this distinction between clock-time and lived time needs greater specification than provided here. To do so I draw here on the distinction within the philosophy of time between the A- and the B-series of time (McTaggart 1927). I have so far mainly considered the B-series, which is the Aristotelian sense of time as 'before and after'. Events are seen as separate from each other and strung out along the fourth dimension (of time) such that they can be located as either before or after each other (see Gell 1992; Ingold 1993b; Osborne 1994). Each event in the B-series is viewed as separate and never changes its relationship to all other events. Time is taken to be an infinite succession of identical instants, each identifiable as 'before' or 'after' the other. Thus, if we consider event y; this occurred after x, it is still after x and will always be after x, whatever else happens. Statements about such phenomena are thus timelessly true. Many analysts have presumed that the physical world can be examined through the prism of what Benjamin terms the 'empty homogeneous' time of the B-series (loosely analogous to clock-time; Benjamin 1969).

This time can be distinguished from the A-series, the Augustinian sense of time indicated by the relationships of 'past-to-present-to-future'. Here past events are in part retained within the present and then carried forward into the future. Moreover, the present is not seen as an instant but as having duration. Both Husserl and Bergson bring out that the lived present endures. The past is not simply back there but is incorporated into that present, and it also embodies certain expectations of the future, most famously in Heidegger's anticipation of death as the transcendental horizon of human temporality (Osborne 1994). In the A-series, events can be differentiated in terms of their pastness, presentness and futurity; that is, time depends upon context. Various writers have explored aspects of the A-series.

George Herbert Mead adopts a consistently 'temporal' viewpoint (1959). He focuses upon how time is embedded within actions, events and roles, rather than seeing time as an abstract framework. Mead regards the abstract time of clocks and calendars, of the B-series, as nothing more than a 'manner of speaking'. What is 'real' for Mead is the present, hence his major work on time is *The Philosophy of the Present*. As he says: 'Reality exists in the present' (1959: 33). What we take to be the past is necessarily reconstructed in the present, each moment of the past is recreated afresh within the present. So there is no 'past' out there, or rather, back there. There is only the present, in the context of which the past is being continually recreated. It has no status except in the light of the emergent present. It is emergence that transforms the past and gives sense and direction to the future. This emergence stems from the interaction between people and the environment, humans being conceived by Mead as indissolubly part of nature. This emergence is always more than the events giving rise to it. Moreover, while the present is viewed as real, the past and future are ideational or 'hypothetical'. They are only open to us through the mind.

Heidegger likewise was concerned to demonstrate the irreducibly temporal character of human existence. He stresses in *Being and Time* that philosophy must return to the question of 'Being', something that had been obscured by the western preoccupation with epistemology (1962). And central to Heidegger's ontology of the Being is that of time, which expresses the nature of what human subjects are. Human beings are fundamentally temporal and find their meaning in temporality. Being is made visible in its temporal character and in particular the fact of movement from birth towards death. The movement towards death should not be viewed as a kind of perimeter but as something that necessarily permeates one's being. Birth and death are necessarily connected forming a unity. 'Dasein' is the 'between'. Being necessarily involves movement between birth and death or the mutual reaching out and opening up of future, past and the present. The nature of time should not of course be confused with the ways in which it is conventionally measured, such as intervals or instants. Measurable time-space has, he says, been imposed upon being and time in western culture. Feminist critics have argued that this Heideggerian notion of 'being unto death' signifies a masculine approach to time that emphasises the inevitability of movement towards death. Such a view is said to exclude women's concerns such as birth and the apparently time-generating capacity of procreation, and the need to protect the environment for future generations, for the 'children of our children' (see Adam 1995b: 94).

I now consider two writers who adopted a similar position to Heidegger but sought to integrate their analysis of time with that of space. Bergson distinguishes between *temps* and *durée*, the former being the sense of time as quantitative and divisible into spatial units (the B-series discussed above; 1950; 1991). But Bergson argues against such a spatialised conception of time and maintains instead that it is *durée* or lived duration that is thoroughly 'temporal'. *Durée* or time proper is the time of becoming. People should be viewed as in time rather than time being thought of as some discrete element or external presence. Time involves the 'permeation' of the supposedly separate moments of past, present and future; each flows into the other, as the past and future are created in the present.

Furthermore time is inextricably bound up with the body. People do not so much think real time but actually live it sensuously and qualitatively. Bergson argues that one's memory should not be viewed as a drawer or store, since such notions derive from incorrectly conceptualising time in a spatial fashion. Time is not 'spatial'. Memory thus can never be a simple representation of the past but should rather be viewed temporally. It is the piling up of the past upon the past that means that no element is simply present but is changed as new elements are endlessly accumulated.

A 'sociological' twist to Bergson's argument can be found in Halbwachs' examination of collective memory (1992). He emphasises the social, commemorative and festive institutions by which the past is stored and interpreted for the present and especially for the current generation (more generally, on how societies remember the past, see Connerton 1989). And Gurvitch more critically maintains that Bergson fails to develop a theory that elaborated the multiplicity of times that can be deduced from the categories of Bergsonian analysis (1964: 21–4, 1971). Two of these are of particular relevance here. The first is 'explosive time', the time where the past and present dissolve in the creation of an immediately transcended future. The emphasis is upon discontinuity and the contingent, what I term instantaneous time. The second is 'enduring time' – the time of slowed down long duration. The very distant past is projected into the present and the future. He describes this as the time of the ecological and it connects to what I refer to in the next chapter as glacial time (Gurvitch 1964: 31–3).

In Bergson's critique of the 'spatialised' conception of memory as a 'drawer', he privileges time over space and views the latter as abstract and

quantitative (Game 1995; Gurvitch 1964). But Bergson's account of duration is somewhat disembodied and does not deal with the qualitative
nature of space. Bachelard endeavours to remedy this problem in Bergson
through developing a conception of space that is qualitative and heterogeneous, rather than abstract, empty and static (1969). Bachelard seeks to
integrate such a notion of space back within a broadly Bergsonian conception of time. He maintains that such a sense of space as qualitative,
sensuous and lived ought to be central to Bergsonian time. There are three
components to this argument.

First, Bachelard argues that phenomenology is concerned with experiencing an image in its 'reverberations', not in terms of its visual impact. He
thus employs an aural rather than a visual metaphor through the idea of
sound waves. This notion of reverberation points to a movement between
the subject and object that disrupts any clear distinction between the two.
The metaphor implies an immediacy between subject and object that is not
the case with a visual appropriation of memory. Bachelard describes his
work as an ontology of 'reverberation' (1969: xvi; and see Chapter 4
above on the oral sense).

Second, Bachelard specifically considers the nature of the 'house' and
argues that it is not to be seen as a purely physical object. In particular it is
the site within which one's imagination and day-dreaming can take place
and be given free rein (Bachelard 1969: 6). And the home is also a
metaphor for intimacy. Houses are within us and we reside in houses. In
particular, all sorts of spaces, such as the house in which one is born, are
imbued with memory traces. And that belongingness derives from the
materiality of the particular place in question. Hetherington describes this
Bachelardian position: 'The smell of the sheets in the cupboard, the slope
of the cellar steps, the patch of paint picked off the edge of the window-sill
in a moment of childish boredom, all become the material substance
through which our memories are constituted … To dwell … is, through
daydream and memory, to bring back from the past that which has long
been forgotten and live within the reverberations of its remembered intimacy' (1995: 18).

Moreover, Bachelard argues that the very duration of time that is
Bergson's concern is itself dependent upon such spatial specificity. Space is
necessary to give quality to time. Or as Game expresses it: 'Space transforms time in such a way that memory is made possible' (1995: 201). Thus
a space such as a house plays a particularly significant role in the forming
and sustaining of memory. It shelters daydreaming. It is a metaphorical
space within which Bergsonian time operates.

Third, Bachelard presents a notion of memory as irreducibly embodied.
In particular our bodies do not forget the first house that we encounter.
Bachelard talks of a 'passionate liaison' between the body and this initial
house (1969: 15). Its characteristics are physically inscribed in us.

Memories are materially localised and so the temporality of memory is spatially rooted, according to Bachelard. He spatialises the temporality of memory. Houses are lived through one's body and its memories (Game 1995: 202–3). Without lived space the lived time of duration would be impossible.

This powerful set of arguments, which dissolve the boundaries of time and space, of the social and the bodily, of past-present-future, will be mainly considered in the next chapter. The problem with these formulations is that they deal with an exceptionally limited array of social practices – visiting a house, childhood, daydreaming. I seek to develop such notions but in relationship to a much wider variety of social practices and especially to powerful global networks and flows that rewarp social life across massively extended expanses of time and space.

In the next section I turn to one such set of powerful social practices, namely the physical sciences; and in the following section to diverse technologies which are reordering our experiences of the *durée* and especially of past-present-future in remarkable 'timeless' ways. The philosophical formulations discussed in this section remain highly normative and deal insufficiently with the awesome power of changing times and their institutional embodiments.

Natural and social times

Social scientists have insisted on the radical distinction between natural and social time. However, most of what they have seen as specifically social time is in fact generalised throughout nature. What social scientists and phenomenologists of time have treated as the specifically 'human' aspects of time are in fact characteristics of the physical sciences. Adam argues that: 'Past, present, and future, historical time, the qualitative experience of time, the structuring of 'undifferentiated change' into episodes, all are established as integral time aspects of the subject matter of the natural sciences' (1990: 150). Moreover, 'clock time, the invariant measure, the closed circle, the perfect symmetry, and reversible time [are] our creations' (Adam 1990: 150). The one component of time that cannot be generalised throughout nature is in fact clock-time, which is a human creation. But this is the very time which has been taken by the social sciences as the defining feature of natural time, as that time came to be historically separated from social time (see Elias 1992). Social science has thus operated with an inappropriate conception of time in the natural sciences, an almost non-temporal time, which can be described as Newtonian and Cartesian.

It is Newtonian because it is based on the notion of absolute time, that from 'its own nature, [it] flows equably without relation to anything eternal … the flowing of absolute time is not liable to change' (quoted

Adam 1990: 50; see Coveney and Highfield 1990: 29–31). Such absolute time is invariant, infinitely divisible into space-like units, measurable in length, expressible as a number and reversible. It is time seen essentially as space, as comprising invariant measurable lengths that can be moved along, both forwards *and* backwards. And it is Cartesian space because it is premised upon the dualisms of mind and body, repetition and process, quantity and quality, form and content, subject and object and so on.

However, twentieth-century science has transformed our understanding of the time of nature. It is no longer predominantly Newtonian and Cartesian (see Coveney and Highfield 1990). Hawking summarises:

> Space and time are now dynamic qualities: when a body moves, or a force acts, it affects the curvature of space and time – and in turn the structure of space-time affects the way in which bodies move and forces act.
>
> (1988: 33)

The social sciences have failed to see this transformation of time within the 'natural' sciences. Few have therefore followed Elias' argument that if we reflect upon time then we see how 'nature, society and individuals are embedded in each other and are interdependent' (1992: 16). Thus some of the extraordinary insights of twentieth-century natural science are not incorporated literally or metaphorically into the social sciences that rely upon now discredited notions of time.

There are many scientific 'discoveries' of the twentieth century that have transformed the understanding of time in nature (Adam 1990, 1998; Rifkin 1987; Hawking 1988; Coveney and Highfield 1990; Prigogine 1980; Casti 1994; Prigogine and Stengers 1984). First, Einstein showed (at the age of 26!) that there is no fixed or absolute time independent of the system to which it is refers. Time or *Eigenzeit* is thus a local, internal feature of any system of observation and measurement. Further, Einstein showed that time and space are not separate from each other but are fused into a four-dimensional time–space curved under the influence of mass. Amongst other consequences is the possibility of the past catching up with the future, of travelling through time down a wormhole and of the incredible warping of time–space that must have occurred in order to generate the singular event which initially created the universe.

Quantum theory provided further critique of orthodox notions of cause and effect. Quantum physicists describe a virtual state in which electrons seem to try out instantaneously all possible futures before settling into particular patterns. Quantum behaviour is mysteriously instantaneous. The notion of cause and effect no longer applies within such a microscopic indivisible whole. The position and momentum of any electron cannot be known with precision. Indeed the interrelations and interactions between the parts are far more fundamental than the parts themselves. Bohm refers to this as the occurrence of a dance without dancers.

Chrono-biologists have shown that it is not only human societies that experience time or organise their lives through time. Rhythmicity has been shown to be a crucial principle of nature, both within the organism and in the organism's relationships with the environment. And humans and other animals are not just affected by clock time but are themselves clocks. It seems that all plants and animals possess such a system of time that regulates the internal functions on a 24 hour cycle. Recent research indeed has revealed timekeeping genes. Biological time is thus not confined to ageing but expresses the nature of biological beings as temporal, dynamic, and cyclical. Change in living nature involves the notions of becoming and rhythmicity.

More generally, thermodynamics has shown that there is an irreversible flow of time. Rather than there being time-symmetry and indeed a reversibility of time as in classical physics a clear distinction is drawn between what is past and what is future. Thermodynamics is more consistent with the A-series rather than the B-series sense of time. This arrow of time results from how all systems show a loss of organisation and an increase in randomness or disorder over time. This accumulation of disorder is called positive entropy resulting from the so-called Second Law of Thermodynamics; negative entropy involves a thermal disequilibrium characterised by evolutionary growth and increased complexity (see Reed and Harvey 1992; Cilliers 1998: 8). All energy transformations are irreversible and directional.

The clearest example of irreversibility can be seen in the process by which the universe has expanded – through the cosmological arrow of time following the singular historical event of the 'big bang'. But there are many mundane examples of irreversibility in nature, coffee always cools, organisms always age, spring follows winter and so on. There can be no going back, no reabsorbing of the heat, no return to youth, no spring before winter and so on. Laws of nature are historical and imply pastness, presentness and futureness. 'The great thing about time is that it goes on' (Eddington, quoted Coveney and Highfield 1990: 83); while 'irreversibility [of time] is the mechanism that brings order out of chaos' (Prigogine and Stengers 1984: 292; see Chapter 8 below).

Chaos and complexity theories involve repudiating simple dichotomies of order and disorder, of being and becoming. Physical systems do not, it seems, exhibit and sustain structural stability. The commonsense notion that small changes in causes produce small changes in effects is mistaken. Rather there is deterministic chaos, dynamic becoming and non-linear changes in the properties of systems as a whole rather than transformations within particular components. Time in such a perspective is highly discontinuous and investigation takes place of the many non-equilibrium situations in which abrupt and unpredictable changes occur as parameters change over time. Following a perfectly deterministic set of rules, unpredictable yet patterned results can be generated. The classic example is the famous butterfly effect, where minuscule changes at one location produce, in very particular circumstances, massive weather effects elsewhere. Such complex systems are characterised by counter-intuitive outcomes that occur temporally and spatially distant from where they appear to have originated. Complexity theory emphasises how complex feedback loops exacerbate initial stresses in the system and render it unable to absorb shocks in a simple way which re-establishes the original equilibrium. There are very strong interactions seen to occur between the parts of a system and there is a lack of a central hierarchical structure.

The emergence of a certain patterning within an overall disorder results from so-called 'strange attractors' which generate such patterns as a result of thousands or millions of iterations. Such attractors are immensely sensitive in the effects that they generate to slight variations in their initial conditions; as iteration occurs time and time again, so a patterned disorder develops. One such patterned disorder is that of fractals where Mandelbrot demonstrated the geometry of self-similarity, the irregular but strangely similar shapes found in fragmented phenomena at very different scales. Fractals also demonstrate that measurement is inseparable from the metric of measurement, as in the impossibility of definitively establishing the length of Britain's coastline.

In particular, complexity theory has analysed systems as dissipative structures, thermodynamically open and capable of assimilating large quantities of energy from the environment and converting it into increased structural complexity (Reed and Harvey 1992: 360–2). Simultaneously systems dissipate into their environment high levels of residual heat. Once they do this such processes are irreversible. However, such dissipative systems reach points of bifurcation when its behaviour and future pathways become unpredictable. New structures of higher order and complexity then emerge. Dissipative structures thus involve non-linearity, a flowingness of time, no separation of systems and their environment, and a capacity for an autopeitic re-emergence of new order (Capra 1996: 187).

Relatively little social science (or social philosophy) has incorporated these materials into theory or research (see Hayles 1991; Reed and Harvey 1992; Baker 1993; Francis 1993; Zohar and Marshall 1994; Luhmann 1995; Mingers 1995; Keil and Elliott 1996; Eve et al. 1997; Byrne 1998; Cilliers 1998). More generally, Zohar and Marshall elaborate the concept of the *quantum society* (1994). They describe the collapse of the old certainties of classical physics based upon the rigid categories of absolute time and space, solid impenetrable matter made up of interacting 'billiard balls' and strictly determinant laws of motion. In its place there is 'the strange world of quantum physics, an indeterminate world whose almost eerie laws mock the boundaries of space, time and matter' (Zohar and Marshall 1994: 33). They particularly develop analogies between the wave/particle effect and the emergent characteristics of social life: 'Quantum reality ... has the potential to be both particlelike and wavelike. Particles are individuals, located and measurable in space and time. They are either here or there, now and then. Waves are 'nonlocal', they are spread out across all of space and time, and their instantaneous effects are everywhere. Waves extend themselves in every direction at once, they overlap and combine with other waves to form new realities (new emergent wholes)' (Zohar and Marshall 1994: 326). In this book I try somewhat analogously to analyse various global 'waves' which appear to generate 'new emergent wholes' (note Reed and Harvey 1992: 366, on 'societies as peripatetic, boundary-testing entities'). And at the same time there are countless individual particles, that is, humans and social groups, who are resolutely 'located and measurable in space and time'.

Kelly specifically connects complexity back to the metaphor of the network discussed in Chapter 2. He argues that the atom represents the past in physics, while the 'symbol of science for the next century is the dynamical net' (Kelly 1995: 25). Such a network 'channels the messy power of complexity' since it is the only organisation capable of containing 'true diversity working as a whole' (Kelly 1995: 26; Castells 1996: 61; Cilliers 1998: 129). Such notions of a self-making autopeitic system have been employed within the recent analyses of the World Wide Web. Plant argues that:

> No central hub or command structure has constructed it ... It has installed none of the hardware on which it works, simply hitching a largely free ride on existing computers, networks, switching systems, telephone lines. This was one of the first systems to present itself as a multiplicitous, bottom-up, piecemeal, self-organizing network which ... could be seen to be emerging without any centralized control.
>
> (1997: 49)

Thus the main characteristics of such 'complex' systems include:

- a very large number of elements which render formal means of representation inappropriate
- these elements interact physically and informationally over time
- such interactions are rich, non-linear and based upon information carried over a relatively localised range
- complex systems involve positive and negative feedback loops
- they interact dissipatively with their environment
- they operate under conditions which are far from equilibrium, partly because each element responds only to 'local' sources of information

- they have a history which evolves irreversibly through time and where their past is co-responsible for their future

Overall then the social sciences continue to employ incorrect models of how time is conceived of within the natural sciences, and they have neglected notions from within 'science' which could well be relevant to a reconfigured sociology seeking to overcome the division between the physical and social worlds. Comte after all described sociology as 'social physics'; but if so, it is essential to incorporate twentieth-century and not seventeenth-century physics. But this is not to imply that natural science models of time should be directly transplanted into social science. We are now much more aware of the complex relations between models and empirical phenomena. Unforeseen 'chaotic' consequences can result from drawing strict analogies between models of phenomena developed within different domains of inquiry. However, given the necessarily metaphorical nature of social science, we should consider whether some of this new science could generate productive metaphors for the understanding of mobility and time in social life, metaphors to replace the mechanistic, linear and symmetrical notion of clock-time. I examine two such metaphors. In Chapter 6 the metaphor of a slow-moving and sedimented glacial time will be developed – a notion of time that parallels the concept of the dissipative structure embedded within its environment. And in the next section in this chapter I consider the metaphor of instantaneous time – a time characterised by unpredictable change and quantum simultaneity.

Instantaneous time

We have seen that quantum mechanics employs a notion of instantaneous (and simultaneous) time. How might this provide a productive metaphor for a social science of time? In pre-modern societies predominant metaphors were those of various animals, as well as different kinds of agricultural work (many are still powerful today). In modern societies predominant metaphors have been those of the clock, various types of machinery and the photographic lens. While for post-modern societies the hologram would be a productive metaphor. Holography is based upon non-sequentiality, the individual-whole relationship and complexity. Information is not located in a particular part of the hologram. Rather any part contains, implies and resonates information of the whole, what Bohm calls the 'implicate order' (Baker 1993: 142). Hologram means 'writing the whole'. Thus the 'focus here is not on individual particles in motion, crossing time and space in succession, but on all the information gathered up simultaneously' (Adam 1990: 159). The language of cause and effect is inappropriate since the connections are simultaneous and instantaneous. Everything implies everything else and thus it makes no sense to conceive of the separate, if interdependent, 'parts' of any such system. There is some similarity here with the recently newly fashionable views of Leibniz in that each monad in his monadological metaphysics is seen as mirroring the whole, albeit from their particular perspective (Harvey 1996: 69–70).

This metaphor of the hologram can be contrasted with that of the photographic lens that has provided a powerful metaphor for 'modern' epistemology and aesthetics. With a lens there is a one-to-one relationship between each point on the object and each point on the image that shows up on the plate or film. The metaphor of the lens implies sequentiality, the separation between parts and the whole and a relatively extended process through clock-time by which the image comes to be generated. This metaphor is not helpful here.

I turn to some recent changes in the connections of time, space and technology that provide a theoretical and substantive underpinning of instantaneous time. Harvey has sought to show how capitalism entails different 'spatial fixes' within different historical periods (1989). In each capitalist epoch, space is organised in such a way so as to facilitate the growth of production, the reproduction of labour-power and the maximi-sation of profit. And it is through the reorganisation of such time–space that capitalism overcomes its periods of crisis and lays the foundations for a new period of capital accumulation and the further transformation of space and nature through time.

Harvey examines Marx's thesis of the annihilation of space by time and attempts to demonstrate how this can explain the complex shift from 'Fordism' to the flexible accumulation of 'Post-Fordism'. The latter involves a new spatial fix and most significantly new ways in which time and space are represented. Central is the 'time–space compression' of both human and physical experiences and processes. This can be illustratively seen in relationship to corporeal mobility. The journey from the east to the west coast of the US took two years by foot in the eighteenth century; four months by stagecoach in the nineteenth century; four days by rail at the beginning of the twentieth century, and less than four hours by air towards the end of the twentieth century (Giddens 1984: 231). Harvey brings out how this can generate a sense of foreboding, as I noted above when the railway first transformed the countryside. George Eliot, Dickens, Heine, Baudelaire, Flaubert and many others reflected some of the novel ways in which time and space were felt to be different, that there was a trans-formed 'structure of feeling' engendered by this rapidly transformed mobility (Thrift 1996). Harvey argues that as a consequence time and space appear literally *compressed*:

> we are forced to alter ... how we represent the world to ourselves ...
> Space appears to shrink to a 'global village' of telecommunications

and a 'spaceship earth' of economic and ecological interdependencies ... and as time horizons shorten to the point where the present is all there is ... so we have to learn how to cope with an overwhelming sense of *compression* of our spatial and temporal worlds.

(Harvey 1989: 240)

There is the accelerating turnover time in production and the increased pace of change and ephemerality of fashion. Products, places and people go rapidly in and out of fashion at the same time that the same products become instantaneously available almost everywhere, at least in the 'west'. The time-horizons for decision-making dramatically shrink – they are now in minutes in international financial markets. There is a hugely magnified speed of monetary and other transactions (Castells 1996: 434; Thrift and Leyshon 1997). Products, relationships and contracts are increasingly temporary because of short-termism and the decline of a 'waiting culture'. There is the production and transmission of rapidly changing media images and the increased availability of techniques of simulating buildings and physical landscapes from different periods or places. And new technologies of information and communication instantaneously transcend space at the speed of nanoseconds. Interestingly Heidegger in 1950 foresaw much of this speeding up of social life. He talks of the 'shrinking' of the distances of time and space, the importance of 'instant information' on the radio and the way that television is abolishing remoteness and thus 'un-distancing' humans and things (Zimmerman 1990: 151, 209; Chapter 3 above).

However, these dramatic ways in which time and space are compressed, in order that a new round of capital accumulation can be realised, does not mean that places necessarily decrease in importance. Some of course will as a consequence of the 'creatively destructive' power of capital. But more generally people appear to have become more sensitised to what different places in the world contain or what they may signify. There is an insistent urge to seek for roots:

in a world where image streams accelerate and become more and more placeless. Who are we and to what space/place to we belong? Am I a citizen of the world, the nation, the locality? Can I have a virtual existence in cyberspace ...?

(Harvey 1996: 246)

Thus the less important the temporal and spatial barriers, the greater the sensitivity of mobile capital, migrants, tourists, asylum-seekers to the variations of place, and the greater the incentive for places to be differentiated in ways which attract the in-migration of most of the flows discussed in Chapter 2 (Harvey 1989: 295–6, 1996: 246).

Castells elaborates some of the more precise connections of information and time in the network society (1996). Key features of the 'informational society', that developed within north America from the 1970s onwards, include: new technologies are pervasive since information is integral to more or less all forms of human practice; the building blocks are bits of electronically transmitted information; there are complex and temporally unpredictable patterns of informational development; such technologies are organised through loosely organised and flexibly changing networks; the different technologies gradually converge into integrated informational systems (especially the once separate biological and microelectronic technologies); these systems permit organisations to work in real time 'on a planetary scale'; and such instantaneous electronic impulses provide material support for the space of flows (Castells 1996: chap. 1, for the history of such technologies). Such electronic information generates a 'timeless time'. Capital's freedom from time and culture's escape from the clock are both decisively shaped by the new informational systems.

Thus contemporary technologies and social practices are based upon time-frames that lie beyond conscious human experience. While telex, telephones and fax machines reduced the human response time from months, weeks and days to that of seconds, the computer has contracted them into nanoseconds, to event times of a billionth of a second (Adam 1990: 140; Rifkin 1987; Negroponte 1995). Never before has time been organised at a speed that is beyond the feasible realm of human consciousness. Computers make decisions in nanosecond time. Hence the

> events being processed in the computer world exist in a time realm that we will never be able to experience. The new 'computime' represents the final abstraction of time and its complete separation from human experience and rhythms of nature.
>
> (Rifkin 1987: 15)

This instantaneous time stems from what Negroponte describes as the shift from the atom to the bit; that the information-based digital age 'is about the global movement of weightless bits at the speed of light' (1995: 12). The information can become instantaneously and simultaneously available more or less anywhere, although not of course everywhere.

I thus use the term 'instantaneous time' to characterise: first, new informational and communicational technologies based upon inconceivably brief instants which are wholly beyond human consciousness; second, the simultaneous character of social and technical relationships which replaces the linear logic of clock-time characterised by the temporal separation of cause and effect occurring over separate measurable instants; and third, a metaphor for the widespread significance of exceptionally short-term and fragmented time, even where it is not literally instantaneous and simultaneous.

I will now turn to the last of these characteristics, the instantaneous as metaphor. First, there is the *collage* effect, that once events have become more important than location, then the presentation in the media takes the form of the juxtaposition of stories and items that share nothing in common except that they are 'newsworthy' (Giddens 1991: 26). Stories from many different places and environments occur alongside each other in an often chaotic and arbitrary fashion, such stories serving to abstract events from context and narrative. The experience of news is thus a temporally and spatially confused collage organised around instantaneously available stories that are simultaneously juxtaposed.

Second, such a mediated experience involves the 'intrusion of distant events into everyday consciousness' (Giddens 1991: 27). Events often of a tragic character are dramatically brought into people's everyday experience. There is thus time–space compression, as this collage of disconnected stories about famines, droughts, slaughters, nuclear accidents and so on, intrude and shape everyday life. There has been the production of a 'global present' in which seemingly instantaneously people are 'transported' from one tragedy to another in ways that seem out of control. This can be characterised as a world of 'instantaneous ubiquity' (Morley and Robins 1995: 131). The world appears to be particularly risky and there is little likelihood of even understanding the temporally organised processes that culminate in the newsworthy tragedies routinely represented. Such time–space compression magnifies the sense that we inhabit a world of intense and instantaneous riskiness.

At the same time those charged with decision-making have to respond to this exceptionally risky world instantaneously. And as in the case of say the world-wide stock exchange crash in 1987, the effects of individual events upon the rest of the world are hugely magnified, as Wark elaborates in detail (1994). This increasing instantaneity of response has its roots in the early years of this century. Kern notes that new technologies emerging at that time played havoc with the established arts of diplomacy based upon customary times for 'gentlemanly' reflection, consultation and conciliation (1983).

These effects are in turn connected to the development of the so-called three-minute culture. Those watching TV/VCR tend to hop from channel to channel and they rarely spend time in following a lengthy programme. Indeed many programmes are now made to mimic such a pattern, being comprised of a collage of visual and aural images, a stream of 'sound bites', each one lasting a very short time and having no particular connection with those coming before and after. According to Cannon, there can be up to 22 separate images in a 30 second commercial (1995: 32; and see Demos Quarterly 1995, more generally). This instantaneous conception of time could also be re-characterised as 'video-time', in which visual and aural images of the natural world are juxtaposed with multiple images of 'culture'. This is described by Williams in terms of a 'televisual flow' which replaces that of single and discrete events (see Allan 1997; and Chapter 7 below). I also noted in Chapter 3 that instantaneous time may be generating new cognitive faculties. Such 'multi-media' skills based on the simultaneity of time may be more important in the future than conventional skills based upon linear notions of time.

Furthermore, as a result of the need for instantaneous responses, particularly because of the speed implied by the telephone, telex, fax, electronic signals and so on, the future increasingly appears to dissolve into an extended present. It no longer functions as something in which people appear to trust. Qualitative research suggests that almost all groups of British citizens are pessimistic about what is happening in the future and feel that the pace of life and the development of new lifestyles are increasing stress, pressure and short-termism (Macnaghten and Urry 1998: chap. 7; Pahl 1995). There appears to be an increased sense of speed in social life that, according to Virilio, replaces the clear distances of time and space; there is a 'violence of speed' of the military, the media and cities which transcends and may destroy place (1986). He asks rhetorically: 'When we can go to the antipodes and back in an instant, what will become of us?' (quoted Wark: 1994: 11). Recent small-scale research by Cannon suggests that young people conceptualise the future as more or less instantaneous, and becoming even shorter (1995). This generation does not seem to have long-term plans or dreams of the future. It believes that: 'most organisations ... [are] simply incapable of delivering future promises with any certainty ... Barings is just one more name on a long list which convinces young people that mortgaging one's life is a dangerous strategy' (Cannon 1995: 31). Cannon suggests that the younger generation lives in 'real-time', seeing the day as having 24 hours in which to eat, sleep, work, relax and play, a kind of student ordering of time writ into the rest of one's life! Biachini describes the attempts to develop new and imaginative urban timetables that more closely reflect such patterns of social life (1995; Schor 1992, on the US). The development of a rave culture at weekends involves the timing of activities and the use of illegal substances that enable the transcendence of the conventional divisions of night and day (see Mckay 1998).

Finally, instantaneous time also means that the time–space paths of individuals are often desynchronised. There is a greatly increased variation in different people's times that spread, if not over 24 hours, over much longer periods. People's activities are less collectively organised and structured as mass consumption patterns are replaced by more varied and segmented patterns. There are a number of indicators of time–space desynchronisation: the increased significance of grazing, that is, not eating at fixed meal times in the same place in the company of one's family or workmates, and hence of fast-food consumption (see Ritzer 1992, on MacDonaldisation);

the growth of 'free and independent travellers' who specifically resist mass travel in a group where everyone has to engage in common activities at fixed times; the development of flexitime, so that groups of employees no longer start and stop work at the same time; and the growth of the VCR which means that TV programmes can be stored, repeated, and broken up, so that little sense remains of the authentic, shared watching of a particular programme by the whole family.

Instantaneous time

- informational and communication changes which allow information and ideas to be instantaneously transmitted and simultaneously accessed across the globe
- technological and organisational changes which break down distinctions of night and day, working week and weekend, home and work, leisure and work
- the increasing disposability of products, places and images in a 'throwaway society'
- the growing volatility and ephemerality in fashions, products, labour processes, ideas and images
- a heightened 'temporariness' of products, jobs, careers, natures, values and personal relationships
- the proliferation of new products, flexible forms of technology and huge amounts of waste often moving across national borders
- growth of short-term labour contracts, what has been called the just-in-time workforce, and the tendency for people to develop 'portfolios' of tasks
- the growth of 24 hour trading so that investors and dealers never have to wait for the buying and selling of securities and foreign exchange from across the globe
- the increased 'modularisation' of leisure, education, training and work
- extraordinary increases in the availability of products from different societies so that many styles and fashions can be consumed without having to wait to travel there
- increased rates of divorce and other forms of household dissolution
- a reduced sense of trust, loyalty and commitment of families over generations
- the sense that the 'pace of life' throughout the world has got too fast and is in contradiction with other aspects of human experience
- increasingly volatile political preferences

In the box are set out the main characteristics of time as instantaneous, characteristics particularly identifiable in north America and Europe. Instantaneous time appears to transform the powers of nation-states. It was significant in what we used to call 'Eastern Europe'. One set of processes which activating the transformations that took place there more or less simultaneously was the inability of such countries to cope with the intense speeding up of time. Eastern Europe was stuck in modernist clock-time and was unable to respond to the instantaneity of fashion, image and the microcomputer, and the parallel transformations of space. Such societies were caught in a time-warp, in a forced modernisation around clock-time (note of course the appeal of scientific management to Lenin). While all around them, and increasingly criss-crossing their boundaries, were transformations of time that made such islands of modernist clock-time unsustainable. Borneman suggests that time in the GDR was 'petrified' compared with how it had been 'quickening' in the west (1993: 105). There was no incentive to speed it up, time appeared to stand still since 'everything around them becomes motionless, petrified and repetitious' (Keane 1991: 187). There was little or no chance of people acquiring status through instantaneous conspicuous consumption (see Chapter 2 above).

Moreover, the process of German unification demonstrated that East Germany (what had been the GDR) was fundamentally behind in time. Two symbols in West Germany were the growth of travel abroad and the lack of speed limits on the autobahns. By contrast East Germany appeared to be stuck in clock-time, as the west moved into the intensely mobile 'nanosecond [eighties and] nineties', characterised by what Keane calls 'information blizzards' (1991).

Conclusion

In the next chapter I examine some of the effects of instantaneous time upon forms of belonging and travelling within the 'west'. Various forms of dwellingness are analysed, some based upon clock-time and some upon the instantaneous times of various global networks and flows. However, other forms of dwelling are dependent upon what I term 'glacial' time which resists both the clock and the nanosecond.

In Chapter 7 I consider some of the implications of instantaneous time for national regulations and contrasting modes of citizenship within the new world order, while in Chapter 8 some implications of the notions of complexity are examined. I suggest that the intensely unpredictable yet patterned 'global system' can be profitably interrogated through the metaphor of complexity.

Chapter 6

Dwellings

We are in the epoch of simultaneity, the epoch of near and far, of the side by side, of the dispersed.

(Michel Foucault 1986: 22)

Dwellings and communities

I have used the term 'dwelling' at various points in this book. This term indicates an obvious indebtedness to Heidegger and his discussion of dwelling and building (1993: 347–63). He argues that building and dwelling were once more or less the same. To build (*bauen*) involved cherishing and protecting, tilling soil and cultivating vines. Such building involved care and was habitual. But this proper sense of building, that of dwelling, has fallen into oblivion with modern technology. Uprooted modern humanity no longer dwells authentically upon the earth (Zimmerman 1990: 151). Heidegger seeks to ensure how that building and dwelling can be combined again, so that we understand that the essence of building is not abstract technology but the way that any such building permits and facilitates dwelling. He terms this 'letting dwell' (Heidegger 1993: 361).

For Heidegger, dwelling (or *wohnen*) means to reside or to stay, to dwell at peace, to be content or at home in a place. It is the manner in which humans inhabit the earth. He talks of dwelling places, as opposed to other kinds of buildings such as railway stations and bridges. People inhabit these public buildings but they do not dwell within them. Dwelling always involves a staying with things. Thus he argues against the separation of man [sic] and space, as though they stand on opposite sides. Rather to speak of men [sic] is to speak of those who already dwell in and through such spaces: 'To say that mortals *are* is to say that *in dwelling* they persist through spaces by virtue of their stay among things and locales. And only because mortals pervade, persist through, spaces by their very essence are they able to go through spaces' (Heidegger 1993: 359). But people only go through spaces in ways which sustain them through the relationships which are established 'with near and remote locales and things' (Heidegger 1993: 359). When one goes to open the door of a room one is already part of that room. A person is not a separate 'encapsulated body' since such a person already pervades the space of the room they are about to enter. Only because of the form of dwelling is it possible to go through that particular door.

Rather analogous to contemporary actor-network theory, things play a central role in Heidegger's analysis of how it is that people dwell at home and in various locales (although he much more strongly emphasises the unique character of the human *Dasein*). He talks for example of a jug that is not merely an instrument for human ends, but as helping to constitute the world. Zimmerman summarises: 'human existence and [a] thing join together in a mutual dance or play in which a world can maintain itself' (1990: 154).

Heidegger discusses the built object of a bridge that does not connect banks that are already there. The banks only emerge as a consequence of the bridge that now crosses the stream. The bridge causes the banks to lie across from each other and means that the surrounding land on either side of the stream is brought into close juxtaposition. Heidegger argues that the bridge: 'brings stream and bank and land into each other's neighbourhood. The bridge *gathers* the earth as landscape around the stream' (1993: 354; see Pinkney 1991: 66, for a Heideggerian account of doors). Furthermore, the bridge reorganises how it is that people dwell within that area. Bridges initiate new social patterns, forming a locale or connecting different parts of a town, or the town with the country, or the town with 'the network of long-distance traffic, paced and calculated for maximum yield' (Heidegger 1993: 354). A bridge also permits slow movement across it, the 'lingering' ways of people to and fro across the bridge, moving from bank to bank. Elsewhere Heidegger describes the truck driver as being at home on the highway but that the driver does not dwell there; the driver dwells at home.

In this chapter I try to develop in more detail just what we might mean by dwelling, particularly considering some contemporary forms of belonging (beyond the rather limited examples discussed by Heidegger). I will show that, as with Heidegger's bridge and the truck-driver, contemporary forms of dwelling almost always involve diverse forms of mobility. Their examination also necessitates seeing how certain components of such mobilities, such as maps, cars, trains, paths, computers and so on, powerfully reconstruct the relations of belonging and travelling. Unlike Heidegger I do not suggest that there are inauthentic modes of social life, or that the only form of authentic dwelling is a pattern of life rooted in a particular earth and world.

Thus this chapter develops Heidegger's account of the bridge, showing how people dwell in and through being both at home and away, through the dialectic of roots and routes or what Clifford terms 'dwelling-in-travel' (1997: 2; and see Zimmerman 1990: 211). Contemporary social processes have conjured up some strikingly new kinds of dwellingness which only imperfectly map on to national borders. Most social solidarities are more contingent and mobile than how they have typically been seen.

Within sociology the notion of dwelling has normally been conceptualised in terms of 'community', as the way to describe the typical form of life found within rural areas and in certain 'villages' within urban areas (see Frankenberg 1966). Much of this literature has employed the nostalgic conception of the rural community which has often done little more than reproduce ideological conceptions held by those actually living in, or who wished to live in, rural areas (Newby 1979).

To develop a more analytical framework, Bell and Newby distinguish between three different senses of community (1976). First, there is community in a topographical sense. This refers to a particular kind of settlement based upon geographical *propinquity* and where there is no implication of the quality of the social relationships found in such settlements of co-presence. Second, there is the sense of community as a *local* social system in which there is a localised, relatively bounded set of interrelationships of social groups and local institutions. And third, there is *communion*, a human association characterised by close personal ties, belongingness and warmth between its members. The last of these is what is conventionally meant by the idea of 'community'. Bell and Newby maintain that communion is not necessarily produced by any particular settlement type and can result even where those involved do not dwell in close proximity. Geographical propinquity also does not necessitate localness, and localness need not generate communion (this was discussed in Chapter 3 in relationship to 'virtual communities').

Each of these 'communities' can be seen as different forms of dwelling and hence make that notion more analytically complex than Heidegger suggests. But all three conceptions, as employed within conventional sociology, are problematic. First, these conceptions ignore the nature of bodily movement within, and especially through, any such 'community', as well as the ways in which other peoples and objects are sensed over time and space. I showed in Chapter 4 how such senses combine to generate different sensescapes and hence what are in effect different 'places'.

Second, such conceptions of community are over-focused upon people and their interactions and ignore the role of objects, what Hetherington terms the 'materiality of place' (1997b). I show below how a tree and a church can constitute a village as a particular place of dwelling. I also demonstrate the role of objects in relationship to various imagined communities, of printed words and pictures for the imagined communities of nations, and the screen for the imagined community of the global community. In each case such objects carry imagined communities over huge distances, so creating a kind of virtual dwellingness. Generally, sociology has too focused upon specific social interactions between peoples and social groups. In this book I emphasise that we should also analyse those peoples and social groupings with which we do *not* interact on a regular basis but with whom some sense of connection or belonging can be sensed and sustained. We should investigate not only presence and absence, but also 'imagined presence' and the way that diverse objects carry imagined presence across, and into, multiple kinds of dwelling (see Thrift 1996: chap. 7).

Third, community is also a matter of powerful discourses and metaphors. Certain ideals of a supposed *gemeinschaft* are vigorously attached to particular social groupings, especially in recent years in western societies with the supposed general loss of community and its communion-like features. But many places that deploy the notion of community are often of course characterised by highly unequal internal social relations and by exceptional hostility to those who are on the outside. To speak of community is to speak metaphorically or ideologically. The metaphor of community as necessarily involving warm face-to-face relations also plays an important role in the debates about computer-mediated communication.

Although I return to these distinctions of propinquity, localness and communion, I integrate into their analysis diverse mobilities, senses, times, objects and discourses. Hetherington somewhat analogously deploys the metaphor of the ship. Imagine, he says, that places are like ships (1997b: 185–9; Gilroy 1993). They are not something that stays in one place but move around within networks of agents, humans and non-humans. Places are about relationships, about the placings of materials and the system of difference that they perform. Places should be thought of as being placed in relation to sets of objects rather than being fixed through subjects and their uniquely human meanings and interactions.

In similar vein I now consider Ingold's Heideggerian analysis of Peter Bruegel's painting *The Harvester* (1993b; see plate 5.1 in Macnaghten and Urry 1998). For Ingold the 'landscape is constituted as an enduring record of – and testimony to – the lives and works of past generations who have dwelt within it, and in so doing, have left there something of themselves' (1993b: 152). Landscape is neither nature or culture, neither mind or matter. It is the world as known to those who have dwelt in that place, those who currently dwell there, those who will dwell there, and those whose practical activities take them though its manifold sites and journey along its multiple paths.

And any such landscape is a place of memory and temporality. Ingold argues that present events involve some pattern of retention from the past and necessitate projections into the future (A-series time; see Chapter 5). Such interpenetrations of past, present and future revolve around the practices, or the 'taskscape', of any environment. It is this taskscape which produces the social character of a landscape. Such a taskscape only persists as long as people actually engage in the manifold tasks and practical activities of dwelling within, and moving through, that particular environment.

Ingold also argues that landscapes are felt through the senses. They come to be incorporated into our bodily experiences. When looking at Bruegel's painting our eyes are forced to move down and then move up, and as a result we can *feel* the valley as represented in the painting and experience its powerful presence. The contours of the landscape enter into what Bachelard terms our 'muscular consciousness', as though 'the road itself had muscles, or rather, counter-muscles' (Bachelard 1969: 11).

Consider the paths in the painting that were central to the mobilities of that period. Paths show the accumulated imprint of the countless journeys that have been made, as people go about their day-to-day business. The network of paths shows the sedimented activity of an entire community stretching over many generations; it is the taskscape made visible (Ingold 1993b: 167). This explains why the maintenance of the particular network of paths is often strongly desired and campaigned for within a given community (see Macnaghten and Urry 1998). People imagine themselves treading the same paths as countless earlier generations that have lived there or thereabouts. Thus the redirection of a path, or its elimination, will often be viewed as an 'act of vandalism' against that sedimented taskscape, the community and its collective memories and forms of dwelling. Paths that for generations have demonstrated the sedimentation of taskscapes can be overwhelmed by new roads, by instantaneous routes that seem to 'carve' through the landscape, killing trees, paths, dwellings and the existing taskscape. New roads instantaneously destroy the existing taskscape and no amount of re-landscaping makes up for that sudden loss (as opposed to gradual change). And this is partly because roads allow means of movement into the landscape (the car and lorry) that demonstrate no 'muscular consciousness'. Movement is achieved in instantaneous time.

Trees are often significant within places. Ingold suggests that the old pear tree in *The Harvesters* painting partially 'creates' the place. This is because: 'the place was not there before the tree, but came into being with it ... the people, in other words, are as much bound up in the life of the tree as is the tree in the life of the people' (1993b: 167–8). Not far off in the picture is a church and Ingold suggests that it too is a monument to the passage of time (1993b: 169). As with the tree, the church helps to constitute the place as it brings in and unifies the surrounding landscape, especially the taskscape that it exemplifies and supports. The tree and the church have much in common. In both cases 'the form is the embodiment of a developmental or historical process, and is rooted in the context of human dwelling in the world' (Ingold 1993b: 170). This brings out how objects provide affordances to humans (see Chapter 8 below). Sue Clifford from the organisation Common Ground analogously argues that the loss of an orchard involves more than the loss of some trees:

> you might lose fruit varieties particular to that locality, the wild life, the songs, the recipes ... the look of the landscape, the wisdom gathered over generations about pruning and grafting ... In short the cultural landscape is diminished by many dimensions at one blow.
>
> (1994: 2)

There is a loss of what I later discuss as 'glacial time'.

Echoing my argument in Chapter 4, the people represented in *The Harvesters* are not only seen but are heard. We are meant to imagine the sounds that they are making, of talking, eating, snoring, drinking and so on. It is intended that we should reconstruct the senses that they are deploying in producing this particular landscape. The characters in the picture are relating to each other and to their dwellingness through various senses, spanning different times. Ingold argues that the: 'landscape, in short, is not a totality that you or anyone else can look *at*, it is rather the world *in* which we stand in taking up a point of view on our surroundings ... For the landscape, to borrow a phrase from Merleau-Ponty, is not so much the objects as 'the *homeland* of our thoughts' (1993b: 171).

In this painting, propinquity, localness and communion thus coincide. But in the contemporary world they almost never coincide. The emergence of new, often more or less instantaneous, mobilities mean that the patterns of dwelling described by Ingold (and by Heidegger) require extensive reconceptualisation. The modes of dwelling are enormously more complex and diverse than in Bruegel the Elder's world of 1565. In the following I analyse multiple material and cultural transformations which have desynchronised propinquity, localness and communion. I elaborate these relationships with regard to some local and 'neo-tribal' communities in the next section; and in the section following, some elements of national and diasporic communities are briefly examined in the light of the multiple modes of travelling outlined in Chapter 3. I end the chapter by setting out the concept of glacial time that is an important component of many modes of contested dwelling.

This in turn relates to a further theme of this chapter, the links between these forms of contemporary dwelling and a variety of remembering practices. Memory does not seem to be physically locatable in some part of the brain and merely waiting for appropriate activation (see Arcaya 1992; Middleton and Edwards 1990). It appears to be energised through social practices, as people remember together and work at producing their memories within particular social contexts. The production of a memory of an event, place or person necessitates co-operative work, often carried out over considerable periods of time and located within geographically distant contexts. It thus often involves travel to get together or to visit particular sites.

Moreover, there is often a complex rhetoric involved in the articulation of a discourse of memory which may involve a range of senses working across various times and spaces. Proust conveys the embodied character of one's memory of place when he says that 'our arms and legs are full of torpid memories' (quoted Lowenthal 1985: 203). An important form of collective memory is that of institutional commemoration, the 'official memories' within societies. These can have the effect of silencing alternative memories of particular places. Particular landscapes, buildings or monuments are often taken to stand for, or represent the nation, in ways which undercut the memories of other social groups, especially those of women, the working class, subordinate ethnic groups, the young and so on. Many social groups, institutions and whole societies can develop multiple and often contradictory memory practices but these may be excluded from official recognition (Urry 1996).

Further, memories are often organised around objects and particular spaces, such as buildings, bits of landscape, rooms, machines, walls, a smell, furniture, a photograph, a taste, a sound, trees, a hilltop and so on (Radley 1990; as noted in Chapter 4). These different objects and environments can stimulate and structure people's capacities to reminisce about the past, to day-dream about what might have been, or to recollect about how their own lives have intersected with those of others. Benjamin reminds us of the importance that Proust attaches to the *mémoire involuntaire*, a sudden memory intervention that occurs without warning and makes the past seem incredibly vivid within the present. On one occasion Proust's *mémoire involuntaire* was induced by the eating of a particular kind of pastry (Benjamin 1969: 160).

Local belongings

In this section I discuss certain forms of local belongingness, showing in each case the travelling and memory practices involved. I begin with the distinction between *land* and *landscape* as distinct forms of local belongingness (see Milton 1993; land here means what Ingold terms landscape above). The former, land, is the kind of dwellingness revealed in *The Harvesters* as well as in Heidegger. It involves conceptualising land as a physical, tangible resource that can be ploughed, sown, grazed and built upon. It is a place of work that is conceived of functionally (rather than aesthetically). As a tangible resource, land can be bought and sold, inherited and especially left to children, either directly or through the rights established resulting from the use of land over lengthy periods of time. Such land may be directly owned and worked by the 'farmer', or there may be divorce of ownership and control. In many cases farming work, domestic work and leisure all take place in very close spatial proximity. To dwell on a farm is to participate in a pattern of life where productive and unproductive activities resonate with each other and with very particular tracts of land, whose history and geography will often be known in intimate detail. Heidegger's notion of dwelling well-captures the practice of land, where human subjects are apparently united with their environment (1993; Thomas 1993: 27–9). There is a lack of distance between people and things.

The practice of land is quite different from that of landscape, with the latter entailing an intangible resource whose definitive feature is that of appearance or look (Milton 1993; see Chapter 4 above on the visual sense). The notion of landscape emphasises leisure, relaxation and visual consumption by visitors. Writing in 1844, Wordsworth described how the development of the idea of landscape was relatively recent (1984). Earlier travellers to the Alps had made no reference to the beauty of the Alps and their sublime qualities. Wordsworth also quotes a woman from whom he rented a room as a young man who had said that everyone nowadays is 'always talking about prospects: when I was young there never [sic] a thing named' (1984: 188). Well into the eighteenth century barns and other outbuildings were often placed in front of houses 'however beautiful the landscape which their windows might otherwise have commanded' (1984: 188).

However, in the late twentieth century it is commonly thought that landscapes should be communally owned, a 'sort of national property' as Wordsworth expressed it. Such landscapes should be available to all who want to look. There are many ways in which such landscapes are encountered, while walking, driving, climbing, photographing and so on. If people can gain access to the landscape then it is presumed that they should be able to consume that landscape visually. The rights embodied in landscape are also seen to be those of future generations who constitute potential viewers of landscape, and not just those of the current owners of any particular tract of land.

These competing practices, of land and landscape, come into the sharpest contradiction when those seeking to experience landscape try to 'dwell' temporarily on the land. The effects depend upon how such mobile 'landscapers' enter the land, how long they stay, what kinds of sensuous intrusion they effect, what they demand while enjoying the landscape, what practices they generate through the market to service them, how they move across the land, and the kinds of visual gaze that they seek to achieve. Thus land does not provide exclusive rights to ownership and control. Complete strangers may exercise historical rights to walk over agricultural land, often close to places of dwelling, or they may seek to prevent the pursuit of particular leisure practices viewed by locals as part of land and its dwellingness. Thus issues of belonging are intimately bound up with patterns of travelling. In Britain this contradiction of land and landscape is currently seen over the introduction of a policy establishing the general 'right to roam' (or travel) across the countryside even when it is owned by others.

Another way of conceiving this distinction of land and landscape is posed by O'Neill who asks why successive generations of farmers did 'improve the land, even given that they knew they would not reap the benefits?' (1993: 39). His answer is that land had been seen as the common property of particular families or communities stretching across successive generations in glacial time. Each generation possessed a sense of dwellingness over time with the previous and future owners. There was a strong sense of temporal continuity and people saw themselves as implicated in a set of projects from the past, through the extended present and into the future. The planting and growing of trees is a good example of how successive generations of family members participated in a very long-term collective process in 'glacial time'. The growing of trees has been a key element in how families dwelt in a particular place, often over many generations.

Three features of instantaneous time disrupt this continuity of dwellingness: global agricultural competition which emphasises instantaneous monetary returns; the replacement of family by corporate owners who treat the land as more or less like any other factor of production; and the increased mobility of land ownership which has effectively destroyed the long-term links between generations and the sense that anyone really *owns* the earth (O'Neill 1993: 40–1). Further disrupting changes include the rapid increases in the turnover of new products, the ways in which products are transported almost everywhere in the increasingly global market place, and the importance of *look* for vast numbers of visitors as 'land' is turned into 'landscape'.

I now turn to some more general features of many 'local' communities (see Massey 1994; Urry 1995; Macnaghten and Urry 1998). First, following the previous chapter, different local communities are to be seen as organised in and through different temporalities. Partly this means that communities carry traces of the memories of very different social groups who have lived in or passed through that place historically. All sorts of contestation over those memories mark off each such place. Further, places can be distinguished in terms of whether they are temporally rich or poor. Sennett for example says that some 'places [are] full of time' and it is this that makes them brim with cosmopolitan opportunity (1991: Chapter 7). Other places exhibit a 'drudgery of place', the sense of being inexorably tied to that place and where time seems fixed and unchanging. Such places remain heavy with time. Furthermore, different times seem to be embedded within different places. I suggested in Chapter 5 that much of

Eastern Europe before 1989 was organised around clock-time. Some places get left behind in the 'slow lane' of clock-time. Other places are based upon instantaneous time, a time induced by the dazzling disorientation of Virilio's 'speed' (1986).

Second, time is not necessarily progressive (as opposed to the supposedly static quality of space). Time may or may not presuppose movement, change and transformation, just as places are not necessarily static and unchanging (see Massey 1994: 136–7). Places involve process and such processes involve combining the more local and much wider sets of social relations. What I have termed localness is a 'distinct mixture together in one place [which] produce[s] effects which would not have happened otherwise' (Massey 1994: 156, 138). Places can be loosely understood therefore as multiplex, as a set of spaces where ranges of relational networks and flows coalesce, interconnect and fragment. Any such place can be viewed as the particular nexus between, on the one hand, propinquity characterised by intensely thick co-present interaction, and on the other hand, fast flowing webs and networks stretched corporeally, virtually and imaginatively across distances. These propinquities and extensive networks come together to enable performances in, and of, particular places.

Third, objects are very significant in this construction of localness. In *The Harvesters*, a tree and a church served to constitute the village as a particular place of dwelling. Such natural or physical objects can carry memory-traces which signify glacial time. Various kinds of object, or activity or media images may constitute the basis of such an 'imagined presence'. They carry that imagined presence across the members of a local community, although much of the time members of such a place may not be conscious of this imagined community (see Massey 1994: 138). Various objects can function in this way – and not just the immense monuments of place and community analysed by Lefebvre (1991: 220–6). Oldenburg has described the significance of informal casual meeting places, bars, cafés, community centres, spaces under pear-trees and so on. He calls these 'third places' beyond work and households where communities come into being and neighbourhood life can be sustained (1989; and see Diken 1998, on the gendering of café life amongst Turkish migrants in Denmark).

Fourth, many places whose members may describe themselves as part of a 'community' are characterised both by highly unequal local social relations (divided by class, gender, ethnicity, age) and by hostility to those on the outside. Indeed the opposition to the outsider, the stranger, is often part of the mechanism by which those unequal local relations are established and sustained. Those inequalities are moreover reinforced by the use of the term 'community' which can falsely imply that the locality is based upon warm, consensual, face-to-face relations of communion. Diken shows the power of such a 'violent hierarchy' of the community of Danes opposed to non-Danes, especially Turks, that has the effect in Denmark of excluding and marginalising the latter (1998: 41). Dicks shows the ways in which narrative functions within the Rhondda Heritage Park to construct a story organised around the trope of the 'mining community'; the narrative reaches closure with the story of how mining has ended. It is a story that minimises the inequalities especially of gender rife within such 'communities' (Dicks 1997).

Fifth, local communities are places of consumption, such as raw materials or eighteenth-century buildings or lakeside views. Places provide the context within which various goods and especially services are compared, evaluated, purchased and used. Moreover, places are themselves in a sense consumed, through deploying the various senses discussed in Chapter 4. Places are both part of, and help to constitute, various sense-scapes, including especially those mediated through the normally hegemonic visual sense (see Massey 1999, on various local landscapes of sense in one's place of upbringing). But also part of the experience of many such places is that they are constituted as places which are consumed by various others, whose sights, noises, smells and touch can attract or repel.

Finally and most importantly, even those communities which are based around geographical propinquity depend upon diverse mobilities (as noted in Chapter 3 above). There are countless ways of reaffirming a sense of dwelling through movement within a community's boundaries, such as walking along well-worn paths. But any such community is also interconnected to many other places through diverse kinds of travel. Raymond Williams in *Border Country* is 'fascinated by the networks men and women set up, the trails and territorial structures they make as they move across a region, and the ways these interact or interfere with each other' (Pinkney 1991: 49; Williams 1988; Cresswell 1997: 373). Massey similarly argues that the identity of a place is derived in large part from its interchanges with other places that may be stimulating and progressive. Sometimes though such notions depend upon gender-unequal relationships to the possibilities of travel. Massey discusses how 'mum' can function as the symbolic centre to whom 'prodigal sons' return when the going elsewhere gets tough (1994: 180).

Also in *Border Country* Williams describes how during the 1926 General Strike in Britain different kinds of network were differentially powered. There was the rich network made possible by the trucks and wirelesses of the state and the bosses, compared with the much thinner networks constituted by the bikes and telegrams of the strikers (1988; Pinkney 1991: 51). More generally, Williams' novels demonstrate the paradoxical interaction of spaces, of the intensely specific and locally loved places and multinational global spaces. Such a yoking of localism-and-internationalism means the 'bypassing the territory of the old nation-state' (Pinkney 1991: 141, 32; and see Graham and Marvin 1996: 58–9, on hub and spoke urban networks). Macdonald makes a similar point by recounting a common story she heard told on the apparently remote Isle of Skye in Scotland:

> There was an old woman ... living in township X. One day a couple of tourists come by and start asking her questions. 'Have you every been outside this village?' ... 'Well, yes. I was at my sisters in [neighbouring township]' ... 'But you've never been off the island?' 'Well, I have, though not often I suppose'. 'So, you've been to the mainland?' She nods. 'So you found Inverness a big city then?' 'Well, not so big as Paris, New York or Sydney, of course ...
>
> (1997: 155)

The *bund*

I turn now to some different kinds of 'communities', most of which do not involve geographical propinquity, or at least not 'ascribed' geographical propinquity. Sometimes they involve an 'achieved' geographical propinquity at 'sacred moments' of kairological time (see Parsons and Shils 1951: 82–4, on the achievement-ascription pattern variable). The 'neo-tribal' communities include self-help groups, direct action organisations, community groups, ethnic groupings, women's groups, travellers, leisure groups, gay/lesbian groups, voluntary organisations, environmental NGOs and so on (see Maffesoli 1996, on the 'time of the tribes'). Each such group involves a particular intersection of belonging and travelling. Many are premised upon cultures of resistance, a kind of horizontal extension of the networks of civil society, both within and especially beyond the boundaries of nation-states. These resistant networks 'defend their spaces, their places, against the placeless logic of the space of flows characterizing social domination in the Information Age' (Castells 1997: 358). For Castells human subjects 'are not built any longer on the basis of [national] civil societies, that are in the process of disintegration, but as prolongation of communal resistance' (1997: 11: emphasis removed).

Hetherington argues that these loose sociations should be conceptualised as *bunds* (1994). The early German youth movement, the *Wandervogel*, conceived of themselves as *bund*-like. In this period there were no youth hostels, no well-travelled routes, no established techniques of roaming through the countryside. So *bund*-like *Wandervogel* developed to facilitate the mobility of young German men into the countryside. The *Wandervogel* were small groups forming a mobile communion and seeking through their fellowship as they roamed Bohemian forests an authentic recreation of a lost *Gemeinschaft*.

This notion of the *bund*, as an idealised form of mobile sociation, provided the inspiration for Schmalenbach who adds this third term to the conventional *Gemeinschaft-Gesellschaft* distinction (1977). The *bund* involves community but this is a community that is conscious and freely chosen on the basis of mutual sentiment and emotional feeling. And *contra* Weber the affective basis on such a *bund* is not irrational and unconscious. Affective commitment to the *bund* is conscious, rational and non-traditional. Such bünde, unlike *gemeinschaftlich* communities, are not permanent or necessarily stable. Hetherington argues:

> Bünde are maintained symbolically through active, reflexive monitoring of group solidarity by those involved, in other words, they are highly self-referential ... the Bund is self-enclosed and produces a code of practices and symbols ... Bünde involve the blurring of public and private spheres of life of their members.
>
> (1994: 16)

Some contemporary examples involve groupings organised around food, gender, animals, vegetarianism, DIY, pets, alternative medicine, local place, spirituality, the countryside, festivals, road protests, dance culture, and an array of highly specialised leisure practices (Szerszynski 1993). Such practices point to the important role of relatively informal and overlapping networks defined culturally, rather than politically or socially in terms of a national civil society (Lash *et al.* 1996). Such *bunds* or sociations are normally joined out of choice and people are free to leave. Indeed people will rapidly enter and leave such sociations. They remain members in part because of the emotional satisfaction that they derive from common goals or shared social experiences, albeit of a temporary sort. These sociations enable people to experiment with new kinds of dwellingness which are often temporary and involve diverse mobilities. They may empower people, providing relatively safe places for identity-testing and the context for learning new skills. These sociations vary as to the degree of decentralisation of power from a centre, the degree of formal specification of the organisational structure, the level and forms of participation at the local level, the types of action which are entered into by the membership, and the degree to which the membership is linked into networks criss-crossing national borders and involving diverse modes of travel (Urry 1995: chap. 14; Hetherington 1998).

Other writers have described some of these groups as 'collective enthusiasms' (Hoggett and Bishop 1986; Abercrombie and Longhurst 1998: chap. 5). Such enthusiasms carry out a great deal of 'work' that is normally done in what is people's formal 'leisure' time. These leisure activities are often more engaging than people's actual [paid] work experiences. The members of the enthusiasm work through reciprocity and mutual aid. Members of such sociations are self-organised and particularly resentful of outside experts instructing them how to act or to manage themselves.

Much emphasis is placed upon acquiring through networks arcane forms of knowledge and skill. And there is often strong resistance to the commodification of either products, or of the forms of labour involved. Many outputs are produced, including the artistic, written, sporting, spoken, visual and on. These outputs are mainly consumed by the membership itself or by the family and friends of members (Hoggett and Bishop 1986: 42). People's activities within such enthusiasms involve communication, networking and moments of emotional satisfaction at particular events located at particular moments within the yearly calendar. There are obviously tens of thousands of such enthusiasms within advanced societies, ranging from highly mediatised fan organisations, through various cults, to the purer collective enthusiasms such as 'hot-rodding' or environmental NGOs (see Abercrombie and Longhurst 1998: 132–4, on these distinctions).

Mckay emphasises four further features of these sociations or enthusiasms involved in communal resistance (1996; 1998). First, they construct 'their own zones, their own spaces'. Normally such spaces enjoy a local situatedness, a sense of the previous forms of dwelling that occurred in that place, such as fairs, markets, houses, workshops and so on (Mckay 1996: 39). They are also 'living spaces, vibrant and imaginative', separate from, and in one way or another, defined against those of the rest of society (Mckay 1996: 71). These zones of dwelling are liberated, 'temporary autonomous zones' or 'heterotopias of deviation'. These are places of 'alternative ordering' characterised by unsettling and often shocking juxtapositions of incommensurate objects. Such heterotopic sites are transgressive, marginal, incongruous and hugely contested (Foucault 1986; Hetherington 1997a: chap. 7).

Dwellings are often impermanent. They are characterised, according to one participant, by 'their shared air of impermanence, of being ready to move on ... re-locate to other universities, mountain-tops, ghettos, factories, safe houses, abandoned farms' (quoted Mckay 1996: 8). There is a sense of movement, of continuous acts of transgression, as happens in the case of a peace convoy. Their dwelling spaces are constituted through various routeways and specific often sacred nodes, rather than the permanent forms of dwelling described in the case of the practices of *land*. Emotionally intense communion through likeness and friendship takes place within specific nodes at particular moments in the year. Dwelling is intense, impermanent and mobile.

Further, these spaces are not only defined visually but also in terms of other senses, especially sound. Mckay quotes the original organiser of the Stonehenge Free Festival who said that' 'Our temple is sound, we fight our battles with music, drums like thunder, cymbals like lightning ...' (1996: 8). Smells and tastes also constitute the dwelling-places of many of these cultures of resistance. Indeed part of the resistance of such groups involves challenging the orthodox sense-scapes based upon visuality (see Chapter 4). However, these cultures of resistance do not necessarily feel 'at home' within the same sense-scape. The Dongas, for example, object to outdoor raves because of the noise pollution that such modernist sound technology generates.

Finally, these cultures of resistance are constituted as 'a *network* ... of *independent collectives and communities*' (Albion Free State Manifesto of 1974, quoted Mckay 1996: 11). Such groupings form a 'loose network of loose networks', such as those involved in free festivals, rural fairs, alternative music, hunt saboteurs, road protests, new age travellers, rave culture, poll tax protest, peace convoys, animal rights and so on (Mckay 1996: 11). These networks are reinforced by various patterns of corporeal travel in which there is a kind of resistant mapping of key events, places, routeways and so on. A member of the Donga tribe, which first came to prominence at the Twyford Down protest, expresses well both the impermanent and changing nature of the Dongas as *bund*, and the significance of particular spatial and temporal nodes to their intermittent sense of communion:

> The Tribe itself has grown and diversified in that time with some people now working full-time in the grassroots protest movement which has sprung up, or in related areas such as tree-planting and permaculture. A small group continues to live a nomadic lifestyle, moving from hillfort to hillfort with horses, donkeys and handmade carts to transport personal and communal possessions. We remain in close contact and meet up often at major seasonal celebrations and feel bound together through our experiences and shared vision.
>
> (quoted Mckay 1996: 143)

One particular network are travellers, self-styled groupings of young people who choose to spend at least some of the year moving irregularly in convoy through the countryside (Mckay 1996: chap. 2; Hetherington 1998). Such travellers live in brightly painted makeshift lorries, buses and caravans that constitute their places of dwelling. But they also dwell in this punctuated movement, their map and timetable being constituted through various free festivals, sacred heterotopic sites and magical routes. They claim rights of squatting en route irrespective of existing places, land or landscape. These traveller festivals and campsites are normally seen as visually polluting by local people, by visitors who temporarily dwell through what I termed 'landscape' and by those who permanently dwell on the 'land'.

That travellers might stay and pollute the places of dwellingness can provoke intense hatred and the reassertion of existing communities against the travelling intruder. More generally communion is often formed in hostile opposition to such strangers, to those who are mobile, to gypsies going to horse fairs, to travellers to free festivals, to tourists to honeypot holiday centres, to commuters whose cars pollute small villages and so on. Particularly intense hostility can be expressed against those who might dwell for a while in their midst. Hetherington summarises the response to such an 'invasion': as 'has been the case with Jews and gypsies down the centuries, the "New Age travellers" are hated not because they are always on the move but because they might stay and "contaminate" through their ambivalence' (Hetherington 1992: 91; 1998).

More generally, a largely unintended effect of a highly individualised and marketised society has been the intensification of social practices which 'systematically evade the edicts of exchange value and the logic of the market' (Berking 1996: 192). Such networked practices are often based upon reciprocal relations including gift-giving, voluntary work, self-help networks and even friendship. They acquire symbolic value as sites of resistance to a world perceived to be structured and regulated by global relations, self-interest and dominant market relations (see Keck and Sikkunk 1998: 8–9 on networks). Castells in turn sees almost all contemporary sociations as both resistant to globalisation while at the same time using the objects of the global (1997; and see Mckay 1998).

The importance of 'activists beyond borders' has been more generally analysed by Keck and Sikkunk who describe how they are organised into 'transnational advocacy networks' (1998). Most strikingly there have been enormous increases in the number of such networks over the post-war period. 'International non-governmental social change organisations' (which are a kind of 'official proxy' for the more inclusive category of transnational networks) have increased from 102 in 1953 to 569 in 1993, more than a five-fold increase (Keck and Sikkunk 1998: 11). Some areas have shown astonishing increases: the number of 'development' groups has risen ten-fold and 'environmental' groups forty-five-fold over this forty-year period. Together groups working on human rights, the environment and women's rights account now for over half of such transnational networks. Other estimates suggest that there are nearly 5,000 international NGOs of all sorts (Billig 1995: 131).

The growth of these transnational networks resulted from the availability of cheap air travel, new communications technologies that provide informal connections between members of the network, and the creation of a broader global public that was a legacy of the 1960s. Keck and Sikkunk summarise:

> Both the activism that swept Western Europe, the United States, and many parts of the third world during that decade, and the vastly increased opportunities for international contact, contributed to this shift. With a significant decline in air fares, foreign travel ceased to be

the exclusive privilege of the wealthy. Students participated in exchange schemes. The Peace Corps and lay missionary programs sent thousands of young people to live and work in the developing world.

(1998: 14–15)

One important consequence of new instantaneous flows of image, information and the bearing of witness by such transnational networks is that states and corporations can no longer monopolise the information available to the public. Especially important are these flows into and from the developing world which in the past were organised on the basis of slow-moving and unreliable mail systems. Now information and image can flow along dense communications networks linking these transnational networks. And with links into competitive media so these networks can subject states and corporations to suitable shaming (Keck and Sikkunk 1998: 21; see Chapter 7 below). Particularly significant are the flows of image and information on the occasion of world meetings concerned with the environment, human rights, development, women's issues and so on. For example, at the World Conference on Human Rights held in Vienna in 1993, there were representatives from 1,500 NGOs. According to Keck and Sikkunk, what is emerging is a 'transnational civil society as an arena of struggle, a fragmented and contested area', as I discuss further in Chapters 7 and 8 (1998: 33).

Heritage, nation and diaspora

In this chapter I have considered diverse forms of contemporary dwelling-ness. I have emphasised that objects are often central to such forms of dwelling; that each dwelling involves various combinations of belonging and of travelling; that these forms of dwelling often involve loose network-like patterns; and that their effect has been to shrink and disarticulate national civil societies. I now turn to the issue of the nation more directly and consider some of the mundane practices by which national identity has been historically established, sustained and subject to contestation. I will return briefly to the notion of 'banal nationalism' encountered in Chapter 1, consider the diverse ways in which a unique and exclusive national heritage has been produced and remembered, and analyse a diverse set of transformations of nationhood and nationalism.

I previously noted the importance of the 'imagined presence' of others who share much in common with oneself and of the role of vernacular nationalism that is part of who people are and their identity. Central to any such nation is its narrative of itself. National histories tell a story, of a people passing through history, a story often beginning in the supposed mists of time (Bhabha 1990). Each incredibly slow-moving glacial time of a national history is seen as unique – it is a time peculiar to that particular nation and shared by all its members (Billig 1995: 70–4). One can suggest that such a 'banal nationalism' and the very particular history of each nation is something like a fractal. Banal nationalism comprises the irregular but strangely similar shapes found in fragmented phenomena at very different scales of the body social, from each person, through each local level, right up to and into the centre of the society.

However, it is also clear that such a fractal is by no means 'natural'. Much of any society's history of its national traditions and icons has been both invented and resulted as much from forgetting the past as from remembering the past (McCrone 1998: chap. 3). Late nineteenth-century Europe was a period of remarkable invention, of national traditions focused upon specific times and places that came to be sacralised. Nairn demonstrates the powerful English nationalist invented traditions working through the 'enchanted glass' of the monarchy (1988). While in France, Bastille Day was invented in 1880, La Marseillaise became the national anthem in 1879, July 14th was designated the national feast in 1880 and Jeanne d'Arc was only elevated from obscurity by the Catholic Church in the 1870s (McCrone 1998: 45–6). More generally, the idea of France which began as an elite concept was extended 'by a process akin to colonisation through communication (roads, railways and above all by the newspapers ...) so that by the end of nineteenth century popular and elite culture had come together' as a result of diverse corporeal and imaginative mobilities (McCrone 1998: 46). Importantly part of this process was the mass production of public monuments of the nation especially in re-built Paris, monuments that were travelled to, seen, talked about and shared through paintings, photographs and later films.

This sense of collective participation and the more general nation-inducing role of travel had been initiated in 1851 with the Great Exhibition held at London's Crystal Palace. This was the first-ever national tourist event. Although the British population was only 18 million, an extraordinary 6 million visits were made to the Exhibition, many people using the new technology of the railway to visit the national capital for the first time. Many of these trips were organised by the eponymous Thomas Cook who declared in 1854 that 'all the world is on the move' (quoted Lash and Urry 1994: 262). In the second half of the nineteenth century similar mega-events took place across Europe with attendances at some reaching 30 million or so (Roche 1999). There was a world-wide movement to develop these mega-international expositions. The development of these international events, which were premised upon mass transportation and tourism and a certain cosmopolitanism, meant that national identity was increasingly conceived of in terms of a location within, and on, a European stage. It was that staging which facilitated both corporeal and imaginative travel to and within such mega-events (Roche 1999).

Centennial celebrations were held in the US in 1876 and Australia in

1888 (Spillman 1997). In the USA the central event in a year-long celebration was the Centennial Exhibition in Philadelphia seen by over 8 million visitors. It is thought that one in twenty Americans visited the exhibition, while many of those unable to do so were pleased to see photographs of the event (Spillman 1997: 38–9). In Australia in 1888 a Centennial International Exhibition was organised in Melbourne, while there was a wide array of events held in Sydney. It is thought that an extraordinary two-thirds of the Australian population attended the exhibition in Melbourne (Spillman 1997: 51). For both countries an international exhibition was seen as the best way of expressing and confirming national identity since it invited the gaze of the rest of the world, confirming status, achievement and distinctiveness. Visitors from home and abroad were able to confirm that nation's particular achievements and characteristics (although neither set of events was without controversy at the time: Spillman 1997: chap. 3).

Corporeal mobility is thus importantly part of the process by which members of a country believe they share some common identity bound up with the particular territory that the society occupies or lays claim to. Since the mid-nineteenth century travel to see the key sites, texts, exhibitions, buildings, landscapes and achievements of a society has singularly developed that cultural sense of a national imagined presence. Particularly important in the genealogy of nationalism in most societies has been the founding of national museums, the development of national artists, architects, musicians, playwrights, novelists, historians and archaeologists and the location of the nation's achievements in world exhibitions (McCrone 1998: 53–5; Harvey, P. 1996: 56–7). Many artists and intellectuals became synonymous with the emergence of a national culture and of events and places that had to be visited.

Thus even the apparently simple English culture has been assembled together out of many different components and elements, including the historical patterns of travel and exchange within the countries and cultures of 'Empire' (Hall 1990; Gilroy 1993). Moreover, within England corporeal travel has been centrally involved in establishing and sustaining the sense of what is English national identity. People travel to the culture's sacred sites (such as Buckingham Palace, the English countryside); to the location of the central written or visual texts (the Lake District, Stratford-upon-Avon); to places where key national events took place (Hastings, the Civil War); to see particularly noteworthy individuals or their documentary record (the monarch, 'Shakespeare'); and to view other cultures so as to reinforce national superiority (such as the rest of 'Europe' or former colonies).

Nationalism has been historically bound up with the valorisation of certain features of the physical landscape. In England Lowenthal argues that because there are few other signs of national identity such as a national costume, flag or national holiday, there developed a strong scenic essence to English identity:

> One icon in heritage has a distinctly English cast. This is the land-scape. Nowhere else is landscape so feted as legacy. Nowhere else does the very term suggest not simply scenery and *genres de vie*, but quintessential national virtues ... rural England is endlessly lauded as a wonder of the world.
>
> (1991: 213; 1994; see also Condor 1996: 42–3)

Central to this social spatialisation has been the English village. Hilaire Belloc believed that the true heart of (southern) England lay in the village that acquired almost mythological status as the archetypal English community. In the interwar period, Baldwin, who described himself as the man in a field-path, played an exemplary role in developing this English ideology of ruralism and in much more sharply distinguishing between the town and country as social spatialisations. Constable's *Hay Wain* for example became popular in the inter-war period as a particular icon of Englishness. Miller suggests that it was the growth of national radio broadcasting in the 1930s that helped to develop and sustain this increasingly national ideology of ruralism, a ruralism specifically intended for national consumption mainly of course by those living within urban areas (1995).

This English countryside abounds with monuments to past achievements, including especially domination over the other nations of the UK. By comparison, the countrysides of Ireland, Scotland and Wales are littered with memorials to lost causes and especially to lost battles (Lowenthal 1991: 209–10). As with other colonised societies, Irish nationalism in valorising the pictorialised Irish countryside has internalised components of the very colonial culture that it sought to contest. Thus Ireland reflects what Pratt more generally calls auto-ethnographic expression. These involve the colonised, collaborating with and appropriating the idioms of the conquering 'seeing-man' whose imperial eyes have looked out and possessed so much of the globe (Pratt 1992).

Different features of the landscape are of course differentially celebrated as nationally iconic: Alpine altitude and air in Switzerland, fjords in Norway, bogs in Ireland, Wild West wilderness in the US, heaths in Denmark, geysers in New Zealand and so on (Lowenthal 1994). Sometimes it is the very complexity of landscapes that is nationally emblematic, as in France (Lowenthal 1994: 19). Also the same kind of physical feature can signify very different notions across different nations. Schama shows this in the case of woods where extraordinarily powerful and different myths have come to be woven into the roots and branches of various cultures (1995: Part 1). In Germany, forests have long been viewed as representing the spirit of militarism; an embodied memory which the modernising Nazis deployed and developed. In England, the forest has long stood for the idea that liberty against the despot could be attained by those who lived under the greenwood tree (as in the Robin Hood myth). In France forests have represented the passion for order and the intervention of the state. In Poland forests have stood for the enduring struggle for national freedom. In the US, the Big Trees of California were seen as an American godsend, the revelation of the uniqueness of America and of the chosen character of the American people.

I have so far presumed that what has normally been understood and remembered as 'national heritage' in a society is both unchanging and is representative of, and congruent with, the interests of its national élites. For example, in England the houses and estates of the mostly agrarian-based landed class living in the south of England have been those which have been mainly 'saved for the nation' by the National Trust and other preservationist organisations. It is these houses, estates and consequential forms of upper class life that have been presumed to constitute the national heritage and to define Englishness (see Wright 1985; Lowenthal 1985; Samuel 1994: part 3). Similar examples can be cited in the case of other national identities. However, there are three important sets of trans-formations of such a single and exclusive national heritage. These transformations are interconnected, since they involve corporeal and imag-inative mobilities that undermine a single and definitive sense of what constitutes the nation and the national heritage.

First, the recent period has seen the development of a global public stage upon which almost all nations have to appear, to compete and to mobilise themselves as spectacle. This placement upon such a stage partic-ularly occurs through the media. In the next chapter I discuss this in terms of what I call the shift from public sphere to public stage, or what one might term, the universal performativity of the global public stage in which even nations have to effect performances. This placement particu-larly operates through mega-events such as the Olympics, World Cups and Expos which people visit as well as view through the media.

The Universal Exhibition at Seville in 1992 offers an invaluable prism into these processes. As I have noted, such exhibitions operate as a tech-nology of nationhood, providing narrative possibilities for the imagining of national cultures (P. Harvey 1996: chap. 3). Through powerful images, symbols and icons, nation-states are represented as repositories of stability, continuity, uniqueness and harmony. However, Seville was also a place of international capital, funding various national displays, the Expo as a whole and their own exhibition spaces, especially with communicational and informational advances that transcend national borders. In these displays the emphasis is placed upon consumer desire, individual choice, cosmopolitanism and the freedom of the market to cross national borders (the tourist crossing of borders is also to be found in collecting stamps in the Exhibition Passport). Universal Exhibitions are places to celebrate global scapes and flows and of the companies that mobilise such mobilities; while nations are principally there as spectacle and sign in the instantaneous tourism that such Expos construct and celebrate.

This in turn relates to Maier's argument that the very nature of nationality has shifted (1994: 149–50). It was once based upon a homogeneous and mapped national territory, in which law was defined, authority claimed and loyalty sought within that territorial boundary. Now as frontiers are permeable and much cultural life is interchangeable across the globe (through for example Expos) so 'territory is less central to national self-definition' (1994: 149). What in turn are central to nation are specific places and landscapes, icons of the nation. But we may further add that it is the signs of such places and landscapes that are central to nation since these are endlessly circulated and recirculated on the global stage of the mass media and mega-events.

Second, there is the emergence of diverse, often localised, sociations seeking to save 'their history' and especially the signs and memories of their former modes of dwelling. This vernacular contestation of the power of national élites was reflected in the intense debates over the nature of the Australian bicentennial held in 1988 (see Spillman 1997: chap. 4). There was very strong Aboriginal opposition to the celebrations; they termed Australia Day, 'Invasion Day'. As a result of this contestation over memory and history the organisers of the bicentennial minimised public events which celebrated the founding moment of 'Australia' two hundred years before. They emphasised not this moment, nor particular events over the past two centuries, but a variety of vernacular traditions and processes of what was constructed as an inclusive Australian culture. Indigenous protest and vernacular traditions thus left their mark.

In Britain Samuel has most effectively outlined the nature of the rediscovery of such vernacular traditions (1994). He summarises the new democratic, familial, workerist, femininist, consumerist and domestic heritages that various sociations have documented, laid out for display, and sought to bring in visitors to see, touch, hear and remember:

> the 'heritage' which conservationists fight to preserve and retrieval projects to unearth, and which the holiday public or museum visitors are invited to 'experience' – is in many ways a novel one. Though indubitably British ... it departs quite radically from textbook versions of 'our island story'. It has little to do with the continuities of monarchy, parliament or British national institutions ... It is the little platoons, rather than the great society, which command attentions in this new version of the national past.
>
> (1994: 158)

Since the early 1960s many new heritage sites have proliferated, started and run by enthusiasts who contest once-dominant traditions, enthusiasts who are extending and elaborating civil society horizontally, disrupting what and who is in the nation. Examples of forms of preserved dwelling-ness by the 'little platoons' include railway engines, canals, industrial archaeology sites, docks, ancient languages, trees, steam traction engines, cottages, mills, derelict coalmines and so on (Corner and Harvey 1991; Dicks 1997). There are now nearly thirteen thousand designated ancient monuments, a new museums open every fortnight, there are 78 museums devoted to railways and 180 water and wind mills are open to the public (Samuel 1994: part 2).

One interesting 'little platoon' or *bund* established the Aros Heritage Centre on the Isle of Skye in Scotland (see Macdonald 1997). Its two founders had been involved in various projects based on reviving the use of Gaelic language. They thought that establishing such a Centre would strengthen Gaelic language and culture. Aros possesses few 'authentic' exhibits – it mostly consists of 'reproductions' since this was a poor culture with few physical remnants. More important is the 'story' that it tells which links together the decline of Gaelic culture with the history of resistance of the people both to the English and to Scottish clan chiefs (Macdonald 1997: 162–3). Aros is subtitled [in translation] 'the heritage of the Island' [of Skye]. Heritage is viewed as 'more intangible matters of nature, character and duty' which are inalienable and cannot be transmitted from seller to buyer (Macdonald 1997: 173). But this inalienable heritage does not presuppose a pristine, untouched and unchanging culture. Gaelic heritage is rather a story of contact and relations with numerous outsiders – and such a story highlights resilience, resistance and the appropriation of elements from way beyond Gaelic culture. Thus Gaelic heritage is necessarily hybridised and one that never existed in some pure state before visitors began to arrive. It has moreover been extended and elaborated through this Gaelic-speaking *bund* that has developed new ways of belonging and travelling within an increasingly profitable and autonomous Scottishness (see McCrone *et al.* 1995, on developing *Scotland – the Brand*; Edensor 1997).

Scotland is a powerful example of the rise of 'neo-nationalism' in many of the advanced societies of North America and Western Europe. Such developments are recent, born out of relative wealth rather than poverty, with the emphasis upon civic rather than ethnic nationalism. The nationalism is broadly progressive rather than reactionary and the movement occurs within nations which have in some way possessed 'coherent civil societies' (see McCrone 1998: chap. 7). Most importantly, such a neo-nationalism is characterised by multiple identities, that there is no longer one 'true national self' but that one can possess multiple identities; between half and two-thirds of those living in

Scotland consider themselves both Scottish and British (McCrone 1998: 140).

Third, the literature on diasporas show further ways in which a single and exhaustive national heritage has become less sustainable. Post-colonial writings have more generally demonstrated that all cultures are in a sense inauthentic, contrived and constituted through their complex interchanges with other cultures. Gurnah for example brings out how colonial cultures, in his case in Ethiopia, are not simply oppressive: 'they rarely replaced our organic culture, but they also significantly contributed to our developing world view ... once absorbed, aspects of the processed "foreign" cultures became ours' (1997: 121). Such cultures have thus been made and remade as a consequence of the flows of peoples, objects and images, backwards and forwards across borders. These corporeal and imaginative mobilities resulted from the different patterns of colonial administration, work-induced migrations, exile/asylum patterns, individual travel and mass tourism, popular culture and the mass media, the complex relationships of exchange in post-colonialism, 'myths of return' and so on (Bhabha 1990). For example, in that area delimited by the continents of Africa, Europe and the Americas, Gilroy argues that: 'In opposition to ... ethnically absolute approaches, I want to develop the suggestion that cultural historians could take the Atlantic as one single, complex unit of analysis ... and use it to produce an explicitly transnational and intercultural perspective' (1993: 15). Connected with this is his employment of the powerful metaphor of the ship (see Chapter 2 above).

The creolisation or hybridisation culture results from complex, uneven and unequal processes of social interchange often over many centuries, processes of interchange which have proliferated many 'societies' in the world. While there are now 200 states, there are thought to be at least 2,000 'nation-peoples', all of which may suffer various kinds of displacement and ambiguous location (see Cohen 1997: ix–x). Only a minority of 'societies' in some minimal sense are therefore constituted as separate nation-states-societies. Most societies are not nations, let alone nation-states. Perhaps the most striking of such non-nation-state societies are the 'overseas Chinese' with a membership calculated as between 22 and 45 million (Cohen 1997: chap. 4).

Many of these 2,000 societies can indeed be viewed as diasporic, once the concept of diaspora loses its particular association with intense victim, forced loss and traumatic suffering which has been paradigmatically associated with the Jewish experience. Cohen advocates a more varied typology: of victim disaporas (such as Africans via the slave trade), labour diasporas (such as Italians in the US), trade diasporas (such as the Lebanese), imperial diasporas (such as Sikhs) and cultural diasporas (what Gilroy terms the 'Black Atlantic', 1993; Cohen 1997; Van Hear 1998). Diasporas entail the notion that 'the old country' where one is no longer living, exerts some claim upon one's loyalties, emotions and identity. Such an old country can be defined in terms of language, religion, customs or folklore. All diasporic communities are thus in part cultural.

Such diasporic societies cannot persist without much corporeal, imaginative and increasingly virtual travel both to that homeland and to other sites of the diaspora (Kaplan 1996: 134–6). Clifford summarises the means of mobility: 'dispersed peoples, once separated from homelands by vast oceans and political barriers, increasingly find themselves in border relations with the old country thanks to a to-and-fro made possible by modern technologies of transport, communication, and labour migration. Airplanes, telephones, tape cassettes, camcorders, and mobile job markets reduce distances and facilitate two-way traffic, legal and illegal, between the world's places' (1997: 247).

The sacred places and the family and community members to be visited, corporeally or imaginatively, are located in various 'societies'. They are linked through 'structured travel circuits' (Clifford 1997: 253). Such modes of travel and exchange, what Clifford terms the 'lateral axes of diaspora', reorganise the very sense of what is a social group's 'heritage' that is never simply fixed, stable, natural and 'authentic' (1997: 269). The cultures that get produced are curious hybrids, constructed and reconstructed through heterogeneity, difference and diverse mobilities. Diken demonstrate the unsettling character of such hybrid identities in the case of the Turkish diaspora in Denmark (1998: chap. 5). He suggests that 'There is no hybrid in the Union Danish' would effectively characterise the Danish search for purity and order and their hostility to Turkish cultural hybridity.

Imaginative travel through TV images has become particularly salient to the heritage and identity of some groups (Samuel 1994: 25). One dramatic example of a diasporic heritage being remade through imaginative travel is that of Irish culture. Though literature, arts, drink, dance, sport, the concept of the Celtic Tiger and so on, signifiers of Irishness have become a powerful component of a contemporary globalising culture (see Peillon and Salter 1998). Irishness no longer signifies poverty, drunkenness and labourers. In entering the global stage, Irishness has been remade. This can be interestingly seen in the case of *Riverdance*, a classic cultural hybrid. *Riverdance* has its roots loosely at least within Irish dance; but simultaneously with its emphasis upon stunning spectacle, visual exhilaration and the aural technologising of the body, it is quintessential 'global dancing' (O'Connor 1998). The leading dancers of *Riverdance* have, together with a variety of other global celebrities, become 'diasporic heroes' within Ireland. They are part of a diasporic élite, the members of which have been able to create their own biographical narratives in and through global flows and networks. Corcoran notes that: 'our diasporic heroes are drawn precisely from those spheres of life which are deeply implicated in global information and communication structures – transnational media systems, international sport and publishing' (1998: 136; a similar story could be told about the diasporic heroes of the Black Atlantic).

Cohen indeed goes on to suggest that there is an elective affinity between what we might term the processes of 'diasporisation' and the proliferation of global networks and flows. This is because:

> Deterritorialized, multilingual and capable of bridging the gap between global and local tendencies, diasporas are able to take advantage of the economic and cultural opportunities on offer ... As diasporas become more integrated into the cosmopoli, their power and importance are enhanced.
>
> (1997: 176)

Especially the close-knit family, kin, clan and ethnic connections within a diaspora enable the flows of migrants and income across national borders and the more general organisation of diasporic trade. Also the tendency for diasporas to live within major 'global' cities means that they particularly contribute to, and profit from, the increasingly cosmopolitan character of such thriving places (see Hannerz 1996). Thus a Chinese investor in San Francisco stated that he could live anywhere in the world as long as it was near an airport (Clifford 1997: 257)! The significance of certain nodes in any given diaspora is indeed to be seen in the case of overseas Chinese who have generated Chinatowns in many major cities across the globe. The largest is in New York and is a strikingly recent phenomenon. In the 1960s there were only 15,000 residents but over the next twenty years it grew twenty-fold with a staggering array of services, workshops and increasingly professional trades. Chinatowns have of course become key nodes within the routeways of 'global tourism' since they sell authentic 'ethnic quaintness', a quaintness cleaned up and repackaged for the international tourist gaze (Cohen 1997: 93).

Finally, we should note that there appears to be some development of other kinds of transnational identification. Across the countries of the European Union two-thirds of people claim to feel 'European' although few associate the EU itself with that feeling (Leonard 1998: 19). There is an apparently increasing sense of European-ness. Habermas suggests that this might result in a European civil society if it were possible to develop a European public sphere (1998: 7, 1992). Such a public sphere may develop through talk about EU matters, through increasing information about Europe, through common cultural and sporting events, through extensive corporeal travel and so on (see Stevenson 1997: 57; Morley and Robins 1995). However, there are clear divisions of class with regard to this European-ness, with capitalists, managers and professionals being the most European, although they also appear the most global (see Mann 1998: 195–6; Roche and van Berkel 1997; Axtmann 1998).

I have thus elaborated three kinds of disruption of nations and national heritage. There is the emergence of various global 'stages' for the spectacle-isation of nation and identity. Multiple forms of alternative memory and heritage have been developed by the 'little platoons' rather than by and for national élites. And economically and culturally innovative diasporas and transnational identities have emerged from, and have in turn generated, complex mobilities. In Chapter 7 I explore some of the citizenship conse-quences of these processes, of how they disrupt the ability of nation-states to produce for their national race an exclusive citizenship based upon a unique bounded space. Cohen notes that there is an enhanced scope for multiple affiliations, both to and beyond the nation-state. There is a 'chain of cosmopolitan cities and an increasing proliferation of subnational and transnational identities that cannot be easily contained in the nation-state system' and in the notion of clearly given and exclusive national citizen-ship (Cohen 1997: 175).

Conclusion

There are therefore a variety of ways of dwelling, but that once we move beyond that of land, almost all involve complex relationships between belongingness *and* travelling, within and beyond the boundaries of national societies. People can indeed be said to dwell in various mobilities; bell hooks writes: 'home is no longer one place. It is locations' (1991: 148). I have also noted some ways in which instantaneous time transforms contemporary modes of belonging and travelling. Current time is 'like an ever-shrinking box, in which we race on a treadmill at increasingly frenetic speeds'; this allows us only 'the very briefest experience of time' (Macy 1993: 206; see Virilio 1986).

In conclusion I will elaborate a mode of time and forms of dwellingness that I have referred to at various points in this chapter. This glacial time resists instantaneous time and seeks to slow down time down to 'nature's speed' (see Macnaghten and Urry 1998: chap. 5). This metaphor of the glacier indicates a number of characteristics. First, glacial time is extremely slow-moving and ponderous, de-synchronised from both clock and instan-taneous times. Change therefore occurs over generations and indeed can only be observed inter-generationally. Such change depends upon the glacier's context or environment. A glacier cannot be separated from its environment where it can be said to dwell. In that location it requires long-term care and monitoring. It is impossible to predict what will happen over such the very long-term because small changes in the glacier's 'envi-ronment' can transform its long-term viability. In turn its condition significantly impacts upon this 'environment'. The time of the glacier is part of its existence qua glacier and is not something to be imposed via particular measuring devices.

So glacial time is slow-moving, beyond assessment or monitoring within the present generation. It involves the relating of processes within their context and imagining what will happen over many generations. It is a time intrinsic to its mode of dwelling, thus mimicking the enormously long 'timescapes' of the physical world. Such timescapes include the thousands of years it takes soil to regenerate, for radioactive contamination to dissipate, or for the impact of genetically modified organisms to be clearly evident (Adam 1998: 145–9; Sullivan 1999).

Various writers and environmentalists have begun to articulate such a time and to argue that humans should organise their lives in accordance with the glacial temporalities of the physical world. Griffiths, for example, says that we should reject the obsession with speed, to walk and cycle rather than to drive or fly, and to see how slowly nature works and to tailor actions to the slowness of time's nature (1995). Likewise Macy argues that it is necessary to 'break out of this temporal trap' caused by current instantaneous time. She advocates inhabiting 'time in a healthier, saner fashion. She talks of opening up our experience of time in organic, ecological or even geological terms and in revitalising relationships with other species' (1993: 206). Road protestors, according to Mckay, sought to replace linear notions of time (what I call clock-time) with those that are cyclical, cosmological and bodily (1996: 139). Adam shows how gardening involves knowing and caring about the future, where every action is marked by multiple, simultaneous time-horizons (1998: 95–6). She also argues for locally grown and seasonal foodstuffs to be a basic citizenship right which supermarkets should satisfy (Adam 1998: 157). More generally, there is an increasing reflexive awareness of the long-term relationship between humans, animals and the rest of 'nature'. It moves back out of immediate human history and forwards into an unspecifiable and unknowable future.

Generally, it seems that the more the future impinges on and predefines the present the more intense becomes the concern about the past – in print, television and electronic records, in museums and heritage parks, in collecting art and artefacts, through the dating of species and so on (Adam 1996: 139). Huyssen describes the significance of the importance of memory as: 'an attempt to slow down information processing, to resist the dissolution of time … to claim some anchoring space in a world of puzzling and often threatening heterogeneity, non-synchronicity and information overload' (1995: 7).

Glacial time can be seen in various forms of resistance to the 'placelessness' of instantaneous time. The organisation *Common Ground* seeks to remake places as sites for 'strolling' and 'living in', and not just for passing through 'instantaneously'. It has developed the idea of community-based 'parish maps'. Clifford summarises it as the 'belief that local people together know more and care more than they are ever credited with; that they can make brave decisions, guide change and keep the strands of history and richness of nature healthy and vibrant' (1994: 2). This slowing down of place, or the capturing of place by its 'community', presupposes glacial time. People feel the weight of history, of those memories and practices within that very particular place, and to believe that it can and will still be there in its essence in many generations' time. For *Common Ground* such places can be anywhere, not merely those places which have the right look. Clifford summarises the determinants of local distinctiveness as 'the patina and detail which makes up ordinary places giving them identity and particularity' over the long-term, stimulating our diverse senses (1994: 3). Thus the appreciation of the detail of certain localities presumes glacial time, as opposed to the clock-time of the national state and the instantaneous time of much corporeal, imaginative and virtual travel.

Such a glacial time can develop in relationship to where one was born or brought up, to one's place of current residence or work, or to where one has visited or even where one might visit corporeally or imaginatively. This can however produce conflicts over different glacial times. Lee shows in her discussion of Yew Tree Tarn in the Lake District the conflicts between two such 'glacial times' (1995). There is first, that of aesthetic beauty which in England is mobilised through the National Trust and seeks to preserve the permanent *look* of the tarn for future generations. This visual preservation will be effected through a clear interference with nature. And second, there are the underlying geological and geomorphic processes which will 'naturally' dry out the tarn and transform it into a meadow and hence will not preserve it for viewing by future generations. In this second sense there are *invisible* long-term natural processes at work. Which glacial time wins out depends upon a struggle that is in part between different sensuous regimes.

It is also argued that women are often more able to develop glacial time. This is partly because they have had to develop shadow times, times that develop in the shadow of clock-time but are partially distinguishable from it (Adam 1990: 94). Davies shows that the time of a 'carer' is open-ended, outside commodified clock-time which is much more men's time (1990; men can of course be carers and may thus develop such a notion). Women as carers are not only in time but also have to give time (Adam 1990: 99). But also because of women's role in the 'natural' activities of childbirth and childrearing, they may develop alternatives to clock-time: 'As such it [clock time] is clearly at odds with the rhythms of our body and the "natural" environment where variations and the principle of temporality are a source of creativity and evolution' (Adam 1995: 52). Fox argues that a woman in labour is: 'forced by the intensity of the contractions to turn all her attention to them, loses her ordinary, intimate contact with clock time' (1989: 127). More generally, because of the role of many women in the activities of procreation, childbirth and childrearing, women are often more likely to be tied into time as inter-generational (Adam 1995: 94).

In the final chapter of this book I return to these questions of nature and time, particularly within the context of developing a 'sociology-with-nature'. Before that I consider in more depth the scapes and flows that cross borders, that remake contemporary forms of dwelling and the resulting rights and duties of citizenship with regard to the environment and to the globe more generally. Chapter 7 is about some remakings of citizenship in relation to different dwellings in various times.

Citizenships

The Vietnam War, the revolutionary changes in eastern and middle Europe, as well as the war in the Persian Gulf are the first world political events in a strict sense. Through the electronic mass media, these events were made instantaneous and ubiquitous … The arrival of world citizenship is no longer a phantom, though we are still far from achieving it.

(Jürgen Habermas 1995: 279)

Introduction

I begin by briefly considering a mid-1990s newspaper article entitled 'Iran bans Baywatch with purge on "Satan's dishes"' (Temourian 1995). 'Satan's dishes' turn out to be the satellite dishes that enable TV programmes transmitted from outside Iran to be received inside. The Islamic leaders see these dishes as causing a 'cultural invasion of world arrogance' from the west, against which the country need to be 'immunised' in order to maintain the purity of Islam. From April 1995 onwards anyone using such a dish faced imprisonment or a heavy fine. The Islamic leadership is described in the article as continuing 'to set its face against the world'. The world here comprises certain global flows, including foreign news and entertainment programmes such as Baywatch, which are relayed through satellites located in territory that belongs to no particular society. The 'world' is not therefore the two hundred and sovereign societies, each being able to determine what its population should see and hear; the 'world' in this article is taken to comprise the global scapes and flows discussed in previous chapters.

There are two further points to note about this article. First, the proposed removal of the satellite dishes will eliminate particular sets of relationships that have connected Iranians with the global media. The satellite dishes are crucial since they effectively complete the hybrid network of peoples and objects that ensure that CNN or Baywatch is exactly the same in Iran as in say Italy (apart from sub-titles or dubbing).

Cheap satellite dishes are all that stands between Iranians and a wide array of global flows. They are the final link in a global chain of connections.

Second, we are clearly meant to read this article as implying that globalisation is good and that the outlawing of these dishes constitutes an infringement of the rights of Iranians to watch global TV. This right is clearly meant to hold even where what can be watched are trivial programmes such as Baywatch. Temourian implies that it is a *right* of Iranians to see such programmes made outside Iran and which describe patterns of life and representations of sexuality and gender mostly foreign to those within Iran. Particularly important in this elaboration of the rights of 'global citizen' are certain rights of the senses, especially in this case of men to be able to see extensive images of western consumerism and especially female sexuality. Such rights to participate in a global society are presumed in this article to be more or less natural, as opposed to the unfair rights of the Iranian state to prevent Iranians from participating within the globalised world. It is presumed that societies should not be able to close their borders to global flows.

This brief example illustrates some of the paradoxical connections of citizenship and globalisation. As process and as discourse, both citizenship and globalisation have swept much else before them in recent years. In the case of citizenship, movements to demand rights of national citizenship have been enormously powerful in one continent after another (see Huntington 1991, on 'democratization'). This demand for the rights of citizenship and for the institutions of civil society occurred most strikingly within the former Eastern Europe. The year 1989 in many ways represents the year of the citizen, two hundred years after the subjects of Paris took to the streets demanding to be citizens (Murdock 1992). In 1989 peoples in many diverse societies: 'wanted to be citizens, individual men and women with dignity and responsibility, with rights but also with duties, freely associating in civil society' (Garton Ash 1990: 148).

And yet 1989 is when the discourse of globalisation took off. Exponential growth in analyses of the global suggested that there might be a putative global reconstitution of economic, political and cultural relationships. The struggles for citizenship and democracy, most strikingly in 1989 with the fall of the Berlin Wall and the Pro-Democracy movement in China, were instantaneously transmitted throughout the world. We have seen that global money markets, world travel, the Internet, globally recognised brands, global corporations, the Rio Earth summit, 'global celebrities' living as global citizens and so on, all speak of social experiences which partially transcend the nation-state, the national citizen and a nationally organised civil society.

So just at the moment that everyone is seeking to be a citizen of a society, so global networks and flows appear to undermine what it is to be a national citizen. Does globalisation mean that nationally-based forms of citizenship have become, or will become, redundant? Does it entail the withering away of society and its unique citizens formed within its policed national borders? What rights do states have to regulate these global flows? Does globalisation imply a notion of universal human rights and duties? Are there indeed citizens of the 'globe'?

In conventional debates a major issue is whether citizenship is seen as a property of individuals or whether it is collective. A rights-based approach is conventionally criticised as overly individualistic, one response being to emphasise the social practices that could be thought to generate or underpin any such rights (see Turner 1993a: 2). In this chapter I adopt a collective approach but show that the collective practices involved are diverse and not confined to those that occur within a particular society. I show the connections of diverse mobilities with new diverse notions of citizenship.

Contemporary citizenship can also be described as 'post-modern'. In some places there is no modern rational-legal state, with a clear monopoly of power, able to deliver unambiguous rights and duties to its citizens who comprise a nation of strangers. And elsewhere global networks and flows restructure social inequalities and transform many states into 'regulators' of such flows. Corporations, brands, NGOs and multinational 'states' have emerged more powerful than nation-states. While we saw in the previous chapter the important development of 'societies', such as the overseas Chinese, which are non-coterminous with the boundaries of nation-states. Overall the hybrid character of many apparent societies in a post-colonial period results in a disjunctive, contested and inconsistent citizenship, which Yuval-Davis terms a 'differential multi-tiered citizenship' order (1997: 12; and see Bauböck 1994).

There are then many social organisations delivering different kinds of rights and duties to different kinds of citizens over very different geographical reaches. Citizenship is contested not just within a nation-state over the access of different social groups to rights such as personal property, a job or health-care. There is a more fundamental contestation over what are the appropriate rights and duties of citizens living within, and moving around, the contemporary world; over what entities should be providing citizenship; and over what mechanisms should adjudicate between the different complexes of rights and duties over very different temporal and spatial scales.

In the next section I elaborate some of the limitations of the existing citizenship literature, especially T.H. Marshall's society-centric formulation which has hugely influenced debates across the globe. Following that I consider certain implications of the 'environment' for the nature of contemporary citizenship. I then elaborate the concept of global citizenship through the prism of hazards, rights and duties, reporting on some research relating to the mass media and global imagery. I show the paradoxical entanglements of citizenship and consumerism in the contemporary cosmopolitan and mobile order.

Citizenship debates

The sociology of citizenship within Britain takes the concept of the bounded society as central. Each society is presumed to be a sovereign social entity with a state at its centre that organises the rights and duties of each member. Most major sets of social relationships are seen as flowing within the territorial boundaries of each society. The state possesses a monopoly of jurisdiction over the territory of the society. It is presumed that economies, social class relations, politics, culture, gender, ethnicity and so on, are societally structured. In combination such relations constitute the social structure that determines the life-chances of each member of that society. This concept of society has been central to western notions of what it is to be a human being, someone enjoying the rights and duties of citizenship. To be human has meant that one is a member of a particular society.

Brubaker summarises how there has been a emergent duality of humans and society: 'the articulation of the doctrine of national sovereignty and of the link between citizenship and nationhood; the substitution of immediate, direct relations between the citizen and the state for the mediated, indirect relations characteristic of the ancien régime' (1992: 35). It was thought that most economic and social problems or risks were produced by, and soluble at, the individual society. The concerns of each were to be dealt with through national policies. Societies involved the concept of the citizen who owed duties to, and received rights from, their society.

The most important formulation of this societal conception of citizenship was Marshall's lectures delivered during the heyday of British welfare state formation (in 1949: reprinted in Marshall and Bottomore 1992; see Bulmer and Rees 1996). Marshall articulates this relationship between society and citizenship: 'the claim of all to enjoy these conditions [of civilised life] is a claim to be admitted to a share in the social heritage, which in turn means a claim to be accepted as full members of the society, that is, as citizens' (Marshall and Bottomore 1992: 6).

Marshall shows how inequalities of social class can co-exist with the formal equalities of citizenship. He says that citizenship was established in England over a number of centuries: civil rights being acquired in the eighteenth century, political rights during the nineteenth century, and social rights in the first half of the twentieth century (Marshall and Bottomore 1992: 17). By the middle of the current century people in Britain had been mostly constituted as full members or citizens of their society. Citizenship is a status bestowed on those who fully participate in their society (Marshall and Bottomore 1992: 18). Societies are constituted through its citizens who over some centuries came to enjoy common rights, as well as some limited common duties.

Marshall describes citizenship as a 'developing institution' that creates an image against which achievement can be measured and towards which people can aspire for further gains. It is thus partly normative – that citizenship ought 'to embrace the majority of the population in a supportive system of social security' (Turner 1993b). Like social class, citizenship is a product of capitalist social relations. During the twentieth century social class and citizenship have been at war with each other. Marshall suggests that classes experienced reducing differentials of income and wealth during the twentieth century as a result of the enriching of citizenship rights which challenged some of the hugely unequal consequences of class (Marshall and Bottomore 1992: 45). Such citizenship was based upon multitudinous forms of 'nationalised' expertise which *in toto* managed the 'social' (Rose 1996).

There have been both many objections to, and elaborations of, Marshall's arguments. First, he erroneously projects the continued growth of citizenship into the foreseeable future and does not consider how attacks on, and reversals of, citizenship could occur (Marshall and Bottomore 1992: 57; Runciman 1996: 54). Thatcherism in Britain could be viewed as a partially successful attempt to contest some of the social rights acquired in the previous half-century. Also Marshall's periodisation is especially confusing with regard to the 'civil' rights achieved by the trade union movement. Even in Britain they were gained much later than the eighteenth century and are more 'collective' in character than more individualistic civil rights (Mann 1993; Rees 1996: 11–13). Also the British state is multinational and citizenship rights have been more restricted within Scotland, Wales and Ireland/Northern Ireland (especially for Catholics), as compared with England (see McCrone 1992, on Scotland). Rights have been less fully established and there have been extensive struggles to force the dominant-England nation to establish full rights of citizenship elsewhere within the UK. Marshall's account mostly applies to England. It is less relevant to other 'western' countries, let alone to those countries which were parts of empires which were run by the societies of the 'west' (Mann 1996; Hewitt 1996).

Marshall's account is strikingly weak in relationship to inequalities of gender and sexuality. He really only analyses the spread of citizenship to able-bodied white, adult males (see Rapoport 1997, on the lack of citizenship rights of many categories of Americans until very recently). Women became citizens in a pattern different from that of men, most obviously because women remained seriously short of rights for much of the period. The obtaining of citizenship seems significantly differentiated by gender in part because, for women, political rights are a precondition for the achievement of their basic civil rights, and not the other way round as for men (Walby 1997; Rees 1996: 10–11; Richardson 1998). Thus there is no single moment of nation-state formation when citizenship is achieved for all adults (Walby 1997: 171). Also gay men and lesbians still remain only partial citizens even in the 'west', since they do not possess many civil and political rights (Richardson 1998). Marshall also provides little explanation of how citizenship comes to develop and in particular he ignores military conflicts and their resulting mobilisations of the citizenry (Mann 1993). Marshall neglects the hugely important role of class, gender, ethnic, gay, disabled and other forms of social mobilisation in the very processes of acquiring citizenship rights 'from below' (Turner 1986, on citizenship from below).

I shall though develop some rather different kinds of criticism. First, citizenship has been conceived of within the west in terms of national risks that may face anyone living within a given territory, national rights that those possessing full membership should receive, and national duties that are appropriate for all such citizens of a society. Underlying such notions has been the prism of social governmentality: 'Government from "the social point of view" ' (Rose 1996: 328). In the British context:

> codifiers such as Beveridge and Marshall constructed a vision in which security against hardship, like hardship itself, was social and to be provided by measures of benefit and insurance that, in name at least, were to be termed 'universal', including all within a unified 'social citizenship'
>
> (Rose 1996: 345)

In focusing upon occupation, income and class, Marshall presumes that social citizenship is the ultimate stage of societal achievement.

However, with globalisation and the re-emphasis upon the category of the community, there is a more general collapse of the power of the social and the development of what Soysal terms 'post-national' citizenship (1994; Rose 1996). She argues that national citizenship is losing ground to a more universal model of membership located within an increasingly deterritorialised notion of a person's universal rights (1994: 3; Bauböck 1994). This post-national citizenship is especially connected with the extensive growth of guest-working across many different societies. It is also related to greater global interdependence, increasingly overlapping memberships of different kinds of citizenship, and the emergence of universalistic rules and conceptions regarding human rights formalised by various international codes and laws (UN, UNESCO, ILO, EU, Council of Europe, Geneva Conventions, European Human Rights Convention and so on). Overall there is an increasing contradiction between rights, which are universal, uniform and globally defined, and social identities, which are particularistic and territorially specified.

This growth of post-national citizenship and more globally reinforced notions of human rights thus stem from an array of new processes and institutional arrangements stretching across different societies. There are a wide variety of citizenships developing in the contemporary world. These include first, cultural citizenship involving the right of all social groups (ethnic, gender, sexual, age) to full cultural participation within their society (Stevenson 1997). Second, there is minority citizenship involving the rights to enter another society and then to remain within that society and to receive appropriate rights and duties (Yuval-Davis 1997). Third, ecological citizenship is concerned with the rights and responsibilities of the citizen of the earth (van Steenbergen 1994). Fourth, there is cosmopolitan citizenship concerned with how people may develop an orientation to other citizens, societies and cultures across the globe (Held 1995). Fifth, consumer citizenship is concerned with the rights of people to be provided with appropriate goods, services and information by both the private and public sectors (Urry 1995). Finally, there is mobility citizenship concerned with the rights and responsibilities of visitors to other places and other cultures (Bauman 1993a).

Each of these citizenships suggests the limitation of Marshall's civil-political-social trilogy. That trilogy is organised around the citizenship of stasis, of the rights and duties attributed to, and available to, those living and working within a given territory by virtue of their long-membership of that society. By contrast these alternative conceptions are citizenships of flow, concerned with the mobilities across various borders, of risks, travellers, consumer goods and services, cultures, migrants and visitors, and of the rights and duties that such mobile entities should enjoy. Such flows involve both threats to, and forms of resistance around, civil, political and social elements that cannot be distinguished from each other. Citizenship of flow de-differentiates civil, political and social rights and responsibilities.

There is a further problem with the way that Marshall conceives of the citizen at the level of the nation-state-society. Citizenship does not in fact entail a specific spatial form (see Pierson 1996: 129). Focusing upon the societal/national level as Marshall does, is to adopt a historically specific form of citizenship. In other literature the classical locus of citizenship was the agora of the Greek city-state. The word citizen is a combination of *cité* and *sein* (Turner 1993b: 177). The spatial 'boundaries' of citizenship are inherent within the very constitution of what it is to be a citizen and are not historically invariant. Those boundaries are not necessarily those of the nation-state (Pierson 1996: 128–30).

In 1949 Marshall's focus upon the nation-state boundary of citizenship could have been justified. But contemporary citizenships are implicated in processes which, in by-passing the borders of the nation-state, imply contradictions between different notions and conceptions of citizenship.

Some rights and duties are derived from, and owed to, both peoples and objects which lie outside the boundaries of each particular society and to some degree 'outside' all societies (Giddens 1996). Marshall's conception of the citizen is overly state-ist and insufficiently economic *and* cultural. In the next section I consider the role of the global media and changing forms of travel and consumption in fostering new modes of putative global citizenship, as novel 'communities of taste, habit and belief become detached from national contexts' (Stevenson 1997: 44). Contradictions develop between national rights and duties *à la* Marshall and these citizenships of flow.

Marshall also mainly concentrates upon the rights involved in citizenship and says little about the duties of citizenship (unlike the more duty-based citizenship notions of the ancient world). Recently the notion of the 'active citizen' advocated by new communitarians have sought to redress the balance of duty and right, partly by emphasising that within a community one's person's duties are an important source of rights for another person (Etzioni 1993). Also much of power of the environmental movement lies in its advocacy of a revived ethics of care towards the one earth, an ethics of responsibility which insinuates itself into almost every mundane decision that is made (such as which washing powder to buy). Thus there are some significant duties involved in contemporary citizenship; as can be seen in each of the citizenships of flow listed above. Moreover, these duties increasingly constitute obligations, not only for ordinary citizens in their day-to-day lives, but for states, corporations and international organisations. There are tentative moves to extend the duties of citizenship to any legal entity whether individual or collective (Pierson 1996: chap. 5).

Citizenship and the environment

I now discuss those new forms of citizenship that are particularly related to issues of the environment since this demonstrates the weakness of the society-nature divide. I begin with Turner's definition of citizenship: 'that set of practices (juridical, political, economic and cultural) which define a person as a competent member of society, and which as a consequence shape the flow of resources to persons and social groups' (1993a: 2). This definition brings out that citizenship is not simply juridical; that it is cultural as well as social; that it involves the flows of resources, power and inequalities; that it involves social practices; and that the rights and duties concern competent societal membership and not atomised individuals.

However, given the processes outlined in previous chapters, what does it now mean to say that someone is a competent member of 'society'? Turner elsewhere outlines a theory of human rights, noting the significance of the UN Charter of Human Rights as a central aspect of 'globalisation' (Turner

1993b; Robertson 1990). And more generally, the growth of cultural glob-alisation, the UN, the EU, the European Court of Human Rights, the world refugee problem, OECD, aboriginal rights and so on, suggest that the 'nation-state is not necessarily the most suitable political framework for housing citizenship rights' (Turner 1993b: 178).

Moreover, implicit in Turner's definition above is a human-centric focus, namely that it is only humans who should be the bearers of rights. His theory of human rights is based upon the notion of the need to compensate for human frailty – that humans typically exist under condi-tions of scarcity, disease and danger. Also in the modern world the institutions which supposedly protect humans are often the cause of new risks to human survival. Citizenship is not always protected by societal institutions since such institutions frequently reinforce the conditions of human frailty (Beck 1992).

But this theory of human precariousness ignores how there might also be 'rights of nature' since nature too is particularly frail (see Turner 1993b: 184–5). Until recently of course people in the west assumed that nature (including animals) had no rights and non-humans only existed to serve humans. There was a utilitarian relationship between humans and nature. There was no sense of an inclusive ethical community (Nash 1989: 17). Recently it is argued that at least some animals do possess rights because of their exceptional frailty and catastrophic dependence upon humans (as with British cattle!). Nash points out that the notion of *natural* rights has been powerful within the US in facilitating the claims to 'citizenship' of animals (see 1989: chap. 6 on 'liberating nature'). As Worster declared in 1980: 'It is now nature's turn to be liberated' (1980: 44). The failure to provide basic rights to living organisms often now generates intense campaigns to establish the rights of certain animals to freedom or liberty (see Anderson 1997: chap. 5, on the media panic engendered by the 1988 seals epidemic). In recent years, domestic, some wild and many laboratory animals have begun to have such rights championed, campaigned for and integrated within a restructured civil society (see Macnaghten and Urry 1998: 66–8). Petulla noted in 1980 that: 'The Marine Mammal Protection Act [and] the Endangered Species Act [embody] the legal idea that a listed nonhuman resident of the United States is guaranteed, in a special sense, life and liberty' (cited in Nash 1989: 161).

More generally Roszak wrote in the 1970s of the rights of inanimate nature: 'We are finally coming to recognize that the natural environment is the exploited proletariat, the downtrodden nigger of everybody's industrial system … Nature must also have its natural rights' (cited in Nash 1989: 13; and see Newby 1996, on environmental citizenship). The Brundtland Commission Report on *Our Common Future* states: 'All human beings have the fundamental right to an environment adequate for their health and well-being' (quoted Batty and Gray 1996: 154). Various American states have affirmed the ecological rights of their citizens, while ecological rights are written into the newly drafted South African constitution (Batty and Gray 1996: 153).

However, most global institutions are problematic for the environment because they are organised into nation-states, such as the General Assembly of the UN with delegates from 184 countries. This structure of the UN leads to the ignoring of issues which do not fit into particular nation-states; it takes limited account of regional blocs such as ASEAN or the EU; it neglects powerful internal regions such as Silicon Valley; it fails to represent other organisations which claim to represent global interests such as Greenpeace; and it generally evades consideration of the causes and consequences of global networks and flows. Newby considers whether a green Leviathan will be necessary to intervene against individual nation-states so as to protect the global commons. Without a Green Leviathan we are all 'pre-citizens' with regard to the global environment (Newby 1996).

Van Steenbergen advocates three extensions of rights: to future generations of humans, to animals and to 'natural' objects (1994; see Batty and Gray's discussion of the human rights to an adequate environment: 1996). Such new duties towards animals and objects reconstruct human beings as possessors of special powers and responsibilities. Ecological citizenship thus comprises a set of rights (such as reasonable quality of water and air) and a set of duties (such as not consuming CFCs). However, this formulation is too mechanistic. Ecological rights and duties involve the implosion of the supposedly separate civil, political and social rights. Indeed the globalisation of risk highlights the artificiality of Marshall's differentiations and how contemporary social life involves simultaneous experiences that subsume and fuse these apparently different bases of citizenship. Batty and Gray maintain that, although there may be a duty to protect the environment, there is no corresponding right to an adequate environment which can be seen as analogous to the conventional civil, political and social rights (1996; and see Jagtenberg and McKie 1997: 188–90).

Some of this complexity of environmental rights and duties can be illustrated by the story of British beef in the 1980s and 1990s (see Macnaghten and Urry 1998: chap. 8; Adam 1998). BSE highlights the huge difficulties that a nation-state has in managing risks in a world of global flows, especially when large-scale farmers and corporations take no responsibility for outcomes in glacial time. It seems that a small and largely unnoticed change in the rendering practices of British abattoirs produced a remarkable chain of events that cost the British taxpayer £4 billion and partially threatened the viability of the EU. BSE is thus an explosive reminder of the inability of nation-states to predict, manage and control risk in a chaotically interacting world of hybrids. As Beck argues:

Politicians say they are not in charge: they at most regulate developments. Scientific experts say they are merely creating technological
opportunities but not deciding how they are taken up. Businesses say
they are just responding to consumer demand ... Our society has
become a laboratory with nobody responsible for the outcome of the
experiment.

(Beck 1996)

Eating beef has been peculiarly significant within British culture. Roast
beef and Yorkshire pudding signify middle-class suburban taste that has
become generalised. Roast beef is normally consumed within the family; it
stands for family life. It is thought that roast beef is good for one; to
consume roast beef is a right of the British. But during the 1980s British
people were placed in a laboratory in which cattle were turned into carnivores and on occasions into cannibals, and where there was no secure
knowledge of the outcomes of this laboratory experiment (Adam 1998:
chap. 5).

Risks in such a laboratory are not open to the senses (see Chapter 4
above). Bad beef could not be sensed as bad and hence people were hugely
dependent upon expert systems to provide guarantees across time and
space. But it is just those guarantees that cannot be provided in the case of
something so indeterminate as BSE. With such hybrids science is often
unable to provide the baseline of 'fact' about the external world. Current
knowledge is not only open-ended and uncertain but also contingent upon
sociological assumptions such as the practices of abattoir workers. A
decade or more after the notification of the disease the origins of BSE, the
nature of the infectious agent, its host range, its means of transmission and
its relationship with CJD in humans remain mostly unknown. Attempts by
the British state to protect the rights of its present and future citizens by
relying upon 'science', as if science can provide incontestable evidence, has
proved hugely problematic.

BSE also shows that there is a wide concern over the 'industrial' practices of the global food industry that infringe the rights of people to
control the most private aspects of their lives. The realisation that farmers,
sanctioned by the state, were treating 'natural' herbivores as carnivores,
confirmed the 'unnatural' character of modern agriculture that does not
respect the rights of animals. CJD in humans appears to confirm that
'nature' knows how to strike back against such apparently 'unnatural'
infringements of those rights. The saga of the mad cow seems to show the
power of 'nature' to extract its revenge upon the human species when its
rights have been so undermined.

The controversies surrounding BSE thus demonstrate the complexity of
contemporary citizenship. How can nation-states govern nature and guar-
antee the rights of their citizens in a world of global flows with many of

the rights-affecting hazards operating in glacial time? The chaos of BSE occurred where the state could not rely upon scientific experts to provide definitive and uncontestable results about what is safe for its citizens. Nation-states possess limited scope to deal with the risks that affect citizens within their national borders. There is no global network that provides immutable test-procedures. Moreover, risk is not a technical or scientific problem but is interlinked with wider political, social and moral processes. Public attention results from media images often flowing in from abroad and which can scandalise publics and occasionally shame nation-states.

I have so far used the language of 'risk' to characterise the rights and duties of citizenship. However, there are contemporary threats to rights which differ from the risks we are familiar with, such as driving a car or having one's house burgled (see Adam 1998: chap. 2 on the following). These are side-effects of otherwise reasonable actions and can be subject to a local calculation of appropriate odds. There is a fairly direct relationship between actions occurring within a particular time and space and the outcomes that occur. But BSE is less a risk and more a hazard resulting from the intrinsic character of the global economy. Instantaneous market forces created a hazard that seriously infringes the rights of both animals and peoples, including those who are historically and geographically distant. They result in no-choice hazards for animals and peoples; in the case of BSE, British cows and the consumers of British beef within and beyond the borders of Britain. Therefore people are subjected to large-scale, often invisible manufactured hazards organised outside local contexts of action. As contemporary economies and societies treat the world as a laboratory, many new hazards are generated. Citizenship is thus intricately intertwined with knowing about, avoiding or minimising the impacts of such massive hazards upon the rights of humans, animals and the rest of 'nature'.

Global citizens

I now turn to the global issue directly, through a further aspect of van Steenbergen's argument, namely that there are a number of different global citizens whose socio-spatial practices highlight, or secure or threaten various rights and duties (1994). Extending his analysis we can suggest at least seven such types of 'global citizen' (see Falk 1994).

First, there are global capitalists who seek to unify the world around global corporate interests that are increasingly 'de-nationalised' and borderless. Such capitalists employ the increasingly internationalised sciences in ways that can result in new hazards being unpredictably generated (Martin and Schumann 1997). Second, there are various kinds of global reformers who use large-scale international organisations to moderate and regulate global capitalism, often using science to legitimate their interventions which often deploys the discourses of rights (organisations include UNESCO, ILO, World Bank, IMF, WHO). Third, there are those working within such organisations as global managers, who seek to implement managerial, scientific and technical solutions to ameliorate various hazards.

Then there are the global networkers discussed in previous chapters who set up and sustain work, professional or leisure networks constituted across national boundaries through imagined or virtual travel (Castells 1997). Fifth, there are 'earth citizens' who seek to take responsibility for the globe through an ethics of often highly localised care (Sachs 1993). Sixth, there are global cosmopolitans who develop a stance and an ideology of openness towards certain 'other' cultures, peoples and environments, often resulting from extensive corporeal travel. A subset includes 'global celebrities' such as the late Princess Diana who have been described as the 'new mobility' or cultural chameleons (McRae 1997). Finally, there is the global green backlash that, in the post-communist era, uses 'environmentalists' and believers in 'political correctness' as the new global scapegoats which can be critiqued and attacked. This occurs through anti-environmentalist demonstrations, the use of the media and physical intimidation (see Rowell 1996).

Obtaining future rights for the world's population depends upon the balance of forces between these different global hybrids and the degree to which any is able to achieve some kind of global hegemony. Each practice articulates one or more notions of citizenship and gives rise to a reconfiguration of hazards, rights and duties, or what I termed a citizenship of flow. This is implied in Stevenson's description of changes in citizenship produced by 'new cultural contexts defined by the movement of people and images through the dimensions of time and space' (1997: 51; see Therborn 1995). I now set out the lineaments of global citizenship in terms of hazards, rights and duties.

First then, hazards have developed which at the putative global scale include (Davis 1990; Beck 1992; Sachs 1993; Rotblat 1997b; Macnaghten and Urry 1998; Adam 1998):

- environmental or health 'bads' resulting from the treating of the earth as a scientific laboratory and from 'global' environmental change
- cultural homogenisation which may destroy aspects of local culture (so-called 'cocacolonisation' of culture)
- the development of diseases carried across national borders by travellers (Aids)
- the intermittent collapse of world markets particularly for agricultural commodities

- financial meltdowns and their devastating effects upon economic and social life within particular places, especially in the developing world
- the proliferation of hugely insecure, unpoliced and out of control 'wild zones' (such as the former Yugoslavia, Somalia and inner-city USA)
- the dependence of people upon expert systems (for travel, environmental protection, medical support, safe food and so on) which they may not trust since such systems contradict day-to-day social experiences and forms of lay knowledge

With regard to the rights to participate within a putative global community, these include the rights (according to Ohmae 1990; Bauman 1993a; Soysal 1994; Bauböck 1994; Held 1995; Kaplan 1996; Pierson 1996; Rotblat 1997a, 1997b; Yuval-Davis 1997; McRae 1997; Castells 1997; Stevenson 1997):

- to migrate from one society to another and to stay at least temporarily with comparable rights as the indigenous population; to be able to return not as stateless and with no significant loss of rights
- to be able to carry one's culture with one and to encounter elsewhere a hybrid culture containing at least some elements of one's own culture
- of all social groups to full cultural participation within the world society (to possess information, representation, knowledge, communication)
- to be able to buy across the globe the products, services and icons of diverse other cultures and then to be able to locate them within one's own culture which incrementally changes
- to be able to form social movements with citizens of other societies to oppose particular states (France's nuclear testing), sets of states (the North), corporations (News Corporation), general bads and so on; such movements often involve branding, advertising and commercialisation and are not necessarily progressive even if oppositional
- to migrate for leisure purposes throughout most of the countries on the globe and hence to 'consume' all those other places and environments (including those *en route*). With the elimination of many formal barriers to leisure travel contemporary citizens expect to consume places anywhere and everywhere (especially those deemed of global significance such as UNESCO-designated World Heritage Sites)
- to be able to inhabit environments which are relatively free of risks to health and safety produced by both local and distant causes; to sense the quality of each environment directly rather than to have to rely on expert systems which are often untrustworthy; and to be provided with the means by which to know about those environments through multi-media sources of information, understanding and reflection

Duties within the putative global community include the responsibilities:

- to find out the state of the globe, both through national sources of information and image and especially through sources which are internationalised (see Ohmae 1990, on the borderless world where states are increasingly unable to control flows of information)
- to demonstrate a stance of cosmopolitanism towards other environments, other cultures and other peoples. Such cosmopolitanism may involve either consuming such environments across the globe; or refusing to consume such environments because of a concern for its wider impact (see Bell and Valentine 1997, on how to 'cook global', as opposed to 'cooking for a small planet')
- to engage in forms of behaviour with regard to culture, the environment and other places which are consistent with the various conceptions of how to live sustainably; to be an ethical visitor (Shiva 1989; Wood and House 1991; Bauman 1993a: 241, on the 'world as the tourists' oyster')
- to respond to images, icons and narratives which address people as highly differentiated citizens of the globe rather than as citizens of a particular nation, ethnie, gender, class, generation (such as Benetton advertising the colours of the world; see Szerszynski and Toogood 1999)
- to seek to convince others that they should also seek to act on part of the globe as a whole which is suffering collectively, rather than in terms of shared identity interests. Such persuasion will involve both informational and image-based media (Hansen 1993a, 1993b; Rotblat 1997b)
- to act in terms of the global public interest rather than in terms of local or national interests (Turner 1993b: 177)

I have set out some of the hazards, rights and duties of global citizenship. The formulation is schematic and only indicative of its possible components, and especially the links between cosmopolitanism and citizenship (see Stevenson 1997: 44). Obviously different social groups will be variably positioned with regard to various modes of citizenship. I will begin with women who have always been slower to receive the citizenship rights and duties derived from a nation-state. This exclusion is systematic, stemming from forms of male power over the national project (such as men being viewed as the earners of the 'family wage'). Women's rights in most societies have been contested by the dominant religion that has resisted the movement of women out of the home and into public spheres of activity. Such religions have normally emphasised women's national role as childbearers and child-rearers. Women have been mostly excluded from the military aspects of national citizenship – only recently in a few countries have they been allowed to join front-line troops. It also seems that women are more likely to be pacifist and concerned with the non-military aspects of their society (see Enloe 1989; Walby 1997: chaps 9 and 10). A pacifist famously states in Virginia Woolf's *The Three Guineas*: 'as a woman I have no country. As a woman I want no country. As a woman my country is the whole world' (1938: 109). Some women will be likely to be nomadic global citizens since they are more likely to oppose wars (see Shaw 1994: 127, on the Gulf War), to find the maleness of the symbols of national power troubling (Yuval-Davis 1997), to be particularly interested in conservation and environmental issues (Anderson 1997: 174), and to seek to convince others of the superiority of a relatively countryless notion of citizenship (Shiva 1989; Billig 1995; Braidotti 1994: 240; Kaplan 1996; Walby 1997).

Some scientists have also begun to develop notions of global citizenship. For example, Nobel Prizewinner Joseph Rotblat argues that we must develop an allegiance to 'humanity' rather than to the 'nation' (1997a: x–xi). The huge size of the world's population is not a problem; the USA with 256 million people and huge ethnic diversity generates a strong sense of national belonging. Rotblat maintains that it is the interdependence between the world's population that is the key to developing an allegiance to 'humanity' rather than to national identities:

> The fantastic progress in communication and transportation has transformed the world into an intimately interconnected community, in which all members depend on one another for their well-being. We are now able to observe instantly what is going on in any part of the globe and provide help where necessary … We must exploit the many new channels of communication to bring us together and form a truly global community. We must become world citizens.
>
> (Rotblat 1997a: x–xi)

Rotblat argues that nation-states should give up their current conception of sovereignty. This should be replaced with a split notion, of autonomy operating within certain spheres, and responsibility to higher level organisations operating elsewhere (see Leonard 1998, for an analogous argument about the EU). At the same time national citizenship should only be based upon permanent *residence*. The so-called 'natural' bases of citizenship such as race, ethnicity or religion, should be eliminated by nation-states (Rotblat 1997a: 8).

One trend which reinforces the development of global citizenship is the 'increasing role that communities that cut across national boundaries play in the lives of ordinary people' (Rotblat 1997a: 9). To some extent scientists (and other groups of academics) can be thought of as 'quasi-nations', with their own system of globally recognised rewards (through Nobel and other prizes). And as modern communications develop, so these quasi-nations will become more important and widespread. More generally, electronic communications already 'help geographically dispersed groups of people to form close ties ... Electronic communities have no territorial grounding' (Rotblat 1997a: 16). These communications can diminish or even eliminate older forms of identity based upon territory (see Chapter 6 above). Some scientists indeed see the global village replacing the nation-state, as electronic communication supplants written communication and as the 'whole earth' replaces the 'territory with borders'.

Other scientists have reflected upon the imaginative consequences of space travel. The astronaut William Anders has famously commented:

> The earth appeared as a small, blue-green sphere like a beautiful ornament, very delicate and limited ... The ancestral home of mankind did not appear vast, unlimited and indestructible ... It seemed much more like a delicate and fragile ornament that you must preserve and protect with appropriate care. Looking back, I saw no national boundaries, no dividing the earth into separate states, each with a different colour as you see on a globe in a schoolroom, a globe divided by man [sic] but obviously not by nature.
>
> (quoted Menon 1997: 28; see also Rotblat 1997b; Cosgrove 1994)

One interesting consequence of space travel and the perception of the fragile character of each planet was the treaty adopted in 1979 that made the moon a common heritage of humankind. This was in the same year that the Antarctica Treaty preserved this area in the common interest of humankind and exclusively for peaceful purposes. Other examples from the same period were the Convention for the Protection of the World's Cultural and Natural Heritage in 1972 and the Law of the Sea Convention in 1982 (Menon 1997: 32–3). Menon argues that modern science in its symbiosis with technology: 'has demonstrated that the Earth is a lonely fragile spaceship that is the only home for all humanity, however riven by divisions based on nationality, religion, colour, community or ethnicity; how it has made the world a small place with the capabilities now available for movement of ideas, information, people, goods and services; how it has demonstrated the fundamental and essential oneness of all living systems' (1997: 35–6). More generally, Vaclav Havel talks of how the 'perspective of a better future depends on something like an international community of citizens ... standing outside the high game of traditional politics ... will seek to make a real political force out of ... the phenomenon of human conscience' (quoted Rapoport 1997: 97). This is analogous to Albrow's suggestion that globality entails a new kind of 'performative citizenship' constructed from below and involving duties developed on the basis of conscience. Such a citizenship is not imposed by national statutory bodies (Albrow 1996: 178).

There is little sophisticated empirical information on how significant such a citizenship currently is. The World Value Survey conducted in 1990 asked a similar sample within about twenty societies whether they belong to the world, or to their country or to the locality or town where they currently live (see Mlinar 1997). In most societies around half identified themselves as 'localist'. What is interesting though is the ratio between what the researchers describe as 'cosmopolitans' and 'nationalists'. This ratio was low in most of Scandinavia and in the former Eastern Europe (about 1: 3). But in western Europe the ratio was more like 1:1.5–2. In Belgium, Italy and Germany almost as many people saw themselves as cosmopolitans as nationalists. This suggests that significant numbers of people do imagine themselves as citizens of transnational entities.

Specifically, with regard to the environment many appeals encouraging people to act in some way on its behalf do depend upon a shared concept of global citizenship. Such a putative global citizenship is itself a kind of culture. Just as national cultures need cultural resources – symbols, narratives, rituals – from which a sense of common destiny can be woven, so too does a culture of cosmopolitanism and global responsibility. The shifts of concern from the local and immediate to the global requires the creation, circulation and consumption of the cultural resources and a glacial sense of time which is necessary to create an 'imagined community' at the global level, and the translation of this community into actions. It may be that through the global media, people may have begun to imagine themselves as part of a single 'community' and indeed even to share some conditions in common with those of non-human animals (Wark 1994). Beck argues: 'With nuclear and chemical contamination, we experience the "end of the other", the end of all our carefully cultivated opportunities for distancing ourselves and retreating behind this category' (1992a: 109).

The Pugwash Conference on Science and World Affairs expect the global media to play a particularly significant role but not because they carry cognitive information across the globe. Rather cultural work is carried through media *images* that are able to engender 'an emotional response to the world events that they portray', they heighten the awareness of regional and global interdependence and they put pressure on offending governments to moderate their often offensive actions (Rotblat 1997a: 14).

Citizenship has always necessitated processes of communication and the distribution of symbolic resources (Murdock 1992: 20–1). Printing, especially of newspapers, was particularly significant in the nineteenth century development of the imagined community of the European nation and the growth of the nation-state. While in the development of twentieth century notions of national citizenship, publicly owned radio broadcasting was particularly significant. As Murdock notes: 'Where commercial broadcasting regarded listeners as consumers of products, the ethos of public service viewed them as citizens of a nation state. It aimed to universalise the provision of the existing cultural institutions' (1992: 26–7). By addressing its listeners as families who would be grouped around the radio set, it cemented powerful imaginative links between home and country, father and fatherland.

In particular, BBC radio broadcasting in inter-war Britain helped to develop the increasingly national ideology of Englishness. Hall argues that the BBC 'was an instrument, an apparatus, a "machine" through which the nation was constituted. It produced the nation which it addressed: it constructed its audience by the ways it represented them' (1993: 32). In developing a National Programme Service, the BBC 'marginalised or repressed the situated cultural formations generated by labour, ethnicity, and locality' which did not fit into this dominant constitution of the nation (Murdock 1992: 29).

There are two main ways in which peoples, places and images can represent a nation (see Billig 1995: 98). First, depiction, that certain words, images or phenomena depict the core features or essential characteristics of the nation in question. Particular landscapes often represent or depict the nation in this sense (see Lowenthal 1994). Second, someone or some institution speaks for that nation. Governments are often said to represent the nation in this sense, speaking, acting and arguing on its behalf. Obviously these two modes of representation are closely connected – speaking for the nation can entail speaking to the nation and characterising its key features.

I consider below what might constitute the 'global' correlates of these two senses of representing the nation? How can the globe be depicted and how can it be spoken for? What role does the mass media play in these two modes of representing the globe? Is there in any sense the emergence of a global 'public sphere'? (Keane 1991; Cohen 1996; Thompson 1995)

The public sphere, as elaborated in Habermas, involves unrestricted debate, the wide availability of public forums, freedom of expression and discussion, and rational persuasion and argumentation (Cohen 1996; Cottle 1993). Especially in his early writings he saw the mass media as inimical to such a public sphere because of how they eliminated the possibility of a reasoning critical public (Habermas [1962] 1989).

But in later formulations Habermas elaborated how radio and television were in fact the 'media of the public sphere' being themselves dependent upon the resources of the 'lifeworld' (1974: 49). In particular the mass media; 'free communication processes from the provinciality of spatio-temporally restricted contexts and permit public spheres to emerge, through establishing the abstract simultaneity of a virtually present network of communication contents far removed in space and time' (Habermas 1987: 390). Such media enjoy 'ambivalent potential', generating a variety of countervailing tendencies to the commodification, centralisation and homogenisation which were emphasised in older Frankfurt-analyses of the media (Habermas 1987: 390; Cohen 1996; Cohen and Arato 1992). As Habermas comes to emphasise the plural character of the public sphere, so this in part is comprised of the multiple mass media which can allow for decentralisation, competition between messages, the influence of journalistic ethics and a resistance to straight manipulation by the media (1992; see Cohen 1996).

In the following I suggest however that the mass media do in fact make an enormous difference to the public sphere which gets turned into a 'public stage'. The media alter the very possibilities of interaction and dialogue, remaking the public sphere through highly mediated forms of quasi-interaction, producing new ways of conceiving of self and identity and generating fundamentally new performativities (see especially Szerszynski and Toogood 1999; Gitlin 1980; Meyrowitz 1985). Central to such a global public stage are various images, as well as face-to-face conversation and more straightforward informational flows.

This public stage involves images of events, spectacles and personal performances. A large array of personalities are placed on the public stage and brought into the home so that people feel that they know them as individuals (Scannell 1996: 165). Television personalises discourse, favouring informal and back region styles of address and performance (Meyrowitz 1985: 106). The formal language of political discourse becomes informalised and familiar. TV makes public much of what once had been private. Before broadcasting 'public life was not "for me"'. It was beyond one's reach.

Images play a central role because many sources of cognitive information are not trusted. Indeed media images can provide more stable forms of meaning and interpretation in a globalising culture in which, as we saw in previous chapters, 'seeing is believing', especially when those images are repeated time and time again (see Morley and Robins 1995: 38–9, on TV and images). These images can connect local experiences with each other and hence provide powerful sources of hermeneutic interpretation to make sense of what would otherwise be disparate and apparently unconnected events and phenomena. It also seems that images are important because, according to Ramonet: 'the objective is not to make us understand a situation, but to make us take part in an event' (quoted Morley and Robins 1995: 195). Too much information may not be desired, partly because of information overload (Keane 1991: 182–6). Morley and Robins discuss the 'desire not to know' since thinking can be disturbing. Or more prosaically, 'Becoming informed is tiring' (Ramonet, quoted Morley and Robins 1995: 194). The most that people want is to be a small part of the imagined community concerned about the plight of the Amazonian rainforest, the war in Bosnia, the famine in Ethiopia, but not cognitively to understand the nature of such events or what might be seriously done to eliminate them. Images constitute a cumulative process of what has been termed 'cultivation', of the way that people are exposed over time to various consistent and compelling symbolic streams (see Anderson 1997: 26).

The mass media are thus important because they publicly stage what might otherwise remain private. All individuals and social institutions can be put on to that stage and subject to exposure. Meyrowitz describes how electronic media leave no time for preparation behind the scenes. There is little that can be kept secret and remain private. Nothing much will for long remain backstage and kept away from the prying eye of the increasingly borderless media. The transformation of the public sphere into a public stage de-differentiates the previously separate spheres of the private and the public (see Cohen and Arato 1992).

Meyrowitz describes the fascination with exposure, with how the act of exposure seems almost more exciting than what is exposed (1985: 311–20). And one exposure leads on to the desire for further exposure in an escalating desire to reveal, to shame, to produce yet another scandal for global circulation. This exposing of the misdeeds of the powerful can of course happen to every person and every institution. No-one is necessarily exempt from this shaming culture, especially not powerful figures or institutions. A person's 'good name' (Clinton), the 'brand' of a state (France and its nuclear testing) or the 'brand' of a corporation (British banks involved in the pensions mis-selling scandal), all constitute particularly vulnerable symbolic capital. In just one week, Rio Tinto, Shell, P & O, Premier Oil, Nestlé and ICI all held Annual General Meetings in which groups of protesters mobilised the world's media to expose and to shame the companies for their perceived misdeeds (often in countries far away from where the meeting is held). The brand can be threatened with exposure and shame and it can rapidly evaporate. There is a right of global scrutiny conducted by the media, especially at certain keynote moments (such as big public meetings; see Stevenson 1997: 46). Such scandals are instantaneously transmitted across the globe. Scandals threaten 'reputation' and reputation functions as symbolic capital or power that increasingly flows across national borders waiting to be undermined (Thompson 1997). It is said that the example of Nike, and the threatening of its brand because of the 'slave wages' paid to its workforce, shows that 'public shaming and consumer pressure can have a mighty impact upon mighty manufacturers' (Dionne 1998).

Media events also reveal themselves as visibly staged. They entail performances in which almost everything can be brought into public staging. Albrow notes the importance of global events in which the world views itself. It is the event placed upon the world's stage. Examples include the globally broadcast Live Aid concert, the release from prison of Nelson Mandela, the dramatic death and subsequent funeral of Princess Diana, the Olympics Games, the Millennium and so on (Albrow 1996: 146; Anderson 1997: 172–3). In each of these striking images came to be globally circulated, recognised and consumed, images which have become central to the iconography of global citizenship. Such images can be seen as both depicting the globe and speaking to the globe.

Of course many such visual images are accompanied by written or by spoken text which contextualise these images. Within an electronic age there are many possible relations between speakers and audiences. Thus such texts will involve 'a complex deixis of little words' which imaginatively connect the speaker to particular audiences (Billig 1995: 106). The little words involved here include 'I', 'you', 'we', 'they', 'here', 'now', 'this' and 'that'. They are all used deictically, they point to various contexts of the utterance. When Clinton points to 'this, the greatest country in human history', the 'this' evokes a national place of belonging, an habitual nation which will implicitly understand that the 'this' in Clinton's speech refers to the US (Billig 1995: 107). All Americans will understand the deixis here, that the US is 'the greatest country in human history'. 'We' typically means not just the speaker and the immediate listeners but the imagined nation that is the site of routine obligation and connection (Stevenson 1997: 45).

But does this deictic pointing occurs not just to the nation, but to wider imagined communities stretching beyond its borders (although see Stevenson 1997)? Billig cites Mandela who refers to 'the people of South Africa and the world who are watching' (1996: 107). The 'we' in his speeches almost always evokes those beyond South Africa who are watching on the global media and have collectively participated in the country's rebirth. When Mandela states that 'we are one people' he is pointing both to South Africa and to the rest of the world. Likewise at Princess Diana's funeral much of the deictic pointing from the television commentators to the collective 'we', was in fact to the estimated 2.5 billion people watching the event from around the world.

I now turn briefly to some research on the scale and impact of various 'global images'. What evidence does this provide of what, following Billig, we might term 'banal globalism'. Are there ways through depiction and speaking that the globe is represented? What are the main forms that this takes? These questions were researched through a 24-hour survey of all the visual images available on a variety of TV channels within Britain (see Toogood 1998; Szerszynski and Toogood 1999). The following array of 'global' images was found during this 24-hour period, deployed within advertising as well as on regular programming. Numerous examples of images in each of the following categories were found over a 24-hour period:

- images of the earth, including the mimetic blue earth, but also including a football as indexical of the globe where soccer is conceived of as the iconic game of the global citizen
- long, often aerial images of generic environments (a desert, an ocean, a rainforest) which are taken to depict the globe (and threats to it) rather than depicting particular nations
- images of wildlife – especially auratic animals (lions), persecuted species (seals) and indicator species which index the overall state of the environment (eagles)
- images of the family of man where it appears that people from almost all the cultures of the globe can all be happily in one place (a sports stadium) or share one global product (Coke)
- images of relatively exotic places and peoples (beaches, native dancers, ski slopes), often taken with unusual camera perspective, which suggests the endless possibilities of global mobility, communication and cosmopolitanism
- images of global players who are famous in and through the world's media and whose actions (and in cases misdeeds) are endlessly on display to the whole world (OJ Simpson, Madonna, Queen Elizabeth II)
- images of iconic exemplars who, through their setting and costume, demonstrate global responsibility – they are seen as speaking and acting for the globe (Mandela, Princess Diana as the 'queen of hearts', Ken Saro-Wiwa)
- images of those engaging in actions ultimately on behalf of the global community, this being represented by a montage of different cultures or places, or of people encountering the needy, the starving, the sick and so on (Red Cross, UN Volunteers, Special Constables)
- images of corporate actions conducted on behalf of the globe and of its long-term future (water companies cleaning up the environment, drug companies spending billions on new medical research)
- images of global reportage which is shown to be present, live and staffed by iconic figures able to speak, comment and interpret the globe (Kate Adie [BBC], Christiane Amanpour [CNN], John Pilger [ITV])

The widespread availability of these images demonstrates a number of features about contemporary citizenship. First, it is intertwined with a wide variety of representations of the globe within the contemporary media, such representations being associated with diverse kinds of cosmopolitanism and mobility. These images imply that to be excluded from free mobility and full access to the global market-place are infringements of one's rights (see Stevenson 1997: 51). Second, these global images involve both the depiction of the globe and speaking for the globe; in some cases the same media item contains both aspects. Princess Diana in some ways was an icon of the globe and especially of its cosmopolitanism *and* had the authority to speak on the globe's behalf. Third, these images are constitutive of contemporary culture that is increasingly bound up with questions of citizenship (see Stevenson 1997: 56–7). Global citizenship is inextricably connected with cultures and with modes of cultural access and equality. And finally, many of these global representations occur within advertisements, thus demonstrating that global networks and flows often involve curious hybrids of the once-separate public and private spheres. There is increasing overlap between these spheres and hence between issues of citizenship and of contemporary consumerism, which I now explore a little further.

Citizenship and consumerism have been opposed practices and discourses. Citizenship was to do with service, the public, the state – while consumerism involved the private, the market, the customer. But now they overlap and clear boundaries cannot always be drawn around what is 'public' citizenship and what is 'private' consumerism. A number of processes have dissolved such boundaries: the development of consumer rights with the transformation to a post-Fordist mode of production/consumption; the increasing significance of the quality of 'service delivery' to users within many economic sectors; the increased array of 'services' which are deemed relevant to the forming of the citizen-ship of flow; and changes in the nature of the state away from direct provision to the regulation of goods and services provided by diverse private, voluntary, quasi-public and public agencies (see Chapter 8 below). Stevenson maintains that:

> people are increasingly becoming citizens through their ability to be able to purchase goods in a global market: hence citizenship became less about formalized rights and duties and more about the consump-tion of exotic foods, Hollywood cinema, Brit pop CDs and Australian wine. To be excluded from their commercial goods is to be excluded from citizenship (full membership) in modern Western societies.
>
> (1997: 44)

This de-differentiation entails a major shift from public citizenship, mostly provided by the nation-state on the basis of compulsory taxation and insurance, to 'consumer citizenship' provided by many institutions, global organisations, nation-states, corporations, NGOs, consumer organisations, the media, voluntary groups and so on. The role of the state shifts to a regulatory one concerned with monitoring performance and achieving common standards.

Advertising and branding are central components of contemporary citi-zenship. There is a de-differentiation between public information and private advertising, between education and entertainment (hence edu-tainment), and most importantly between textual information and visual imagery. Part of what constitutes contemporary citizenship are the objects and services that can be bought, both within and across national borders. In Chapter 2 I discussed the significance of consumerism and of 'tourist shopping' in the development of citizenship rights in the later years of 'Eastern Europe'.

Meijer also discusses how branded products and advertising provides resources whereby people can conceive of themselves as global (1998). She even suggests that Coca-Cola could be seen as 'an expression of a new way of living and understanding global cultural values' (Meijer 1998: 239). Somewhat similarly Burgess describes new forms of culture that involves the duty to purchase particular 'global' goods (1990: 144; and see Albrow 1996: 147, on the global phenomenon of WOMAD). People more gener-ally can imagine ourselves as members (or supporters) of organisations through purchases, wearing the T-shirt, hearing the CD, surfing to the page on the Web, buying the video of iconic figures and so on. Objects can provide for that sense of what can be called vicarious 'network-membership' or consumer citizenship.

This consumerism thus relates to changes taking place in what it is to be a 'member' of organisations in the emergent global age. Membership normally involved joining organisations that then provided various rights *and* duties to their members. Such membership was organised through a relatively clear and formalised hierarchy. Trade unions were the classic example of this model. But many new 'organisations' have developed which are much more networked and mediated. Greenpeace is perhaps the best example of an oppositional organisation skilled at developing and handling its media images (see Hansen 1993a: 157). In the case of the Brent Spar protest:

> the communications deployed were second to none. The protestors had satellite telephones and a Mac computer that downloaded photographs and video footage to a media base in Frankfurt. Greenpeace employed its own photographer and cameraman to capture the images that ensured the story was splashed in papers and television screens across the world.
> (Pilkington *et al.* 1995: 4; see also Macnaghten and Urry 1998: 68–72)

The particular image used by Greenpeace was that they were bearing witness to the destruction of the sea, with the sea having the power to stand for global nature. Greenpeace campaigners waved to the world from Brent Spar and were recorded by the world's media (who were invited by Greenpeace to use their facilities). Many such transnational networks are involved in the bearing of witness, and then in communicating that bearing across the globe (see Keck and Sikkunk 1998: 18–20). Hugo Young summarises the long-term impact of Shell's eventual retreat over Brent Spar: 'There is business, there is government, and there is what Greenpeace would call the citizenry of the world whose interests it represents against the baleful conspiracies of the other two' (1995; and see Rheingold 1994: 265; Castells 1997).

In appearing to speak for the citizenry of the world Greenpeace has developed an iconic brand identity. Other transnational networks are similarly involved in the bearing of witness and the proliferation of image, but except in the case of consumer boycotts, rarely with mass mobilisation (Keck and Sikkunk 1998: 19). Environmentalists can view themselves as *citizens* of Greenpeace or other organisations that bear witness, rather than as citizens of a particular nation-state since their rights and duties derive from their cultural identification with the organisation and especially from its branding, and not necessarily from their national society.

Conclusion

The language of rights and duties has been developed over some centuries to provide grounds for the (generally) progressive extension of citizenship to various new groups of human beings. Although this extension has been hugely contested, uneven, unfair and couched in overly individualistic terms, such extensions have been broadly beneficial and bound up with a general incorporation of populations within inclusive 'societies' which orchestrate such rights and duties (see Batty and Gray 1996: 162). I noted just how extensive has been the demand for citizenship in the recent period across much of the globe; national citizenship has become a key element of a global society. To assert a right is to make a claim that, unless there is some other right which is somehow superior to the one in question, then it is imperative for the given nation-state to ensure that all members of the relevant social category should be in receipt of that right.

In the preceding section I considered some elaborations of such a position, especially considering rights which cannot be simply orchestrated within and by each nation-state but only by some kind of putative global society. However, the organisation of the world into nation-states is seriously problematic for such rights. It may also be problematic for some duties where putative global citizens often find little about nation-states in which they can trust although they may possess a well-developed sense of global responsibility.

Overall new hazards, rights and duties criss-cross the conventional national, conception of citizenship, and the socio-spatial context within which people can imagine themselves as being fellow-citizens may be partly shifting from the nation to the globe. I considered in particular some developments of the mass media that may prefigure a shifting sense of identity, loyalty and attachment. My argument though did not imply that 'national' forms of citizenship have simply evaporated, nor that the 'consumerisation' of citizenship is, in terms of 'social equality', at all desirable, nor that global citizenship is anything but a tender flower whose impact may be very limited.

However, those sceptical about the argument here might though consider again Marshall who argued that 'a shared style of life' was necessary for citizenship. Inequalities of taste and lifestyle should not, he said, 'cut too deep' but occur within a population that is 'united in a single civilisation' (see Hindess 1993: 27). Thus paradoxically it may be that aspects of global homogenisation, consumerism and cosmopolitanism, are necessary conditions for preventing social divisions in the contemporary world from 'cutting too deep' and from preventing any kind of citizenship to persist. Given the extraordinarily heterogeneous character of most national societies, and especially their capital cities (see Therborn 1995), then some 'uniting into a single civilisation' through the power of the global mass media may be paradoxically necessary for the peculiar character of contemporary citizenship.

Chapter 8

Sociologies

Modern bourgeois society, a society that has conjured up such gigantic means of production and exchange, is like the sorcerer who is no longer able to control the powers of the underworld that he has called up by his spells.

(Karl Marx and Friedrich Engels [1848] 1964: 58)

Gardeners and gamekeepers

In this book I have developed three main arguments. First, I have shown multiple ways in which the mobility of people has been sociologically ignored. Incorporating the mundane practices of personal mobility (albeit often technologically assisted) transforms appropriate metaphors and sociological concepts. Social processes have to be rethought as involving multiple mobilities with novel spaces and temporalities. Second, notions of such mobile persons can be transferred, metaphorically and literally, to the mobility of other entities, of ideas, images, technologies, monies, wastes and so on. In each case it is hybrids that are mobile, flowing along various scapes. Such networks comprise 'physical' and 'human' entities whose power derives from their complex mobile combination. And third, I have considered some of the disruptive implications of these mobile hybrids for the nature of a self-reproducing 'society' and hence for the discipline of sociology that has been historically based upon the societal realm as its starting (and finishing) premise.

I begin this chapter by briefly turning to Bauman's famous use of the metaphor of 'gardening' to describe modern societies based upon their careful tendering by the state (1987; Hetherington 1997a: chap. 4). He suggests that a gardening state has replaced earlier states which can be described through the contrasting metaphor of the 'gamekeeper'. Such a gamekeeper state was not bothered to give society an overall shape and was uninterested in detail. By contrast the gardening state presumes exceptional concern with pattern, regularity and ordering, with what is growing and what should be weeded out. Legislators have been central to the gardening state, as using their reason to determine what is and what is not productive of order. The social sciences have been part of that application of reason to society through facilitating the husbandry of societal resources, identifying what is and what is not to be cultivated and determining what are the exact conditions of growth of particular plants.

The new global order involves a return to the gamekeeper state and away from that of the gardener. The gamekeeper was concerned with regulating mobilities, with ensuring that there was sufficient stock for hunting in a particular site but not with the detailed cultivation of each animal in each particular place. Animals roamed around and beyond the estate, like the roaming hybrids that currently roam in and across national borders. States are increasingly unable or unwilling to garden their society, only to regulate the conditions of their stock so that on the day of the hunt there is appropriate stock available for the hunter.

The former East European societies were societies based upon exceptional degrees of very detailed gardening. But these societies were unable to develop dynamically and became surrounded by hordes of 'animals' (consumer goods, images, western ideas and so on) which increasingly crossed into and over the land that had been so carefully husbanded. Their populations chased after the animals and trampled the carefully tended plants to destruction (a different kind of 'animal farm').

In this final chapter I examine a number of ways in which gamekeeping rather than gardening is an appropriate metaphor for contemporary social developments. I advocate a sociology that is able to mobilise powerful theory and research in a post-societal, post-gardening epoch. My arguments are organised around the implications of gamekeeping for four crucial domains, 'civil society', the 'state', 'nature', and the 'global'.

I begin with showing how social inequalities should be seen as spatial and temporal, and are not just inequalities that are within the garden. I consider the development of a *civil society* based upon automobility, in which the ability to roam and to escape the previous fixities of public time and space is central. There is regulation of automobility but not the ability to determine where the herds of cars might travel to or when. In the following section I analyse changes in the character of national and other *states* as the regulation of flows and networks of civil society become central to their constitution. States turn into gamekeepers rather than gardeners, as they regulate the herds moving in and across their land. In the next section I consider how gardening was based upon a strict division between the gardener and the garden, showing how this parallels the historic divide between society and nature, or between sociology and the physical sciences. I argue against this division and explore, through the concept of affordances, some implications of 'natural–social' hybrids for contemporary citizenship. I then return to the herds of interacting, patterned and intensely mobile hybrids that roam the *globe*. I briefly consider whether notions of chaos and complexity can assist with the elaboration of a 'sociology beyond societies', a sociology that is appropriate to gamekeeping rather than gardening. The book concludes with an advocacy of a mobile sociology.

Mobile civil societies

I briefly return to the motor car, arguing that automobility has ushered in some striking changes in the character of civil society; and that it is only by analysing the significance of such mobility that contemporary social life can even begin to be analysed. I am obviously reducing everything here to the car, but in part to use this as a model of analysis that the study of mobility necessitates (and see Chapter 3 above).

It has been seen that automobility is a complex of interlocking machines, social practices and ways of dwelling, not in a stationary home but in a mobile semi-privatised capsule. The hybrid car driver is at home in large-scale movement, transcending considerable distances in order to complete a series of activities within highly fragmented moments of time. Many journeys involve multiple functions juggled together and involving complex monitoring. Automobility makes instantaneous time and new kinds of space central to how social life is configured. People dwell and socially interact via movement in and through their cars. The car is thus not simply an extension of each individual; automobility is not simply an act of consumption because of the way that it reconfigures the modes of sociality. Social life has always entailed various mobilities but the car has transforms these in a distinct combination of both flexibility and coercion. Civil society is thus in part a 'civil society of automobility', a civil society of quasi-objects or 'car drivers', and much less of separate human subjects who can be conceived of as autonomous from their machines. People in effect enter the public sphere in their mobility.

Automobility is a source of freedom, the 'freedom of the road'. Civil society seized on the roads and carriages that had been the province of the élite and turned these into the current systems of mass transportation. The flexibility of the car enables the car driver to roam at speed, at any time in any direction along the complex road systems of western societies that link together most houses, workplaces and leisure sites. Cars therefore extend where people can go to and hence what as humans they are able to do. Much of what many people now think of as 'social life' could not be undertaken without the flexibilities of the car and its availability 24 hours a day. One can travel to and from work, friends and family when one wants to. It is possible to leave late by car, to miss connections, to travel in a relatively time-less fashion. People travel when they want to, along routes that they choose, finding new places unexpectedly, stopping for relatively open-ended periods of time, and moving on when they desire.

Moreover, car-driving is an activity that people enjoy in itself or at least feel that it is part of what it is to be a contemporary citizen. Car-driving is a goal and a set of skills and accomplishments in themselves. Driving a car can be a source of pleasure: of flexibility, skill, possession and excitement. Not to drive and not to have a car is to fail to participate fully in western societies. In research conducted in the 1970s it was reported that the over-whelming majority of employees demonstrated more skill in driving to and from work than in what they actually did while they were at work (Blackburn and Mann 1979). The car is never simply a means of transport. To possess a car and to be able to drive it are crucially significant rights articulated through powerful motoring organisations. States provide the licensing and the infrastructure, of who may roam but not where or when.

The nature of this 'dwellingness' has changed, from 'dwelling-on-the-road' to 'dwelling-within-the-car'. The former was found within inter-war North America and Europe and can be seen in much of contemporary Africa and Asia. The car driver is part of the environment through which the car travels and the technologies of insulation do not exist or have not been repaired. The car driver dwells-on-the-road and is not insulated from much of its sensuousness. This contrasts with the car driver in the contem-porary west who dwells-within-the-car, one effect of which has been to provide much greater safety for the car driver since risks have been exter-nalised on to those outside. Those who dwell within the car are also able not only to prevent the smells and sounds of the outside to enter, but also to effect an environment in which a certain sociability can occur. Car drivers control the social mix in their car just like homeowners control those visiting their home. The car has become a 'home from home', a place to perform business, romance, family, friendship, crime and so on. Unlike 'public' transport, the car facilitates a domestic mode of dwelling. The car driver is surrounded by control systems that allow a simulation of the domestic environment, a home from home moving flexibly and riskily through strange environments.

But at the same time automobility coerces people into this intense flexi-bility. Automobility entails instantaneous time that has to be juggled and managed in a complex, heterogeneous and uncertain fashion (J.G. Ballard in *Crash* refers to this infantile world where any demand can be satisfied instantly; 1995: 4). This instantaneous time is to be contrasted with the official timetabling of mobility that accompanied the development of the railways in the mid-nineteenth century (and which continues with many timetables; see Lash and Urry 1994: 228–9). This was modernist clock-time based upon the public timetable (gardening rather than gamekeeping). Automobility by contrast involves a more individualistic timetabling of one's life, a personal timetabling of these many instants or fragments of time. There is here a reflexive monitoring not of the social but of the self. People try to sustain 'coherent, yet continuously revised, biographical narratives ... in the context of multiple choices filtered through abstract systems' (such as that produced by automobility: Giddens 1991: 6). The objective clock-time of the modernist railway timetable is replaced by personalised, subjective temporalities, as people live their lives in and through their car(s) (if they have one). Automobility coerces almost everyone in advanced societies to juggle tiny fragments of time in order to put together complex, fragile and contingent patterns of social life, which constitute self-created narratives of the reflexive self.

The freedom of the car subjects all of civil society to its power. The shortage of time resulting from the extensive distances that increasingly 'have' to be travelled means that the car remains the only viable means of highly flexibilised mobility. Walking, cycling, travelling by bus, steamship or rail may be relegated to the dustbin of history since these are relatively less effective means of roaming the world (Graham and Marvin 1996: 296–7).

There are three other aspects of a civil society of automobility. First, the hybrid of the car driver is in normal circumstances unnoticeable (Michael 1998). There is a careful, civilised control of the car machine deploying considerable technical and interactive skills. But in situations of 'road rage' another set of scripts are drawn upon, of aggression, competition and speed. But these scripts of the other are always components of automobility. Michael elaborates on this polysemic nature of automobility: encouraging people to be careful, considerate and civilised (the Volvo syndrome) and to enjoy speed, danger and excitement (the Top Gear syndrome). There is multiple scription involved here and hence different kinds of car driver, the careful and the competitive, which are both elements of the hybrid car driver and hence of an automobilised civil society (Michael 1998: 133). In the case of road rage, Michael argues:

> one actually needs to be more skilful, to push both body and machine into quantitatively greater alignment, than in the case where one is a responsible civilized driver ... In order to exercise 'loss of social control', one needs to practice greater technological control.
>
> (1998: 133)

Michael describes this as 'hyperhybridisation' with the human being more or less obscured or immersed within the technology and vice versa. According to motoring organisations such a virulent hybrid must be purified, by changing not the technology but the pathology of the human.

Second, automobility involves contestation. From the 1970s the car began to be viewed as more polluting than the train (Liniado 1996: 28). And most recently new roads 'slicing' through the landscape have provoked intense opposition, including from many 'car drivers'. Automobility produces resistance within civil society. Partly this is because new roads instantaneously destroy the existing taskscape and no amount of re-landscaping compensates for that sudden loss. Also roads allow means of movement into the landscape that demonstrate no *travail* and hence may be viewed as less worthy than walking, climbing or cycling that environment. Overall then, while one may 'love' one's car, the system that it presupposes is often unloved, resisted and raged against. Civil society is significantly being remade through contestations over the power, range and impact of automobility. The same people can be both enthusiastic car drivers as well as active protestors against schemes for new roads. By 1994 there were an estimated 250 anti-road groups in the UK, a movement significantly impacting upon civil society. The array of direct actions has also diversified as protesters have become more expert, through the use of mass trespass, squatting in buildings, living in trees threatened by road programmes, and digging tunnels. They too became more sophisticated in the use of new technologies, including mobile phones, video cameras and the Internet. This has enabled almost instantaneous dissemination to the media, as well as information about actions for a growing band of protesters prepared to travel up and down the country to protest against proposed developments (see Macnaghten and Urry 1998: chap. 2; see details in Mckay 1998).

Third, large areas of the globe now consist of car-only environments – the quintessential non-places of super-modernity (Augé 1995). About one-quarter of the land in London and nearly one-half of that in Los Angeles is devoted to car-only environments, where in a sense the public spaces involved in urbanisation have been swamped by automobility. These car spaces areas exert an awesome spatial and temporal dominance over surrounding environments, transforming what can be seen, heard, smelt and even tasted (the spatial and temporal range of which varies for each of the senses). Such car-environments or non-places are neither urban nor rural, local nor cosmopolitan. They are sites of pure mobility within which car drivers are insulated as they 'dwell-within-the-car'.

Automobility then constitutes a civil society of roaming herds of hybridised 'car drivers' who enter the public realm in their mobility, dwelling-within-their-cars, and excluding those without cars or without the 'licence' to drive such cars. And such a civil society of automobility transforms public spaces into public roads, in which to a significant extent the hybrids of pedestrians and cyclists are no longer part of that public. Only those moving even slowly in cars, buses and trucks are *public* within a system where public spaces have been democratically seized, through notions of individual choice and personal flexibility, and then turned into public roads. A civil society of automobility, or the right to roam where and when one wants, involves the transformation of public space into public roads.

Elsewhere in this book I have elaborated how various other mobilities transform social life. In particular such mobilities often fragment nations as a consequence of the emergence, or the resurgence, of local, regional, sub-national, networked, diasporic and global economies, identities and citizenships. In his wide-ranging review of the economic changes involved in such transformations, Scott argues that there are: 'no longer any territorial coincidence between the political forms of states, the flow of economic transactions, and the cultural and communal boundaries of "societies"' (1997: 253). Especially significant have been the growth of monies, environmental risks, taxation-revenues and information which evade control by national states and whose movements do not coincide with those of national borders. They each pass over those borders in instantaneous time. In the case of the Internet it is almost impossible to determine the point of origin of most transactions. The customer often does not know who the provider is or where they are located. To express this more graphically, there is as yet no tax authority for cyberspace.

These changes transform the analysis of social class that has been historically rooted in both data and arguments derived from the 'golden age' of organised, national capitalism. Up to the early 1970s in north Atlantic rim societies it was reasonable to investigate what could be termed 'national' classes. However, conditions are now very different. Change processes in which national states fragment or are drawn into supranational entities add 'a further potential challenge to the [historic] association between class structures and national states' (Breen and Rottman 1998: 16). Specifically with regard to the capitalist class, Scott argues that 'national capitalist classes themselves are being increasingly fragmented along the lines of the globalized circuits of capital and investment that they are involved in' (1997: 312). Some writers go on to argue that this will result in 'transnational capitalist classes' that become detached from national class situations and will possess a kind of global solidarity and cohesion (see Sklair 1995; Scott 1997: 312–13). Even if this lies a little in the future, there has been the more general growth of many powerful professions whose taskscapes are partially global and who can be said to dwell in many places located along diverse scapes. Reich argues that: 'Barriers to cross-border flows of knowledge, money, and tangible products are crumbling; groups of people in every nation are joining global webs' (1991: 172; see Luke 1996, and Chapter 7 above on scientists).

Connected to this de-nationalisation of management and many professions is the significant de-nationalisation of knowledge and of the more cultural and informational determinants of class. We have seen how information can become instantaneously and simultaneously available more or less anywhere, as knowledge has become 'de-territorialised' and turned into hugely mobile bits of information (Delanty 1998). Determinants of status within a given 'society' are as much derived from these global informational flows as from status processes that are endogenous to each such society.

Central to the historic notion of the nation-state has been a single, stable and exhaustive national identity, a civil society organised around a single nation. It is this that had ensured a coherent and unified nation-state able to striate the space surrounding it, clearly distinguishing those people and institutions inside from those who are outside. Smith summarises:

> Nation-states have frontiers, capitals, flags, anthems, passports, currencies, military parades, national museums, embassies and usually a seat in the United Nations. They also have one government for the territory of the nation-state, a single education system, a single economy and occupational system, and usually one set of rights for all citizens.
>
> (1986: 228)

In this book we have seen many ways which mobilities both within a country through especially automobility and across borders through multiple mobilities and citizenships makes such a the notion of a single, stable and exhaustive national identity implausible. In the next section I examine how states increasingly regulate these diverse mobilities that transform civil societies and the character of nation-states.

Regulating mobilities

Social inequalities are often spatial, resulting from hugely uneven forms of access to, or the effects of, various kinds of mobility. In this section I show how states connect to these diverse mobilities, and examine in particular whether national or supra-national states can ameliorate their often detrimental consequences. The shift in corporeal travel from buses and trains to cars highlights the shift in states that I want to generalise here. The development of twentieth-century automobility has involved a massive reduction in the direct production, control and timetabling of corporeal mobility; at the same time it has involved huge new forms of social regulation of such mobilities. Thus contemporary states are involved in licensing, testing, policing, taxing, building, maintaining and managing, drivers, roads and cars.

Various new mobilities imply parallel changes in the character of contemporary states that, no longer able to garden the world, can only act as gamekeepers. Deleuze and Guattari argue:

> the state has always been in a relation with an outside, and is inconceivable independent of that relationship. The law of the State is not the law of All or Nothing ... but that of interior and exterior. The State is sovereignty. But sovereignty only reigns over what it is capable of internalizing, of appropriating locally.
>
> (1986: 15–16)

And what is outside states cannot be reduced purely to the foreign policies of states. Outside are both huge worldwide machines as well as what they term neo-primitive, tribal societies. Both constitute a *'perpetual field of interaction ... its exteriority in what escapes States or stands against States'* (Deleuze and Guattari 1986: 17).

For Deleuze and Guattari, states are necessarily involved in seeking to regulate the spaces that lie beyond its borders and especially to regulate those numerous mobilities that move in and across such spaces:

> one of the fundamental tasks of the State is to striate the space over which it reigns ... It is vital concern of every State not only to vanquish nomadism, but to control migrations and, more generally, to establish a zone of rights over an entire 'exterior', over all the flows traversing the ecumenon. If it can help it, the State does not dissociate itself from a process of capture of flows of all kinds, populations, commodities, money or capital, etc. ... the State never ceases to decompose, recompose and transform movement, or to regulate speed.
>
> (1986: 59–60)

They talk of how fourteenth-century China, despite its very high level of technology in ships and navigation, 'was unable to react except by a politics of immobility, and of the massive restriction of commerce' (Deleuze and Guattari 1986: 61; the events of 1989 may have resulted from a similar immobility).

More generally, Deleuze and Guattari suggest that there has been a recent shift in western societies away from social relations based upon territory and state – that is, Foucault's disciplinary societies. The move is to societies of control, to social relations based upon numbers and deterritorialisation. Contemporary states are forced to regulate 'the mobile occupant, the movable in smooth space, as opposed to the immovable in striated space' (Deleuze and Guattari 1986: 66). Such smooth deterritorialised spaces, of which the pure number is the paradigm case, creates huge new issues for states. Such flows are smooth and deterritorialised especially because of computerised digitisation: 'what counts is not the barrier but the computer that tracks each person's position' (quoted Thrift 1996: 291).

States thus struggle to striate the space surrounding them, but numerical smooth global fluids cause them singular difficulties. This can also be seen by turning to a more conventional definition of the state: namely, that it consists of that set of centralised and interdependent social institutions concerned with passing laws, implementing and administering those laws and providing the legal machinery to enforce compliance with them. These institutions rest upon the state's monopoly of legitimate force within a given territory, which means that most of the time laws are upheld. The powers of the state ultimately rest upon this threat of legitimate force. Such powers include the ability to make and to enforce laws, to raise very sizeable sums of money through general taxation and to effect redistribution through various benefits, to employ large numbers of people and to produce a variety of especially universal services, to own and control land and its uses, to manipulate various instruments of economic policy, and to act as a 'social regulator' employing a variety of coercive and ideological techniques. No set of private institutions, even the most powerful of corporations, possesses this *range* of powers.

Some writers have proceeded to argue that such nation-states no longer possess the particular domestic combination of capacities to offset the disruptive consequences of global flows and networks, while others argue against such a thesis. I consider this latter 'anti-globalisation' argument initially.

Global sceptics argue that the thesis of globalisation is much overstated and that there are possibilities for societies and governments to control international developments. Hirst and Thompson argue that the present international economy is not as distinct as often argued and that in some ways it is less open than in the period 1870–1914 (1996; and see Weiss 1998). They also maintain that most large companies are based within a given society (Ford as American, Sony as Japanese) and there are relatively few truly international companies. Most investment occurs between the rich countries, especially between the triad of Europe, Japan and North America, and is not equally spread across the globe. They claim that governments are able to intervene and make a difference to their conditions of life of their citizens, since although the economy has become internationalised it has not been globalised. There are three critical comments to make on this thesis. Hirst and Thompson conceptualise gobalisation in the most extreme and implausible form; they over-concentrate upon the economic aspects of globalisation and ignore the many other global processes; and they do not sufficiently consider how some of the phenomena they discuss will develop further in a global direction over the next few decades.

These global sceptics do however make some effective points about contemporary states. Weiss argues that there is not convergence of states in a uniform powerless direction (1998: chap. 7). Rather there is increasing variety as a consequence of their diverse capacity to deal with global flows. States can moreover function as midwives for such flows and not just be subject to them. And states increasingly act as catalysts of networks of countries at the regional or international level and hence function as one class of agencies in a complex system (Hirst and Thompson 1996: chap. 8; Pierson 1996). Moreover, there are many international conferences and events that still involve individual states signing up to international agreements (such as the 1992 Rio Earth Summit).

However, this relatively benign analysis of the enduring power of the nation-state may significantly change if the Multilateral Agreement on Investment (MAI) is implemented. This provides a new set of investment rules that greatly increases the mobility of capital and reduces the capacity of states to striate. These rules include the principles of non-discrimination against foreign investors, no entry restrictions, and no special conditions. The Director-General of the World Trade Organisation states that with the MAI 'we are writing the constitution of a single global economy' (Rowan 1998). Critics of the MAI argue that it will generate a new class of supercitizens, namely the 40,000 transnational corporations worldwide, who will be largely exempt from any obligations to local workforces or environments. Clarke and Barlow describe the MAI as a 'Charter of Rights and Freedoms for transnational corporations against citizens and the earth' (1997: 8).

Thus shifts towards global networks and flows transforms the space beyond each state. It is this space which states have to striate and they are therefore involved in increasing efforts at 'social regulation'. Such regulation is both necessitated, and is only made possible, by new computer-based forms of information gathering, retrieval and dissemination. What states increasingly possess are exceptional information flows, especially databases, which enable performance indicators to be implemented and monitored across extensive geographical areas, within and beyond the borders of the nation-state. Such databases can refer to almost every economic and social institution. It has become possible to assess the efficiency of most aspects of life relevant to those living in or visiting any particular country. Such information flows derive from what Power terms the 'audit society' (1994). Organisations have to justify their accountability to the public (and to consumers) through an explosion of audits and the resulting availability of the data collected. There are increasing quantities of surveys and polls designed to ascertain what people really think and feel about almost all aspects of life. This polling culture is itself part of the shift in the nature of states away from the direct provision of services to the regulation of goods and services provided by state-organisations, public-private partnerships, voluntary organisations, the private sector and so on.

Britain has perhaps led the way in recent 'social regulation' (following the US model in part as well). The Conservative Governments in the 1980s, which were elected as apparent 'deregulators', introduced extensive new forms of regulation (Pierson 1996: 107; THES 1997). There was 're-regulation' of private industries (OFGAS and the gas industry), the environment (the EU Bathing Waters Directive), education (OFSTED schools inspection service), railways (the Rail Regulator), the press (Press Complaints Council), trade unions (the Certification Officer for Trade Unions and Employers' Associations) and so on (see publications from the London-based Centre for the Study of Regulated Industries).

In some of this regulation the national states of Europe are modelling themselves upon the European Union. The EU provides a kind of model of the emergent regulatory state (see Majone 1994, 1996). It is a small state employing few bureaucrats and controlling a modest budget (apart from the Common Agricultural Policy that is a historic legacy of a previous epoch). It was organised around the promotion of various mobilities and as a result of this common market, was designed to ensure peace across Europe in the post-war period. It has sought to develop the four freedoms of movement – of goods, services, labour and capital – and has intervened with national state policies to eliminate barriers to mobility, trade and competition. The EU has also pursued something of a 'social' agenda, especially since the Treaty of Maastricht in 1992, with regard to environmental, health and safety, industrial and equal opportunity policies. European laws take precedence over national laws where they conflict and it is possible for the actions of individual governments to be declared illegal, although the 'common market' remains the EU's primary consideration (see Adam 1998: 112–13).

The EU is a 'regulatory state', mostly involved in the monitoring and regulation of the policies and practices of its individual nation-states. Its Treaties and Directives are particularly powerful. They mean both that governments must bring their own legislation in line with such Treaties, and that individual citizens in the EU can appeal direct to the European Court of Justice when it is believed that national governments have not implemented appropriate policies (see Walby 1999). Such laws are cheap to pass since the costs of implementation are passed on to national governments.

An example of where such regulation has had significant effects is the development of equal opportunity policies, drawing upon Article 119 in the Treaty of Rome, which has provided a more effective legal base than that found in member countries (Walby 1999). The EU insists that there is a fundamental right to social protection, especially for migrant workers and their families when they move to other states in the EU (Meehan 1991). The EU, especially following the establishment of the European Environment Agency in 1990, has developed much environmental protection. In the UK over 80 per cent of environmental legislation emanates from the EU (Lowe and Ward 1998). Ward analyses how the European Bathing Waters Directive has provided legal norms as to what constitutes clean and unclean water. This Directive enables NGOs, such as Surfers Against Sewerage in the UK, to become more knowledgeable about the issues and to be reflexively proactive in their campaigning (Ward 1996). Regular publication of precise official data as to which beaches do not meet the appropriate standards provides the kind of media opportunities for NGOs to shame governments and water companies, as discussed in Chapter 7. Other areas where the EU has developed an extensive regulatory regime include consumer product safety, medical drug testing, financial services and competition. Survey data shows that, although the EU is overall not popular, 60 per cent or so think that the EU should deal with those matters which national governments cannot deal with. Thus 'Europe's citizens do want "problems without frontiers" to be dealt with at a European level' (Leonard 1998: 46; Lowe and Ward 1998: 22).

Thus states in the future, like the EU, will not so much tax and spend on their own forms of economic and social provision. Rather, following the EU, they will increasingly act as legal, economic and social regulators, or gamekeepers, of activities and mobilities that are predominantly provided by, or generated through, the private, voluntary or third sectors. These regulative functions are only achievable because of the emergence of extensive computer-based databases on populations, organisations and enterprises that involve almost continuous auditing. Social regulation involves increased monitoring and surveillance. It also involves heightened mediatisation in order that regulatory failure is brought into the open, made visible and individuals and organisations can be shamed by the ensuing scandals or threat of scandals.

Mobile natures

I have noted how contemporary states are often involved in efforts to regulate various kinds of deleterious impact upon the environment. Such an arena of state action demonstrates the increasing interdependence of what would once have been thought of as either 'domestic' or 'foreign' issues. It also shows the reduced significance of the means of physical coercion to the determination of the powers of states. 'Regulation' of environmental impact involves networks of other states, multilateral agencies, the power of the media to shame, the employment of international science and so on. There is no simple 'national' environment that a national state can order and regulate through its own gardening.

However, when people analyse 'nature' or the 'environment' they both appear certain of what they mean (see Macnaghten and Urry 1998, for much of the following). In different ways they adopt a taken-for-granted sense of nature, which is a singular nature, out there, immobile and waiting to be saved, either through science or through social protest. A clear distinction is drawn between nature or the environment, on the one hand, and society, on the other. Obviously what is taken to be natural differs for these different groups. For scientists the environment is a real entity to be investigated by modern science and from which the social activities and experiences of people are largely absent. To the extent that people are considered, the main issue is how to persuade them with increased information or financial inducements to behave in ways that scientists believe will improve the environment, the nature of which they have scientifically established. In the case of protestors nature is a source of particular values which are seen as especially vulnerable to the debilitating effects of modern science and the modern economy. The environment here is treated as a singular fragile nature that is enormously threatened by the values and practices of science, which treats the globe as a laboratory, and by an increasingly global marketplace.

In Chapter 1 it was shown how sociology as the science of society developed on the basis of the juxtaposition of society and nature. This juxtaposition reached its fullest development in nineteenth-century Europe. Nature was degraded into a realm of unfreedom and hostility that needed to be subdued and controlled. And modernity involved the belief that human progress should be measured and evaluated in terms of the domination of nature by society, rather than through any attempt to transform the relationship between the two. This view that nature is separate from society, and should be dominated by it, presupposed the doctrine of human exceptionalism. This entails a number of beliefs: that humans are fundamentally different from, and superior to, all other species; that societies can determine their own destinies and learn whatever is necessary to achieve such destinies; that a singular nature is vast and presents unlimited opportunities for exploitation by human societies; and that the history of each society is one of unending progress though overcoming the resistances of the natural world (see Glacken 1966; Williams 1972, 1973; Merchant 1982; Schama 1995).

The first difficulty with this formulation is that there have been many attempts to establish 'nature'; normally it is distinguished from both God and 'society'. But what has been regarded as nature has hugely varied over time and across different societies, depending in part with what particular notion of God/society it has been contrasted. Thus there has been no single nature but very different *natures*, which differ from, and often contradict, each other (see Macnaghten and Urry 1998). There is no single authority of 'nature'.

Second, one particular nature is what we now call the 'environment'. But such an environment is not simply out there and analysable either as a set of scientific laws or of human values. The environment is a hybrid, a simultaneous fusion of the physical and the social. Or as Latour maintains 'extrasomatic' resources have been necessary to sustain society. Society on its own does not hold us together but it is what is held together (1993; Diken 1998: 266–7). In the past few decades the emergence of this hybrid 'environment' has resulted from the complex interactions between a diverse mix of social and physical elements. These include environmental science, the media, travel patterns, environmental protest movements, state actions and inactions, the sensing of changes by the public, actions of corporations, various environmental writings, changing technologies, advertisements which use images of the globe, the shaming of states on the public stage and so on. The resulting hybrid of the 'environment' comprises various scientifically determined risks (such as models of climate change), particular texts and images (such as the blue globe), some notable heroic actions and moments of witness (such as Brent Spar), and particular individuals and networks (as at various road protests).

Third, there is a significant paradox about contemporary developments. In most western societies, there is a greatly enhanced focus upon the importance of nature and valuing the natural, purchasing natural products (and even natural products made more natural such as decaffeinated coffee), employing images of the natural in marketing products, policies and organisations, and joining and supporting organisations concerned with the conservation of nature (Strathern 1992: 173). But Strathern argues that culture has been necessary to rescue nature; thus there is 'the conceptual collapse of the differences between nature and culture when Nature cannot survive without Cultural intervention' (1992: 174). The strength of nature in the past lay in the way in which its cultural construction was in fact hidden from view (Latour 1993). But in the contemporary world of uncertainty and ambivalence, this is no longer true. All natures we now can identify are elaborately entangled and fundamentally bound up with social practices and their characteristic modes of cultural representation.

Fourth, different natures are indeed embedded within different patterns of social activity, of belonging and travelling (see Chapters 3 and 6). These practices are patterned over different stretches of time, from the instantaneous to the glacial, and across different spaces, from the local community, to the nation-state and to the global. Social activities are organised in terms of how people dwell within different places, how they sense such places through sight, smell, hearing and touch, how they move across and beyond such places and how much power of agency they possess to transform their lives and their immediate environment. Thus different social practices produce different 'natures'. These include: nature as the open countryside available for upper class leisure; nature as visual spectacle sensed through sketches, landscape paintings, postcards, photographs and the camcorder; nature as sets of scientific laws established especially by environmental science; nature as wilderness away from industry and cities and enabling spiritual and physical refreshment; and nature as undergoing 'global environmental change' rather than isolated localised changes.

I will make a few points about 'global environmental change'. The notion of sustainability was institutionalised at the singular global mega-event of the 1992 Rio Earth Summit. This event, the world looking reflexively at itself, led to the viewing of the environment as global. Rio emphasised global warming, ozone depletion and biodiversity – issues that rely on increasingly sophisticated scientific programmes to determine the impact of social processes upon planetary processes. A new type of science emerged in the fields of atmospheric chemistry, oceanography, climatology and geology, dedicated to establishing the impacts of industrial activities upon the bio-geo-chemical cycles of the planet, and the likely long-term effects of current and predicted trends in industrial growth. Such science has contributed to a 'new global ecological look', the sense that environmental problems may be more global, more serious, more urgent, and much more interconnected than previously imagined (Finger 1993: 40).

This globalisation of nature increases the possibilities of agency on behalf of the planet because of people's increased knowledge as how environmental risks flow across national borders. But at the same time such global flows reduce people's sense of personal agency because of the increased awareness of how states and corporations endlessly disobey their own environmental directives, fuelled by instantaneous economic and political interests. More generally, these flows transform the nature of the 'social'. I have shown various ways in which it shifts from being principally comprised of 'national social structures' to putatively globalising networks and flows (Chapters 1 and 2 above). Such global flows crisscross national borders disrupting the organised coherence of individual national societies. They exhibit spatial unevenness and temporal diversity. And this means that 'nature' becomes less intertwined with each individual national society, with a national 'community of fate', and is much more interdependent with these putatively global and hybrid relations, roaming across societies in ever-more elaborate and 'unnatural' shapes, evading constraints of time and space and of those policies routed within particular nation-states.

At the same time that various natures appear even more out of control, so many people argue that they possess rights of glacial time. However, such rights have been resisted because the context for conventional citizenship has been that of 'society' and not some broader concept of 'society-and-nature' (see Chapter 7 above). Within societies only humans are deemed to possess rights – natural and other apparently inanimate objects are not citizens and do not possess rights. In order then to attribute rights to nature (and other objects) we would have to 'treat "natural" non-humans as autonomous participants ... in the world' (Michael 1996: 135). And this would further mean that nature (and other objects) not only has rights but should also have responsibilities (see Batty and Gray 1996, for a duty rather than a rights-based approach to nature). But to conceive of natural objects, let alone artefacts, as having responsibilities, obviously runs counter to western science and its construction of the object-ness of the external world, a world separate from any sense of subjectivity.

There is one approach though to the notion that objects might be said to have responsibilities, Gibson's analysis of the affordances of the environment (1986: chap. 8; see Michael and Still 1992; Costall 1995). He argues that in the environment out there we do not encounter a set of objective 'things' that we may or may not visually perceive. Rather different surfaces and different objects, relative to the human organism, provide opportunities for lying on, sitting on, leaning against and so on. An affordance is both objective and subjective, it is both part of the environment and part of the organism. Affordances stem from the reciprocity between the environment and the organism (Costall 1995: 475). They derive from the manner in which people are kinesthetically active within their world. Nature provides limits to what is corporeally possible but it does not determine the particular actions that humans may engage in. Affordances do not cause behaviour but constrain it along certain possibilities. Michael summarises: 'there are a range of options ... implicit within a physical milieu and this implicitness is directly connected to the bodily capacities and limits of the [human] organism' (1996: 149).

Affordances can also be said to stem from artefacts as well as from the physical environment (see Costall 1995). Some examples include a path that beckons people to walk along it, a rock that provides a place to hide from the sun, a building that affords a panoramic view, a wood that is a repository of memories, a flat entrance that allows unhindered wheelchair access, the lake that engulfs one with cooling water and so on. It is also important to note various resistances existing within the environment: the heat of the sun that prevents one climbing a mountain, a road that spoils the view of a bay, the low bridge that prevents bus tourists from visiting an up-market beauty spot and so on (see Costall 1995). Thus objects can afford certain possibilities, a 'collection of affordances, that inheres in the ecology of the situation' (Michael and Still 1992: 881), even if western science would tell us that lanes cannot invite, rocks cannot provide viewing places and so on. But they do – or rather they sometimes do because of the particular embeddedness of people, technologies and environments. Given certain past and present social relations then particular 'objects' affords a range of possibilities and opportunities; nature and other physical objects owe certain affordances.

Thus we can consider whether nature possesses not just rights but duties towards humans and other living beings. Can we imagine a responsible nature – a nature that has the duty to provide humans and other animals with appropriate affordances? That this is counter-intuitive stems from the elision of the concepts of citizen and citizenship, as though the only entities that might be involved in citizenship are human citizens. This notion of the unique character of humans is further reinforced by more recent attempts to elaborate universal human rights, as opposed to those particular to a given society (see Soysal 1994; Chapter 7 above).

But while it would indeed be odd to describe nature as a *citizen*, it is surely not so strange to conceptualise nature as embedded within the discourses and practices of *citizenship*. This is addressed in a further reworking of the concept of affordance. Michael seeks to 'draw out some of the ways in which "nice nature" interacts with the body to recover previously suppresses possibilities, where the environment ... potentially enables, rather than constrains, the movement of the body in light of the body's capacities' (1996: 149). 'Nice nature' is, one might say, nature demonstrating good citizenship. Affordance refers to the way in which the array of surfaces and structures in the environment specify a range of possible embodied actions for the organism, and particularly for the human organism.

I conclude with three points to note about nature and this reconfigured sense of citizenship. First, the options afforded to humans should relate to the variety of senses that can be involved in their relationship to the environment and not just to the optic sense that Gibson principally examines (see Chapter 4 above). Nice nature should afford experiences of touch, hearing, smell, taste and movement, as well as vision. If it does not, then humans and other animals are not being provided with full citizenship.

Second, a 'nice nature' is one which maximises the array of affordances for humans, especially that which allows corporeal resources for resistance against various modes of disciplining (Michael 1996: 149–50). Nature acting as a good citizen opens up behavioural vistas. For human organisms a good nature expands the potential range of identities which are available to individuals.

Finally, the niceness of nature does not mean that it should be wholly enabling of all human practices. What should be afforded by nature in citizenship terms might well constitute limits upon immediate, instantaneous human practices, in order that there is a viable longer-term or glacial time built into nature's role. Such practices organised through glacial time involve expanding the concept of affordance. It should apply not just to individuals or to social groups but to the human species as a whole as the species reaches into an indefinite future along some of the enormously lengthy timescapes of nature (see Adam 1998, Sullivan 1999). And that in turn entails some further examination of the relations between social practices and their environment which 'complexity theory' has made possible.

Complex mobilities

In Chapter 5 I discussed how chaotic, unintended and non-linear consequences are generated in systems, consequences that are patterned but unpredictable, distant in time and/or space from where they originate and involving patterns of system bifurcation. These features derive from the 'complex' nature of physical and social systems. They are characterised by a very large number of elements which render formal means of representation inappropriate, such elements interact physically and informationally over time, there are positive and negative feedback loops, such systems interact dissipatively with their environment and they have a history which evolves irreversibly through time.

In this section I will consider whether an emergent level of the 'global' is developing that can be viewed as recursively self-producing, that is, its outputs constitute inputs into an autopoietic circular system of 'global' objects, identities, institutions and social practices. And if there is, what are its complex properties, how are chaos and order combined in the global (see Robertson 1992, on the global; and Byrne 1998, Cilliers 1998, Wallerstein 1998, on recent social science applications of chaos/complexity theory)?

Complexity theory in the physical sciences uses mathematical formulae and powerful computers to characterise the enormously large number of iterative events that occur in any such system. In particular experiments, examining increases in the reproduction patterns of gypsy moths showed, through resulting changes in population size, dramatic non-linear changes in the quality of the system. Changes in the parameter resulted in transformations in the system; in certain contexts, order generates chaos (Baker 1993: 133).

This iterative character of systems is one that has not been sufficiently interrogated in sociology. Partly this stems from the presumed a-temporal character of the social world, rather than the seeing of all social hybrids as necessarily historical (as are physical hybrids). But it has also stemmed from the baleful consequences of the conceptual divide between so-called structure and agency. In sociological thought the millions of individual iterative actions are largely subsumed under the notion of 'structure' (such as that of class structure, or the structure of gender relations or social structure). Such a structure does not then have to be further examined; it is 'ordered' and will be reproduced through continuous iteration. The concept of structure solves the problem of iteration for sociology. Of course social systems do change and the sociological trick is then to draw on the concept of agency, to argue that some sets of agents do somehow manage to escape the structure and change it (see Chapter 1's discussion of Archer's morphogenetic formulation of this structure-agency divide).

Of course some authors have seen the limitations of this formulation. Giddens developed the notion of the 'duality of structure' in order to account for the recursive character of social life (1984). Now recursive sounds much like iteration; and Giddens undoubtedly advances the ways in which we understand how 'structures' are both drawn on, and are the outcome of, countless iterative actions by knowledgeable agents. However, in Giddens' analysis there is insufficient examination of the 'complex' character of these iterative processes, of how order can generate chaos, unpredictability and non-linearity. So although there is recurrence, such recurrent actions can produce non-equilibrium, non-linearity and, if the parameters change dramatically, a sudden branching of the social world.

And this is the crucial point; such complex change may have nothing necessarily to do with agents actually seeking to change that world. The agents may simply keep carrying out the same recurrent actions or what they conceive to be the same actions. But it is through iteration over time that they may generate unexpected, unpredictable and chaotic outcomes, often the opposite of what the human agents involved may seek to realise (see Urry 1995: 50). Moreover, of course, agents are not just human but will be a variety of human and non-human actants that constitute the typical mobile, roaming hybrids.

One clear social science example of complexity thinking is Marx's analysis of the unfolding 'contradictions' of capitalism (see Elster 1978). Marx argues that individual capitalists seek to maximise their profits and hence pay their particular workers as little as possible or make them work increasingly long hours. This 'exploitation' of the workforce will continue unless states, or collective actions by trade unions, prevent it, or workers die prematurely. The consequences of such endlessly repeated actions reproduces the capitalist system since substantial profits are generated, so offsetting what Marx hypothesised as the law of the declining rate of profit. The realisation of such profits has the effect of reproducing the class relations of capital and wage-labour integral to the ordering of the capitalist system.

However, the very process of sustaining order through each capitalist exploiting their particular workers, results in three system contradictions. First, the overall level of demand for the products of the capitalist system is reduced since each worker is minimally paid; hence there will be over-production in relationship to demand and the underemployment of capitalist resources. Second, the workforce will be increasingly unhealthy, inefficient and disgruntled; Marx argues that out of the order of reproduced capitalist relations, the chaos of a revolutionary proletariat will be generated. Third, capitalists will seek to find alternative markets for their products and this will, as he says, smash down Chinese walls, expand capitalism worldwide and generate a revolutionary proletariat stretching across the globe. Thus the outcomes of capitalist order are over time and millions of iterations, the opposite of what capitalists appeared to be reproducing through exploiting their local workforce. Millions of iterations produce chaos out of order, non-linear changes and a catastrophic branching of the capitalist system (see Reed and Harvey 1992).

Much sociology has sought to explain why Marx's famous prognostications have not in fact materialised. However, his inability to predict social revolution can be regarded by contemporary theory as understandable since relatively small perturbations in the system could produce a very different branching from what Marx had envisaged a century or more ago (to post-Fordist consumerism, for example). Moreover, the structure of his analysis illuminatingly brings out the key significance of *local* forms of information. Cilliers summarises how any emergent complex system is the result of a rich interaction of simple elements that 'only respond to the limited information each is presented with' (1998: 5). Thus, according to Marx, each capitalist operates under conditions that are far from equilibrium; they can only respond to 'local' sources of information since relevant information carries across only a limited range. Incidentally local struggles by groups of workers against the conditions of their exploitation had the longer-term effect, through iteration, of reproducing the capitalist system. In the end such struggles prevented such an exploitation of the workforce that revolution would have necessarily resulted. Their struggles, based upon local knowledge, had the effect of re-establishing social order albeit at a higher level.

Capitalism, we now know, has indeed broken down many Chinese walls and has in part gone global. Can complexity provide some illumination into such a global capitalism? First, we can note that billions of individual actions occur, each of which is based upon exceptionally localised forms of information. Most people most of the time act iteratively in terms of local information, knowing almost nothing about the global connections or implications of what they are doing. However, these local actions do not remain simply local since they are captured, represented, marketed and generalised elsewhere. They are carried along the scapes and flows of the emerging global world, transporting ideas, people, images, monies and technologies to potentially everywhere. Indeed such actions may jump the scapes, since they are fluid-like and difficult to keep within any particular channel. Interestingly though some connections can exist between the local and the global and this results from an increased reflexivity about those interconnections partially developed through the media (see Chapter 7).

In general though the consequences for the global level are non-linear, large-scale, unpredictable and partially ungovernable. Small causes at certain places produce large consequences elsewhere. Consider a pile of sand; if an extra grain of sand is placed on top it may stay there or it may cause a small avalanche. The system is self-organised but the effects of local changes can vary enormously (Cilliers 1998: 97). The heap will maintain itself at the critical height and we cannot know in advance what will happen to any individual action or what its consequence will be for the pile of sand.

The emergent global order is one of constant disorder and disequilibrium. The following are some recent examples of where millions of decisions based upon local knowledge have resulted in unpredictable and non-linear consequences at the emergent global level. First, as we saw in Chapter 2 out of the US military there emerged the Internet, the technological invention whose use around the world has grown faster than any previous new technology used by humans. Second, again as we saw in

Chapter 2, in 1989 there was the almost overnight collapse of all of Eastern Europe, once the particular local centre of the Kremlin was seen as unable and unwilling to act. Third, as discussed in various chapters we have seen how the apparently 'rational' decision of millions of individual people to drive has resulted in carbon gases that threaten the long-term survival of the planet. Fourth, the exceptional growth of 'western consumerism' has in part remade most of the world in the image of north American shopping malls and theme parks. And finally, almost everywhere there has been the growth of religious fundamentalisms that oppose much of this emergent global order and its omnipotent consumerism.

Barber has apocalyptically explored the last two of these. He describes the emergent global order as being locked in a major conflict between the consumerist 'McWorld' on the one hand, and the identity politics of the 'Jihad', on the other (1996). There is a 'new world disorder' in which McWorld and Jihad depend upon, and globally reinforce, each other. There is a kind of spiralling global disequilibrium that threatens existing public spheres, civil society and democratic forms. There are of course forms of global governance designed to dampen down some of these forms of disequilibrium, but mostly they are based upon national governments (of which there are now over 200) acting in some particular local context. There is a tendency for states to regulate what can be locally measured rather than what may be globally significant if of course it were ever possible to establish what the latter might be.

Baker has interestingly elaborated on how the relationship between the centre and the periphery, or what he calls the 'centriphery', functions to create both order and turbulence in social life (1993). He suggests that the centriphery functions as an attractor, which is defined as the space to which the trajectory of any particular system is over time attracted (Byrne 1998: 26–9; Cilliers 1998: 96–7). In this case the centriphery is a dynamic pattern that is repeated at many different levels, involving flows of energy, information and ideas that simultaneously create both centres and peripheries. The trajectory of social systems is irreversibly attracted to the centriphery.

Finally, can this concept play a useful role in the analysis of global networks and flows? Baker himself argues that:

> Today, particular multinational industries center vast amounts of human activity, locating specific aspects of their enterprise in different continents. In each of these cases, the exchange of goods and services binds and lubricates a dynamic relationship between the center and the periphery. As centering progresses, it deepens the periphery ... Because centering and peripheralizing involve the transformation of energy and information and, thus, the creation of entropy, the process is irreversible.
>
> (1993: 140)

It might be suggested that a specific form taken by centriphery is that of the 'glocal', whereby there is a parallel irreversible process of globalisation-deepening-localisation. Both are bound together through a dynamic relationship, as huge flows of resources move backwards and forwards between the two. Neither the global nor the local can exist without the other. They develop in a symbiotic, irreversible and unstable set of relationships, in which each gets transformed through billions of iterations worldwide. Small perturbations in the system may result in unpredictable and chaotic branching of such a system (see Brodie 1998, on some likely effects on the local).

Conclusion

In this book I have thus shown that mobilities rather than societies should be at the heart of a reconstituted sociology, following the new rules of sociological method elaborated in Chapter 1. Two concluding points about such mobilities should be highlighted for future examination.

First, Dogan and Pahre show the importance of 'intellectual mobility' for innovation in the social sciences (1990). On the basis of extensive research on twentieth century social science, they demonstrate that innovation does not principally result from those scholars who are firmly entrenched within disciplines, nor from those practising rather general 'interdisciplinary studies'. Rather innovation results from academic mobility across disciplinary borders, a mobility that generates what they call 'creative marginality'. It is this marginality, resulting from scholars moving from the centre to the periphery of their discipline and then crossing its borders, which helps to produce new productive hybridities in the social sciences. These can constitute institutionalised sub-fields (such as medical sociology) or more informal networks (such as historical sociology; see Dogan and Pahre 1990: chap. 21). This creative marginality results from complex, overlapping and disjunctive processes of migration, processes which can occur across disciplinary and/or geographical and/or social borders (in the case of the 'Frankfurt School' it was all three; Dogan and Pahre 1990: 73–4). Intellectual mobilities are good for the social sciences, it would seem (see Diken 1998 as well).

Second, most important developments in sociology have at least indirectly stemmed from social movements with 'emancipatory interests' that have fuelled a new or reconfigured social analysis. Examples of such mobilised groupings have at different historical moments included the working class, farmers, the professions, urban protest movements, student's movement, women's movement, immigrant groups, environmental NGOs, gay and lesbian movement, 'disabled' groups and so on. The emancipatory interests of these groupings were not always directly reflected within sociology; more they have had a complex, refracted impact. But in that sense, sociology has been 'parasitic' upon these movements, thus demonstrating how the 'cognitive practices' of such movements have helped to constitute: 'public spaces for thinking new thoughts, activating new actors, generating new ideas' within societies (Eyerman and Jamison 1991: 161; Urry 1995: chap. 2). Societies were organised through debate occurring within a relatively delimited national, public sphere. The information and knowledge produced by its universities centrally formed those debates and delimited possible outcomes. Disciplines were particularly implicated in contributing knowledge to such a public sphere, and indeed in constituting that sphere as part of a national civil society (Cohen and Arato 1992; Dahlgren 1995: 127).

However, the increasingly mediatised nature of contemporary civil societies transforms this. It is not so much that the mass media reflects what goes on elsewhere, so much as what happens in and through the media *is* what happens elsewhere. The sphere of public life that provided the context for knowledge produced within the academy is now increasingly mediatised (see Dahlgren 1995). Debate is as much concerned with image, meaning and emotion, as it is with written texts, cognition and science. As I discussed in Chapter 7 the global economy of signs is transforming the public sphere into an increasingly visual and emotional public stage.

And on that mediated public stage, many social groupings are appearing, developing partially, imperfectly and contingently, a kind of globalising civil society. The extent of this is summarised in Falk's account of the World Order Models Project. He documents the widespread growth of transnational citizens' associations, world-wide shifts towards democratisation and non-violence, huge difficulties for national states in maintaining popularity and legitimacy, and the more general growth of diverse global trends (1995; and see Archibugi *et al.* 1998). Falk concludes that: 'Such cumulative developments are facilitating the birth and growth of global civil society' (Falk 1995: 35). And it is this set of social transformations that constitutes the social base for the sociology of mobilities that I have elaborated in this book. It is to be hoped that the social basis of a 'global civil society', and of its resulting 'sociology of mobilities', will come to occupy powerful places in the scapes and flows that are re-constituting the complex emergent global domains emerging in the twenty-first century.

Bibliography

Abercrombie, N. and Longhurst, B. (1998) *Audiences*, London: Sage.

Adam, B. (1990) *Time and Social Theory*, Cambridge: Polity.

—— (1995a) 'Radiated identities: in pursuit of the temporal complexity of conceptual cultural practices', *Theory, Culture and Society Conference*, Berlin, August.

—— (1995b) *Timewatch*, Cambridge: Polity.

—— (1996) 'Detraditionalization and the certainty of uncertain futures', in P. Heelas, S. Lash and P. Morris (eds) *Detraditionalization*, Oxford: Blackwell.

—— (1998) *Timescapes of Modernity*, London: Routledge.

Adler, J. (1989) 'Origins of Sightseeing', *Annals of Tourism Research*, 16: 7–29.

Albrow, M. (1996) *The Global Age*, Cambridge: Polity.

Allan, S. (1997) 'Raymond Williams and the culture of televisual flow', in J. Wallace and S. Nield (eds) *Raymond Williams Now: knowledge, limits and the future*, London: Macmillan.

Amin, A. and Thrift, N. (1992) 'Neo-Marshallian nodes in global networks', *International Journal of Urban and Regional Research*, 16: 571–87.

Anderson, A. (1997) *Media, Culture and the Environment*, London: UCL Press.

Anderson, B. (1989) *Imagined Communities*, London: Verso.

Appadurai, A. (ed.) (1986) *The Social Life of Things*, Cambridge: Cambridge University Press.

Arcaya, J. (1992) 'Why is time not included in modern theories of memory?' *Time and Society*, 1: 301–14.

Archer, M. (1995) *Realist Social Theory: the morphogenetic approach*, Cambridge: Cambridge University Press.

Archibugi, D., Held, D., Köhler, M. (eds) (1998) *Re-Imagining Political Community*, Cambridge: Polity.

Arendt, H. (1978) *The Life of the Mind*, New York: Harcourt Brace Jovanovich.

Augé, M. (1995) *Non-Places*, London: Verso.

Axtmann, R. (ed.) (1998) *Globalization and Europe*, London: Pinter.

Aycock, A. and Buchignani, N. (1995) 'The e-mail murders: reflections on "dead" letters' in S. Jones (ed.) *Cybersociety*, London: Sage.

Bachelard, G. ([1942] 1983) *Water and Dreams: an essay on the imagination of matter*, Farrell, TX: Pegasus.

—— ([1958] 1969) *The Poetics of Space*, Boston, MA: Beacon Press.

Baker, P. (1993) 'Chaos, order, and sociological theory', *Sociological Inquiry*, 63: 123–49.

Ballard, J.G. ([1973] 1995) *Crash*, London: Vintage.

Barber, B. (1996) *Jihad vs McWorld*, New York: Ballantine.

Barham, P. (1992) ' "The next village": modernity, memory and holocaust', *History of the Human Sciences*, 5: 39–56.

Barrell, J. (1972) *The Idea of Landscape and the Sense of Place. 1730–1840*, Cambridge: Cambridge University Press.

Barrett, M. (1991) *The Politics of Truth*, Cambridge: Polity.

Barthes, R. (1972) *Mythologies*, London: Cape.

—— (1981) *Camera Lucida*, New York: Hill & Wang

Batchen, G. (1991) 'Desiring production itself: notes on the invention of photography' in R. Diprose and R. Ferrell (eds) *Cartographies*, London: Allen & Unwin.

Batty, H. and Gray, T. (1996) 'Environmental rights and national sovereignty', in S. Caney, D. George, P. Jones (eds) *National Rights, International Obligations*, Boulder, CO: Westview Press

Bauböck, B. (1994) *Transnational Citizenship*, Aldershot: Edward Elgar.

Baudrillard, J. (1983) *Simulations*, New York: Semiotext(e) .

—— (1988) *America*, London: Verso.

Bauman, Z. (1987) *Legislators and Interpreters*, Cambridge: Polity.

—— (1993a) *Postmodern Ethics*, London: Routledge.

—— (1993b) 'The sweet smell of decomposition', in C. Rojek and B. Turner (eds) *Forget Baudrillard?* London: Routledge.

Baym, K. (1995) 'The emergence of community in computer-mediated communication', in S. Jones (ed.) *Cybersociety*, London: Sage.

Beck, U. (1992a) 'From industrial society to risk society: questions of survival, structure and ecological enlightenment', *Theory, Culture and Society*, 9: 97–123.

—— (1992b) *Risk Society*, London: Sage.

—— (1996) *The Reinvention of Politics*, Cambridge: Polity.

Bell, C. and Newby, H. (1976) 'Communion, communalism, class and community action: the sources of new urban politics', in D. Herbert and R. Johnston (eds) *Social Areas in Cities*, vol. 2, Chichester: Wiley.

Bell, D. (1993) 'Framing nature: first steps into the wilderness for a sociology of the landscape', *Irish Journal of Sociology*, 3: 1-22

Bell, D. and Valentine, G. (1997) *Consuming Geographies*, London: Routledge.

Benedikt, M. (ed.) (1991a) *Cyberspace*, Cambridge, MA: MIT Press.

—— (1991b) 'Cyberspace: some proposals', in M. Benedikt (ed.) *Cyberspace*, Cambridge, MA: MIT Press.

—— (1991c) 'Introduction', in M. Benedikt (ed.) *Cyberspace*, Cambridge, MA: MIT Press.

Benjamin, W. (1969) *Illuminations*, New York: Schocken.

Berger, P. and Luckmann, T. (1967) *The Social Construction of Reality*, London: Allen Lane.

Bergson, H. (1950) *Time and Free Will*, London: George Allen & Unwin.

—— (1991) *Matter and Memory*, New York: Zone Books.

Berking, H. (1996) 'Solitary individualism: the moral impact of cultural modernisation in late modernity', in S. Lash, B. Szerszynski, B. Wynne (eds) *Risk, Environment and Modernity*, London: Sage.

Berman, M. (1983) *All That Is Solid Melts Into Air*, London: Verso.

Bhabha, H. (ed.) (1990) *Nation and Narration*, London: Routledge.

Bianchini. F. (1995) 'The 24-hour city', *Demos Quarterly. The Time Squeeze*, 5: 47–8.

Billig, M. (1995) *Banal Nationalism*, London: Sage.

Blackburn, R. and Mann, M. (1979) *The Working Class in the Labour Market*, Cambridge: Cambridge University Press.

Blau, P. (1964) *Exchange and Power in Social Life*, New York: John Wiley.

Boden, D. and Molotch, H. (1994) 'The compulsion to proximity', in R. Friedland and D. Boden (eds) *Now/Here: time, space and modernity*, Berkeley, CA: University of California Press.

Borneman, J. (1993) 'Time-space compression and the continental divide in German subjectivity', *New Formations*, 21: 102–18.

Braidotti, R. (1994) *Nomadic Subjects*, New York: Columbia University Press.

Braun, R., Dessewfly, T., Scheppele, K., Smejkalova, J., Wessely, A. and Zentai, V. (1996) *Culture without Frontiers*, Internationales Forschungszentrum Kulturwissenschaften, Vienna: Research Grant Proposal.

Breen, R. and Rottman, D. (1998) 'Is the national state the appropriate geographical unit for class analysis?', *Sociology*, 32: 1–21.

Brendon, P. (1991) *Thomas Cook: 150 years of popular tourism*, London: Secker & Warburg.

Brodie, J. (1998) 'Global citizenship: lost in space', *Rights of the City Symposium*, University of Toronto, June.

Brubaker, R. (1992) *Citizenship and Nationhood in France and Germany*, Cambridge, MA: Harvard University Press.

Brunn, S. and Leinbach, R. (eds) (1991) *Collapsing Space and Time: geographic aspects of communications and information*, London: HarperCollins.

Bryson, N. (1983) *Vision and Painting*, London: Macmillan.

Buci-Glucksmann, C. (1984) *Baroque Reason: the aesthetics of modernity*, London: Sage.

Buck-Morss, S. (1989) *The Dialectics of Seeing: Walter Benjamin and the arcades project*, Cambridge, MA: MIT Press.

Bulmer, M. and Rees, A. (eds) (1996) *Citizenship Today*, London: UCL Press.

Bunce, M. (1994) *The Countryside Ideal*, London: Routledge.

Burgess, J. (1990) 'The production and consumption of environmental meanings in the mass media: a research agenda for the 1990s', *Transactions of the Institute of British Geographers*, 15: 139–62.

Busch, A. (1997) 'Globalisation: some evidence on approaches and data', *Globalization Workshop*, University of Birmingham Politics Dept, March.

Buzard, J. (1993) *The Beaten Track*, Oxford: Clarendon Press.

Byrne, D. (1998) *Complexity Theory and the Social Sciences*, London: Routledge.

Calhoun, C. (1997) *Nationalism*, Buckingham: Open University Press.

Canetti, E. (1973) *Crowds and Power*, Harmondsworth: Penguin.

Cannon, D. (1995) 'Post-modern work ethic', *Demos Quarterly The Time Squeeze*, 5: 31–2.

Capra, F. (1996) *The Web of Life*, London: HarperCollins.

Carson, R. (1962) *Silent Spring*, Boston, MA: Houghton Mifflin.

Castells, M. (1996) *The Rise of the Network Society*, Oxford: Blackwell.

—— (1997) *The Power of Identity*, Oxford: Blackwell.

Casti, J. (1994) *Complexification*, London: Abacus.

Cerny, P. (1997) 'Globalization, fragmentation and the governance gap: toward a new mediaevalism in world politics', *Globalization Workshop*, University of Birmingham, March.

Chambers, I. (1990) *Border Dialogues: journeys in postmodernity*, London: Routledge.

Chapman, M. (1993) 'Copeland: Cumbria's best-kept secret', in S. Macdonald (ed.) *Inside European Identities*, Oxford: Berg.

Chatwin, B. (1988) *The Songlines*, London: Picador.

Cilliers, P. (1998) *Complexity and Post-Modernism*, London: Routledge.

Clarke, D., Doel, M. and McDonough, F. (1996) 'Holocaust topologies: singularity, politics, space', *Political Geography*, 6 (7): 457–89.

Clarke, T. and Barlow, M. (1997) *MAI. The Multilateral Agreement on Investment and the Threat to Canadian Sovereignty*, Toronto: Stoddart.

Classen, C., Howes, D. and Synnott, A. (1994) *Aroma: the cultural history of smell*, London: Routledge .

Clifford, J. (1997) *Routes*, Cambridge, MA: Harvard University Press.

Clifford, S. (1994) 'Pluralism, power and passion', *BANC Conference*, St Anne's College, Oxford, December.

Cohen, G. (1978) *Karl Marx's Theory of History*, Oxford: Clarendon Press.

Cohen, J. (1996) 'The public sphere, the media and civil society', in A. Sajó and M. Price (eds) *Rights of Access to the Media*, The Hague: Kluwer Law International.

Cohen, J. and Arato, A. (1992) *Civil Society and Political Theory*, Cambridge: MIT Press.

Cohen, R. (1997) *Global Diasporas*, London: UCL Press.

Colson, F. (1926) *The Week*, Cambridge: Cambridge University Press.

Condor, S. (1997) 'Unimagined community? Some social psychological issues concerning English national identity', in G. Breakwell and E. Lyons (eds) *Changing European Identities*, London: Butterworth Heinemann.

Connerton, P. (1989) *How Societies Remember the Past*, Cambridge: Cambridge University Press.

Cooke, P. and Morgan, K. (1993) 'The network paradigm: new departures in corporate and regional development', *Environment and Planning D. Society and Space*, 11: 543–64.

Cooper, R. (1997) 'The visibility of social systems', in K. Hetherington and R. Munro (eds) *Ideas of Difference: social spaces and the labour of division*, Oxford: Blackwell and Sociological Review.

Corbin, A. (1986) *The Foul and the Fragrant*, Leamington Spa: Berg.

Corcoran, M. (1998) 'Heroes of the diaspora', in M. Peillon and E. Salter (eds) *Encounters with Modern Ireland*, Dublin: IPA.

Corner, J. and Harvey, S. (eds) (1991) *Enterprise and Heritage*, London: Routledge.

Cosgrove, D. (1984) *Social Formation and Symbolic Landscape*, London: Croom Helm.

—— (1985) 'Prospect, perspective and the evolution of the landscape idea', *Transactions of the Institute of British Geographers,* 10: 45–62.

—— (1994) 'Contested global visions: *one-world, whole-earth*, and the Apollo space photographs', *Annals of the Association of American Geographers,* 84: 270–94.

Costall, A. (1995) 'Socializing affordances', *Theory and Psychology,* 5: 467–81.

Cottle, S. (1993) 'Mediating the environment: modalities of TV news', in A. Hansen (ed.) *The Mass Media and Environmental Issues*, Leicester: Leicester University Press.

Coveney, P. and Highfield, R. (1990) *The Arrow of Time*, London: Flamingo.

Crary, J. (1990) *Techniques of the Observer*, Cambridge, MA: MIT Press.

Crawshaw, C. and Urry, J. (1997) 'Tourism and the photographic eye', in C. Rojek and J. Urry (eds) *Touring Cultures*, London: Routledge.

Cresswell, T. (1997) 'Imagining the nomad: mobility and the postmodern primitive', in G. Benko and U. Strohmayer (eds) *Space and Social Theory*, Oxford: Blackwell.

Dalhgren, P. (1995) *Television and the Public Sphere*, London: Sage.

Dahrendorf, R. (1959) *Class and Class Conflict in Industrial Society*, Stanford. California: Stanford University Press.

Dale, P. (1997) 'Ideology and atmosphere in the informational society', *Theory, Culture and Society,* 13: 27–52.

Davidoff, L. (1973) *The Best Circles*, London: Croom Helm.

Davies, K. (1990) *Women and Time: weaving the strands of everyday life*, Aldershot: Avebury.

Davis, M. (1990) *City of Quartz*, London: Verso.

de Certeau, M. (1984) *The Practice of Everyday Life*, California: University of California Press.

Debord, G. (1994) *Society of the Spectacle*, New York: Zone Books.

Delanty, G. (1998) 'The idea of the university in the global era: from knowledge as an end to an end of knowledge', *Social Epistemology,* 12: 3–25.

Deleuze, G. and Guattari, F. (1986) *Nomadology*, New York: Semiotext(e).

—— (1988) *A Thousand Plateaus: capitalism and schizophrenia*, London: Athlone Press.

Demos Quarterly (1995) *The Time Squeeze*, London: Demos.

Derrida, J. (1987) *Positions*, London: Athlone Press.

—— (1991) *A Derrida Reader*, Hemel Hempstead: Harvester Wheatsheaf.

Deutsche, R. (1991) 'Boys town', *Environment and Planning D: society and space,* 9: 5–30.

Dickens, P. (1996) *Reconstructing Nature*, London: Routledge.

Dicks, B. (1997) 'The life and times of community', *Time and Society,* 6: 196–212.

Diken, B. (1998) *Strangers, Ambivalence and Social Theory*, Aldershot: Ashgate.

Dionne, E. (1998) 'Swoosh. Public shaming nets results', *International Herald Tribune,* May 15: 11.

Dogan, M and Pahre, R. (1990) *Creative Marginality*, Boulder, CO: Westview Press.

du Gay, P., Hall, S., Janes, L., Mackay, H., Negus, K. (1997) *Doing Cultural Studies: the story of Sony Walkman*, London: Sage.

Durkheim E. ([1915] 1968) *The Elementary Forms of the Religious Life*, London: George Allen & Unwin.

—— ([1895] 1964) *Rules of Sociological Method*, New York: Free Press.

—— ([1897] 1952) *Suicide*, London: Routledge.

Eade, J. (ed.) (1997) *Living the Global City*, London: Routledge.

Eco, U. (1986) *Travels in Hyper-Reality*, London: Picador.

Edensor, T. (1996) *Touring the Taj*, Ph.D, Dept of Sociology, Lancaster University.

—— (1997) 'National identity and the politics of memory: remembering Bruce and Wallace in symbolic space', *Environment and Planning D: society and space*, 29: 175–94.

—— (1998) *Tourists at the Taj*, London: Routledge

—— (1999) 'Moving through the city', in D. Bell and A. Haddour (eds) *City Visions*, London: Longman.

Edholm, F. (1993) 'The view from below: Paris in the 1880s', in B. Bender (ed.) *Landscape: politics and perspectives*, Oxford: Berg.

Elias, N. (1978) *The History of Manners*, Oxford: Blackwell.

—— (1992) *Time. An Essay*, Oxford: Blackwell.

Elster, J. (1978) *Logic and Society*, Chichester: Wiley.

Enloe, C. (1989) *Bananas, Beaches and Bases: making feminist sense of international relations*, London: Pandora.

Etzioni, A. (1993) *The Spirit of Community*, New York: Crown.

Eve, R., Horsfall, S. and Lee, M. (eds) (1997) *Chaos, Complexity, and Sociology*, California: Sage.

Eyerman, R. and Jamison, A. (1991) *Social Movements: a cognitive approach*, Cambridge: Polity.

Eyerman, R. and Löfgren, O. (1995) 'Romancing the road: road movies and images of mobility', *Theory, Culture and Society*, 12: 53–79.

Fabian, J. (1992) *Time and the Work of Anthropology: critical essays, 1971–91*, Chur, Switzerland: Harwood.

Falk, R. (1994) 'The making of global citizenship', in B. van Steenbergen (ed.) *The Condition of Citizenship*, London: Sage.

—— (1995) *On Human Governance*, Cambridge: Polity.

Febvre, R. (1982) *Problems of Unbelief in the Sixteenth Century*, Cambridge, MA: Harvard UP.

Finger, M. (1993) 'Politics of the UNCED process', in W. Sachs (ed.) *Global Ecology: a new arena of global conflict*, London: Zed.

Forster, E.M. ([1910] 1931) *Howard's End*, Harmondsworth: Penguin.

Foucault, M. (1970) *The Order of Things*, London: Tavistock.

—— (1976) *The Birth of the Clinic*, London: Tavistock.

—— (1986) 'Of other spaces', *Diacritics*, 16: 22–7.

Fox, M. (1989) 'Unreliable allies: subjective and objective time', in J. Forman and C. Sowton (eds) *Taking Our Time: feminist perspectives on temporality*, Oxford: Pergamon.

Francis, R. (1993) 'Chaos, order, sociological theory: a comment', *Sociological Theory*, 63: 239–42.

Frankenberg, R. (1966) *Communities in Britain*, Harmondsworth: Penguin.

Friedrich, R. and Boden, D. (eds) (1994) *NowHere*, Berkeley, CA: University of California Press.

Frisby, D. and Featherstone, M. (eds) (1997) *Simmel on Culture*, London: Sage.

Game, A. (1991) *Undoing the Social*, Milton Keynes: Open University Press.

—— (1995) 'Time, space, memory, with reference to Bacheland', in M. Featherstone, S. Lash and R. Robertson (eds) *Global Modernities*, London: Sage.

Gamst, F. (1993) ' "On time" and the railroader – temporal dimensions of work', in S. Helmers (ed.) *Ethnologie der Arbeitswelt: Beispiele aus europäischen und aussereuropäischen Feldern*, Bonn: Holos Verlag.

Garton Ash, T. (1990) *We the People: the revolution of '89 witnessed in Warsaw, Budapest, Berlin and Prague*, Cambridge: Granta Books.

Gault, R. (1995) 'In and out of time', *Environmental Values*, 4: 149–66.

Gell, A. (1992) *The Anthropology of Time*, Oxford: Berg.

Gernsheim, H. (1982) *The Origins of Photography*, London: Thames & Hudson.

Giblett, R. (1996) *Postmodern Wetlands*, Edinburgh: Edinburgh University Press.

Gibson, J. (1986) *The Ecological Approach to Visual Perception*, New Jersey: Lawrence Erlbaum.

Gibson, W. (1984) *Neuromancer*, New York: Ace.

Gibson-Graham, J.K. (1997) 'Postmodern becomings: from the space of form to the space of potentiality', in G. Benko (ed.) *Space and Social Theory*, Oxford: Blackwell.

Giddens, A. (1976) *New Rules of Sociological Method*, London: Hutchinson.

—— (1984) *The Constitution of Society*, Cambridge: Polity.

—— (1987) *Social Theory and Modern Sociology*, Cambridge: Polity.

—— (1991) *Modernity and Self-Identity*, Cambridge: Polity.

—— (1996) 'T.H. Marshall, the state and democracy', in M. Bulmer and A. Rees (eds) *Citizenship Today*, London: UCL Press.

Gilroy, P. (1993) *The Black Atlantic: modernity and double consciousness*, London: Verso.

Gitlin, T. (1980) *The Whole World is Watching*, Berkeley: University of California Press.

Glacken, C. (1997) *Traces on the Rhodian Shore: nature and culture in western thought from ancient times to the end of the eighteenth century*, Berkeley, CA: University of California Press.

Glennie, P. and Thrift, N. (1994) 'Reworking E. P. Thompson's "Time, Work-Discipline and Industrial Capitalism" ', *Time and Society*, 5: 275–300.

Goffman, E. (1968) *Asylum*, Harmondsworth: Penguin.

Gould, S. (1997) *Questioning the Millennium*, London: Jonathan Cape.

Gouldner, A. (1972) *The Coming Crisis of Western Sociology*, London: Heinemann.

Graham, S. and Marvin, S. (1996) *Telecommunications and the City*, London: Routledge.

Graves-Brown, P. (1997) 'From highway to superhighway: the sustainablity, symbolism and situated practices of car culture', *Social Analysis*, 41: 64–75.

Gray, C.H. (1997) 'The ethics and politics of cyborg embodiment: citizenship as a hypervalue', *Cultural Values*, 1: 252–8.

Green, N. (1990) *The Spectacle of Nature*, Manchester: Manchester University Press.

Gregory, D. (1994) *Geographical Imaginations*, Cambridge, MA: Blackwell.

—— (1999) 'Scripting Egypt: Orientalism and the cultures of travel', in J. Duncan and D. Gregory (eds) *Writes of Passage*, London: Routledge.

Griffin, S. (1981) *Pornography and Silence: culture's revenge against nature*, London: Women's Press.

Griffiths, J. (1995) 'Life of strife in the fast lane', *The Guardian*, 23 August.

Grosz, E. (1993) 'Merleau-Ponty and Irigaray in the flesh', *Thesis Eleven*, 36: 37-59

—— (1994) *Volatile Bodies: towards a corporeal feminism*, Sydney: Allen & Unwin.

Guérer, A. le (1993) *Scent: the mysterious and essential powers of smell*, London: Chatto & Windus.

Gurnah, A. (1997) 'Elvis in Zanzibar', in A. Scott (ed.) *The Limits of Globalizaion*, London: Routledge.

Gurvitch, G. (1964) *The Spectrum of Social Time*, Dordrecht: D. Reidel.

—— (1971) *The Social Frameworks of Knowledge*, Oxford: Basil Blackwell.

Habermas, J. (1974) 'The public sphere', *New German Critique*, 3: 49-55

—— (1987) *The Theory of Communicative Action*, vol. 2, Cambridge: Polity.

—— (1989) *The Structural Transformation of the Public Sphere*, Cambridge: Polity.

—— (1992) 'Further reflections on the public sphere', in C. Calhoun (ed.) *Habermas and the Public Sphere*, Cambridge, MA: MIT Press.

—— (1995) 'Citizenship and national identity: some reflections on the future of Europe', in R. Beiner (ed.) *Theorizing Citizenship*, New York: SUNY Press.

—— (1998) 'There are alternatives', *New Left Review*, 231: 3–12.

Halbwachs, M. (1992) *On Collective Memory*, Chicago, IL: University of Chicago Press.

Hall, S. (1990) 'Cultural identity and diaspora', in J. Rutherford (ed.) *Identity: community, culture, difference*, London: Lawrence & Wishart.

Hall, S. (1993) 'Which public, whose service?' in W. Stevenson (ed.) *All Our Futures: the changing role and purpose of the BBC*, London: British Film Institute.

Hannerz, U. (1996) *Transnational Connections*, London: Routledge.

Hansen, A. (1993a) 'Greenpeace and press coverage of environmental issues', in A. Hansen (ed.) *The Mass Media and Environmental Issues*, Leicester: Leicester University Press.

—— (ed.) (1993b) *The Mass Media and Environmental Issues*, Leicester: Leicester University Press.

Haraway, D. (1989) *Primate Visions*, New York: Routledge.

—— (1991) *Simians, Cyborgs, and Women*, London: Free Association Books.

Harley, J. (1992) 'Deconstructing the map' in T. Barnes and J. Duncan (eds) *Writing Worlds: Discourse, Text and Metaphor in the Representation of Landscape*, London: Routledge.

Harvey, D. (1989) *The Condition of Postmodernity*, Oxford: Blackwell.
—— (1996) *Justice, Nature and the Geography of Difference*, Oxford: Blackwell.
Harvey, P. (1996) *Hybrids of Modernity*, London: Routledge.
Hassard, J. (ed.) (1990) *The Sociology of Time*, London: Macmillan.
Hawkes, T. (1972) *Metaphor: the critical idiom*, London: Methuen.
Hawking, S. (1988) *A Brief History of Time*, London: Bantam.
Hayles, N.K. (ed.) (1991) *Chaos and Order*, Chicago, IL: University of Chicago Press.
Heidegger, M. (1962) *Being and Time*, Oxford: Blackwell.
—— (1977) *The Question Concerning Technology and Other Essays*, New York: Harper Torchbooks.
—— (1993) *Basic Writings*, ed. D. Farrell Krell, London: Routledge.
Heim, M. (1991) 'The erotic ontology of cyberspace', in M. Benedikt (ed.) *Cyberspace*, Cambridge, MA: MIT Press.
Held, D. (1995) *Democracy and the Global Order*, Cambridge: Polity.
Hempel, C. (1966) *Philosophy of Natural Science*, Englewood Cliffs, NJ: Prentice Hall.
Hetherington, K. (1994) 'The contemporary significance of Schmalenbach's concept of the bund', *Sociological Review*, 42: 1–25.
—— (1995) 'Technologies of place', *Labour of Division Conference*, Keele University.
—— (1997a) *The Badlands of Modernity*, London: Routledge.
—— (1997b) 'In place of geometry: the materiality of place', in K. Hetherington and R. Munro (eds) *Ideas of Difference*, Oxford: Blackwell/Sociological Review.
—— (1998) *Expressions of Identity: space, performance, politics*, London: Sage.
Hewison, R. (1993) 'Field of dreams', *Sunday Times*, 3 January.
Hewitt, P. (1996) 'Social justice in a global economy?', in M. Bulmer and A. Rees (eds) *Citizenship Today*, London: UCL Press.
Hewitt, R. (1997) *The Possibilities of Society*, Albany: SUNY Press.
Hibbitts, B. (1994) 'Making sense of metaphors: visuality, aurality, and the reconfiguration of American legel discourse', *Cardozo Law Review*, 16: 229–356.
Hindess, B. (1993) 'Citizenship in the modern west' in B. Turner (ed.) *Citizenship and Social Theory*, London: Sage.
Hirst, P. and Thompson, G. (1996) *Globalisation in Question*, Cambridge: Polity.
Hoggett, P. and Bishop, J. (1986) *Organizing Around Enthusiasms*, London: Comedia.
Homans, G. (1961) *Social Behaviour: its elementary forms*, London: Routledge.
hooks, b. (1991) *Yearning: race, gender and cultural politics*, London: Turnaround.
—— (1992) *Black Looks: race and representation*, London: Turnaround.
Huntington, S. (1991) *The Third Wave*, Norman: University of Oklahoma Press.
Huyssen, A. (1995) *Twilight Memories*, London: Routledge.
Ihde, D. (1976) *Listening and Voice*, Athens, OH: Ohio University Press.
Ingold, T. (1993a) 'Globes and spheres: the topology of environmentalism', in K. Milton (ed.) *Environmentalism*, London: Routledge.
—— (1993b) 'The temporality of the landscape', *World Archaeology*, 25: 152–74.
Irigaray, L. (1978) 'Interview with L Irigaray', in M.-F. Hans and G. Lapouge (eds) *Les Femmes, La Pornographie et L'Erotisme*, Paris: Minuit.

—— (1985) *The Sex Which Is Not One*, Ithaca, NY: Cornell University Press.

Isajiw, W. (1968) *Causation and Functionalism in Sociology*, London: Routledge.

Jagtenberg, T. and McKie, D. (1997) *Eco-Impacts and the Greening of Postmodernity*, California: Sage.

Jarvis, R. (1997) *Romantic Writing and Pedestrian Travel*, London: Macmillan.

Jay, M. (1986) 'In the empire of the gaze: Foucault and the denigration of vision in twentieth-century French thought', in D. Hoy (ed.) *Foucault: a critical reader*, Oxford: Blackwell.

—— (1992) 'Scopic regimes of modernity', in S. Lash and J. Friedman (eds) *Modernity and Identity*, Oxford: Blackwell.

—— (1993) *Downcast Eyes*, Berkeley, CA: University of California Press.

Jenks, C. (1995a) 'The centrality of the eye in western culture' in C. Jenks (ed.) *Visual Culture*, London: Routledge.

—— (ed.) (1995b) *Visual Culture*, London: Routledge.

Jokinen, F. and Veijola, S. (1997) 'The disoriented tourist: the figuration of the tourist in contemporary cultural critique', in C. Rojek and J. Urry (eds) *Touring Cultures*, London: Routledge.

Jones, S. (1995a) 'Understanding community in the information age', in S. Jones (ed.) *Cybersociety*, London: Sage.

—— (ed.) (1995b) *Cybersociety*, London: Sage.

Kaplan, C. (1996) *Questions of Travel*, Durham, US: Duke University Press.

Keane, J. (1991) *The Media and Democracy*, Cambridge: Polity.

Keat, R. and Urry, J. (1982) *Social Theory as Science*, London: Routledge.

Keck, M. and Sikkunk, K. (1998) *Activists Beyond Borders*, Ithaca, NY: Princeton University Press.

Keil, L. and Elliott, E. (eds) (1996) *Chaos Theory in the Social Sciences*, Ann Arbor, MI: University of Michigan Press.

Kelly, K. (1995) *Out of Control: the rise of neo-biological civilization*, Menlo Park, CA: Addison-Wesley.

Kern, S. (1983) *The Culture of Time and Space (1880–1918)*, London: Weidenfeld & Nicolson.

Kopytoff, I. (1986) 'The cultural biography of things: commoditization as a process', in A. Appadurai (ed.) *The Social Life of Things*, Cambridge: Cambridge University Press.

Kornblum, W. (1988) *Sociology in a Changing World*, New York: Holt, Rinehart & Winston.

Körner, S. (1955) *Kant*, Harmondsworth: Penguin.

Kuhn, T. (1962) *The Structure of Scientific Revolutions*, Chicago, IL: Chicago University Press.

Laclau, E. and Mouffe, C. (1985) *Hegemony and Socialist Strategy*, London: Verso.

Lakoff, G. and Johnson, M. (1980) *Metaphors We Live By*, Chicago, IL: Chicago University Press.

Lash, S. (1995) 'Risk culture', *Australian Cultural Studies Conference*, Charles Sturt University, NSW, Australia, December.

Lash, S. and Urry, J. (1987) *The End of Organized Capitalism*, Cambridge: Polity.

—— (1994) *Economies of Signs and Space*, London: Sage.

Lash, S., Szerszynski, B. and Wynne, B. (eds) (1996) *Risk, Environment and Modernity*, London: Sage.

Latour, B. (1987) *Science in Action*, Milton Keynes: Open University Press.

—— (1990) 'Drawing things together', in S. Woolgar and M. Lynch (eds) *Representation in Science*, Cambridge, MA: MIT Press.

—— (1993) *We Have Never Been Modern*, Hemel Hempstead: Harvester Wheatsheaf.

Law, J. (1994) *Organizing Modernity*, Oxford: Basil Blackwell.

Law, J. and Hassard, J. (eds) (1999) *Actor Network Theory and After*, Oxford: Blackwell/Sociological Review.

Lee, K. (1995) 'Beauty for ever', *Environmental Values*, 4: 213–25.

Lefebvre, H. (1991) *The Production of Space*, Oxford: Blackwell.

Leonard, M. (1998) *Rediscovering Europe*, London: Demos.

Levin, D. (1993a) 'Decline and fall: ocularcentrism in Heidegger's reading of the history of metaphysics', in D. Levin (ed.) *Modernity and the Hegemony of Vision*, Berkeley, CA: University of California Press.

—— (1993b) *Modernity and the Hegemony of Vision*, Berkeley, CA: University of California Press.

Levinas, E. (1985) *Ethics and Infinity*, Pittsburgh: Duquesne University Press.

Lewis, N. (2000) 'The climbing body, nature and the experience of modernity', *Body and Society*, 6.

Leyshon, A. and Thrift, N. (1997) *Money/Space*, London: Routledge.

Light, A. (1991) *Forever England: feminity, literature and conservatism between the wars*, London: Routledge.

Liniado, M. (1996) *Car Culture and Countryside Change*, M.Sc Dissertation, Geography Department, University of Bristol.

Loader, B. (ed.) (1997) *The Governance of Cyberspace*, London: Routledge.

Lodge, D. (1983) *Small World*, Harmondsworth: Penguin.

Lovelock, J. (1988) *The Ages of Gaia: a biography of our living earth*, Oxford: Oxford University Press.

Lowe, P. and Ward, S. (eds) (1998) *British Environmental Policy and Europe*, London: Routledge.

Lowenthal, D. (1985) *The Past is a Foreign Country*, Cambridge: Cambridge University Press.

—— (1991) 'British national identity and the English landscape', *Rural History*, 2: 205–30.

—— (1994) 'European and English landscapes as national symbols', in D. Hooson (ed.) *Geography and National Identity*, Oxford: Blackwell.

Luhmann, N. (1982) *The Differentiation of Society*, New York: Columbia University Press.

—— (1995) *Social Systems*, Stanford, CA: Stanford University Press.

Luke, T. (1996) 'New world order or neo-world orders: power, politics and ideology in informationalizing glocalities', in M. Featherstone, S. Lash and R. Robertson (eds) *Global Modernities*, London: Sage.

Lupton, D. (1998) *The Emotional Self*, London: Sage.

Lury, C. (1997a) *Prosthetic Cultures*, London: Routledge.

—— (1997b) 'The objects of travel', in C. Rojek and J. Urry (eds) *Touring Cultures*, London: Routledge.

Lyon, D. (1994) *The Electronic Eye: the rise of the surveillance society*, Cambridge: Polity.

—— (1997) 'Cyberspace sociality: controversies over computer-mediated relationships', in B. Loader (ed.) *The Governance of Cyberspace*, London: Routledge.

Lyotard, J.-F. (1984) *The Postmodern Condition*, Manchester: Manchester University Press.

—— (1991) *The Inhuman. Reflections on Time*, Cambridge: Polity.

MacCannell, D. (1992) *Empty Meeting Grounds*, London: Routledge.

Macdonald, S. (1997) 'A people's story: heritage, identity and authenticity', in C. Rojek and J. Urry (eds) *Touring Cultures*, London: Routledge.

MacIver, R. and Page, C. (1950) *Society: an introductory analysis*, London: Macmillan.

Macnaghten, P. and Urry, J. (1998) *Contested Natures*, London: Sage.

Macy, J. (1993) *World as Lover, World as Self*, London: Rider.

Maffesoli, M. (1996) *The Time of the Tribes*, London: Sage.

Maier, C. (1994) 'A surfeit of memory? Reflections of history, melancholy and denial', *History and Memory*, 5: 136–52.

Majone, G. (1994) 'The rise of the regulatory state in Europe', *West European Politics*, 17: 77–101.

—— (1996) *Regulating Europe*, London: Routledge.

Makimoto, T. and Manners, D. (1997) *Digital Nomad*, Chichester: John Wiley.

Mallett, P. (1995) 'The city and the self', in M. Wheeler (ed.) *Ruskin and the Environment*, Manchester: Manchester University Press.

Mann, M. (1986) *The Sources of Social Power*, vol. 1, Cambridge: Cambridge University Press.

—— (1993) *The Sources of Social Power*, vol. 2, Cambridge: Cambridge University Press.

—— (1996) 'Ruling class strategies and citizenship', in M. Bulmer and A. Rees (eds) *Citizenship Today*, London: UCL Press.

—— (1998) 'Is there a society called Euro?', in R. Axtmann (ed.) (1998) *Globalization and Europe*, London: Pinter, pp. 184–207.

Marcus, S. (1973) 'Reading the illegible', in H. Dyos and M. Wolff (eds) *The Victorian City: images and reality*, vol. 1, London: Routledge & Kegan Paul.

Marshall, T. and Bottomore, T. (1992) *Citizenship and Social Class*, London: Pluto.

Martin, H.-P. and Schumann, H. (1997) *The Global Trap*, London: Zed.

Marx, K. and Engels, F. (1955) *Selected Works*, vol. 2, Moscow: Foreign Languages.

—— ([1848] 1964) *Manifesto of the Communist Party*, London: Modern Reader.

—— (1976) *Collected Works*, vol. 6, London: Lawrence & Wishart.

Massey, D. (1994) *Space, Class and Gender*, Cambridge: Polity.

—— (1999) 'Living in Wythenshawe', in D. Massey (ed.) *The Unknown City*, London: Routledge.

McClintock, A. (1995) *Imperial Leather*, New York: Routledge.

McCrone, D. (1992) *Understanding Scotland*, London: Routledge.

—— (1998) *The Sociology of Nationalism*, London: Routledge

McCrone, D., Morris, A. and Kiely, R. (1995) *Scotland – the Brand*, Edinburgh: Edinburgh University Press.

Mckay, G. (1996) *Senseless Acts of Beauty*, London: Verso.

—— (ed.) (1998) *DiY Culture*, London: Verso.

McLuhan, M. (1962) *The Gutenberg Galaxy*, London: Routledge.

McRae, H. (1997) 'New York? London? We're all on the move', *The Independent*, 16 July.

McTaggart, J. (1927) *The Nature of Existence*, vol. 2, book 5, Cambridge: Cambridge University Press.

Mead, G.H. (1959) *The Philosophy of the Present*, La Salle, IL: Open Court.

Meehan, E. (1991) 'European citizenship and social policies', in U. Vogel and M. Moran (eds) *The Frontiers of Citizenship*, London: Macmillan.

Meijer, I. (1998) 'Advertising citizenship: an essay on the performative power of consumer culture', *Media, Culture and Society*, 20: 235–49.

Menon, M. (1997) 'Effects of modern science and technology on relations between nations', in J. Rotblat (ed.) *World Citizenship. Allegiance to Humanity*, London: Macmillan.

Merchant, C. (1982) *The Death of Nature*, San Francisco, CA: Harper & Row.

Meyrowitz, J. (1985) *No Sense of Place*, New York: Oxford University Press.

Michael, M. (1996) *Constructing Identities*, London: Sage

—— (1997) 'Hybridising regularity: a characterology and chronology of the hudogledog', *Actor Network and After Conference*, Keele University, July.

—— (1998) 'Co(a)gency and the car: attributing agency in the case of the 'road rage', in B. Brenna, J. Law, I. Moser (eds) *Machines, Agency and Desire*, Oslo: TMV Skriftserie.

Michael, M. and Still, A. (1992) 'A resource for resistance: power-knowledge and affordance', *Theory and Society*, 21: 869–88.

Middleton, D. and Edwards, D. (eds) (1990) *Collective Remembering*, London: Sage.

Miller, D. (1998) *Material Cultures*, London: UCL Press.

Miller, S. (1995) 'Urban dreams and rural reality: land and landscape in English culture, 1920–45', *Rural History*, 6: 89–102.

Milton, K. (1993) 'Land or landscape: rural planning policy and the symbolic construction of the countryside', in M. Murray and J. Greer (eds) *Rural development in Ireland*, Aldershot: Avebury.

Mingers, J. (1995) *Self-Producing Systems*, New York: Plenum.

Mlinar, Z. (1997) 'Globalization as a research agenda', paper given to the European Sociological Association, Colchester, August.

Mol, A. and Law, J. (1994) 'Regions, networks and fluids: amaemia and social topology', *Social Studies of Science*, 24: 641–71.

Morley, D. (1995) 'Television: not so much a visual medium, more a visible object', in C. Jenks (ed.) *Visual Culture*, London: Routledge.

Morley, D. and Robins, K. (1995) *Spaces of Identity*, London: Routledge.

Morris, M. (1988) 'At Henry Parkes Motel', *Cultural Studies*, 2: 1–47.

Morrison, T. (1989) *Song of Soloman*, London: Picador.

Mulvey, L. (1989) *Visual and Other Pleasures*, London: Macmillan.

Murdoch, J. (1995) 'Actor-networks and the evolution of economic forms: combining description and explanation in theories of regulation, flexible specialisation, and networks', *Environment and Planning A* 27: 731–57.

Murdock, G. (1992) 'Citizens, consumers, and public culture', in M. Shovmand and K. Shrøder (eds) *Media Cultures*, London: Routledge.

Myers, G. (1999) *Ad Worlds*, London: Arnold.

Nairn, T. (1988) *The Enchanted Glass: Britain and its monarchy*, London: Radius.

Nash, R. (1989) *The Rights of Nature*, Madison, WI: University of Wisconsin Press.

Negroponte, N. (1995) *Being Digital*, New York: Alfred A. Knopf.

Newby, H. (1979) *A Green and Pleasant Land*, London: Hutchinson.

—— (1996) 'Citizenship in a green world: global commons and human stewardship', in M. Bulmer and A. Rees (eds) *Citizenship Today*, London: UCL Press.

Nguyen, D. (1992) 'The spatialisation of metric time', *Time and Society*, 1: 29–50.

Nowotny, H. (1994) *Time*, Cambridge: Polity.

O'Brien, J., Colebourne, A., Rodden, T., Benford, S. and Snowden, D. (1997) *Informing the design of collaborative virtual environments*, Department of Sociology, Lancaster University.

O'Connor, B. (1998) 'Riverdance', in M. Peillon and E. Salter (eds) *Encounters with Modern Ireland*, Dublin: IPA.

O'Neill, J. (1993) *Ecology, Policy and Politics*, London: Routledge.

Ohmae, K, (1990) *The Borderless World*, London: Collins.

Oldenburg, R. (1989) *The Great Good Places*, New York: Marlowe & Company.

Ong, W. (1982) *Orality and Literacy*, London: Methuen.

Orwell, G. (1937) *The Road to Wigan Pier*, London: Victor Gollancz.

Osborne, P. (1994) 'The politics of time', *Radical Philosophy*, 68: 3–9.

Pahl, R. (1995) *After Success*, Cambridge: Polity.

Parr, M. (1995) *Small World*, Stockport: Dewi Lewis.

Parson, T. and Shils, E. (1951) *Towards a General Theory of Action*, Cambridge, MA: Harvard University Press.

Parsons, T. (1960) *Structure and Process in Modern Societies*, New York: Free Press.

—— (1971) *The System of Modern Societies*, New Jersey: Prentice-Hall.

Peel, J. (1971) *Herbert Spencer: the evolution of a sociologist*, London: Heinemann.

Peillon, M. and Salter, E. (eds) *Encounters with Modern Ireland*, Dublin: IPA.

Peters, T. (1992) *Liberation Management*, London: Macmillan.

Pickering, J. (1997) 'Agents and artefacts', *Social Analysis*, 41: 46–63.

Pierson, C. (1996) *The Modern State*. London: Routledge.

Pilkington, E., Clouston, E. and Traynor, I. (1995) 'How a wave of public opinion bowled over the Shell monolith', *Guardian*, 22 June.

Pinkney, T. (1991) *Raymond Williams*, Bridgend: Seren Books.

Plant, S. (1997) *Zeros and Ones*, London: Fourth Estate.

Plumwood, V. (1993) *Feminism and the Mastery of Nature*, London: Routledge.

Popper, K. (1962) *The Open Society and its Enemies*, London: Routledge & Kegan Paul.

Porteous, J. (1985) 'Smellscape', *Progress in Human Geography*, 9: 356–78.

—— (1990) *Landscapes of the Mind: worlds of sense and metaphor*, Toronto: Toronto University Press.

Power, M. (1994) *The Audit Explosion*, London: Demos.

Prato, P. and Trivero, G. (1985) 'The spectacle of travel', *The Australian Journal of Cultural Studies*, 3.

Pratt, M. (1992) *Imperial Eyes*, London: Routledge.

Prigogine, I. (1980) *From Being to Becoming: time and complexity in the physical sciences*, San Francisco, CA: W.H. Freeman.

Prigogine, I. and Stengers, I. (1984) *Order Out of Chaos*, London: Heinemann.

Radcliffe-Brown, R. (1952) *Structure and Function in Primitive Society*, London: Cohen & West.

Radley, A. (1990) 'Artefacts, memory and a sense of place', in D. Middleton and D. Edwards (eds) *Collective Remembering*, London: Sage.

Rapoport, A. (1997) 'The dual role of the nation state in the evolution of world citizenship', in J. Rotblat (ed.) *World Citizenship: allegiance to humanity*, London: Macmillan.

Reed, M. and Harvey, D. (1992) 'The new science and the old: complexity and realism in the social sciences', *Journal for the Theory of Social Behaviour*, 22: 353–80.

Rees, A. (1996) 'T.H. Marshall and the progress of citizenship', in M. Bulmer and A. Rees (eds) *Citizenship Today*, London: UCL Press.

Reich, R. (1991) *The Work of Nations: preparing ourselves for 21st-century capitalism*, New York: Knopf.

Reid, E. (1995) 'Virtual worlds, culture and imagination', in S. Jones (ed.) *Cybersociety*, London: Sage.

Rex, J. (1961) *Key Problems of Sociological Theory*, London: Routledge.

Rheingold, H. (1994) *The Virtual Community*, London: Secker & Warburg.

Richardson, D. (1998) 'Sexuality and citizenship', *Sociology*, 32: 83–100.

Rifkin, J. (1987) *Time Wars: the primary conflict in human history*, New York: Henry Holt.

Ritzer, G. (1992) *The McDonaldization of Society*, London: Pine Forge.

—— (1995) *Expressing America*, London: Pine Forge.

—— (1997) ' "McDisneyization" ' and "post-tourism": complementary perspectives on contemporary tourism', in C. Rojek and J. Urry (eds) *Touring Cultures*, London: Routledge.

Robertson, R. (1990) 'Mapping the global condition: globalisation as the central concept', in M. Featherstone (ed.) *Global Culture*, London: Sage.

—— (1992) *Globalization*, London: Sage.

Robins, K. (1996) *Into the Image*, London: Routledge

Roche, M. (1999) *Mega-Events and Modernity*, London: Routledge.

Roche, M. and van Berkel, R. (1997) *European Citizenship and Social Exclusion*, Aldershot: Ashgate.

Rodaway, P. (1994) *Sensuous Geographies*, London: Routledge.

Roderick, I. (1997) 'Household sanitation and the flows of domestic space', *Space and Culture*, 1: 105–32.

Rorty, R. (1980) *Philosophy and the Mirror of Nature*, Oxford: Blackwell.

Rose, N. (1996) 'Refiguring the territory of government', *Economy and Society*, 25: 327–56.

Rotblat, J. (1997a) 'Preface, Executive Overview', in J. Rotblat (ed.) *World Citizenship. Allegiance to Humanity*, London: Macmillan

—— (ed.) (1997b) *World Citizenship. Allegiance to Humanity*, London: Macmillan.

Rowan, D. (1998) 'Meet the new world government', *Guardian*, 13 February: 15.

Rowell, A. (1996) *Green Backlash*, London: Routledge.

Roy, A. (1997) *The God of Small Things*, London: Flamingo.

Runciman, G. (1996) 'Why social inequalities are generated by social rights', in M. Bulmer and A. Rees (eds) *Citizenship Today*, London: UCL Press.

Rushdie, S. (1995) *Midnight's Children*, London: Vintage.

Rushkoff, D. (1994) *Cyberia: life in the trenches of hyperspace*, London: Flamingo.

Sachs, W. (ed.) (1993) *Global Ecology*, London: Zed.

Samuel, R. (1994) *Theatres of Memory*, London: Verso.

—— (1998) *Island Stories*, London: Verso.

Sardar, Z. (1996) 'alt.civilizations.faq: cyberspace as the darker side of the west', in Z. Sardar and J. Ravetz (eds) *Cyberfutures*, London: Pluto.

Sardar, Z. and Ravetz, J. (eds) (1996) *Cyberfutures*, London: Pluto.

Scannell, P. (1996) *Radio, Television and Modern Life*, Oxford: Blackwell.

Schama, S. (1995) *Landscape and Memory*, London: HarperCollins.

Schivelbusch, W. (1986) *The Railway Journey: trains and travel in the nineteenth century*, Oxford: Blackwell.

Schmalenbach, H. (1977) *Herman Schmalenbach: on society and experience*, Chicago, IL: University of Chicago Press.

Schor, J. (1992) *The Overworked American*, New York: Basic.

Scott, J. (1997) *Corporate Business and Capitalist Classes*, Oxford: Oxford University Press.

Sennett, R. (1991) *The Conscience of the Eye*, London: Faber.

—— (1994) *Flesh and Stone*, London: Faber and Faber.

Sharratt, B. (1989) 'Communications and image studies: notes after Raymond Williams', *Comparative Criticism*, 11: 29–50.

Shaw, M. (1994) *Global Society and International Relations: sociological concepts and political perspectives*, Cambridge: Polity Press.

Shields, R. (ed.) (1996) *Cultures of Internet*, London: Sage.

—— (1997a) 'Ethnography in the crowd: the body, sociality and globalization in Seoul', *Focaal*, 30/31: 23–38.

—— (1997b) 'Flow as a new paradigm', *Space and Culture*, 1: 1–4.

Shildrick, M. (1997) *Leaky Bodies and Boundaries*, London: Routledge.

Shils, E. (1985) 'Sociology', in A. and J. Kuper (eds) *The Social Science Encyclopaedia*, London: Routledge.

Shiva, V. (1989) *Staying Alive*, London: Zed.

Shove, E. (1998) *Consuming Automobility*, Scenesustech, Sociology Department, Trinity College, Dublin.

Silverstone, R. and Hirsch, E. (eds) (1992) *Consuming Technologies*, London: Routledge.

Silverstone, R., Hirsch, E. and Morley, D. (1992) 'Information and communication technologies and the moral economy of the household', in R. Silverstone and E. Hirsch (eds) *Consuming Technologies*, London: Routledge.

Sklair, L. (1995) *Sociology of the Global System*, 2nd edn, Hemel Hempstead: Harvester.

Smart, J. (1963) *Philosophy and Scientific Realism*, London: Routledge.

Smith, A. (1986) 'State-making and nation-building', in J. Hall (ed.) *States in History*, Oxford: Blackwell.

Smith, J. (1992) 'Writing the aesthetic experience', in T. Barnes and J. Duncan (eds) *Writing Worlds*, London: Routledge.

Sontag, S. (1979) *On Photography*, Harmondsworth: Penguin.

—— (1991) *Aids and its Metaphors*, Harmondsworth: Penguin.

Sorokin, P. (1937) *Social and Cultural Dynamics*, vol. 2, New York: American Books.

Sorokin, P. and Merton, R. (1937) 'Social time: a methodological and functional analysis', *American Journal of Sociology*, 42: 615–29.

Soysal, Y. (1994) *Limits of Citizenship*, Chicago, IL: University of Chicago Press.

Spence, J. and Holland, P. (1991) *Family Snaps: the meanings of domestic photography*, London: Virago.

Spencer, H. ([1876] 1893) *The Principles of Sociology*, vol. 1, London: Williams & Norgate.

Spillman, L. (1997) *Nation and Commemoration*, Cambridge: Cambridge University Press.

Spufford, F. (1996) *I May Be Some Time*, London: Faber & Faber.

Stacey, J. (1997) *Teratologies: a cultural theory of cancer*, London: Routledge.

Stafford, B.M. (1994) *Artful Science*, Cambridge, MA: MIT Press.

Stallybrass, P. and White, A. (1986) *The Politics and Poetics of Transgression*, London: Methuen.

Stevenson, N. (1997) 'Globalization, national cultures and cultural citizenship', *The Sociological Quarterly*, 38: 41–66.

Stone, A. (1991) 'Will the real body please stand up? Boundary stories about virtual cultures', in M. Benedikt (ed.) *Cyberspace*, Cambridge, MA: MIT Press.

Strathern, M. (1992) *After Nature*, Cambridge: Cambridge University Press.

Sullivan, K. (1999) *The New Promethean Fire: radioactive monsters and sustainable nuclear futures*, Ph.D, Department of Sociology, Lancaster University.

Szerszynski, B. (1993) *Uncommon Ground: moral discourse, foundationalism and the environmental movement*, Ph.D, Department of Sociology, Lancaster University.

—— (1997) 'The varieties of ecological piety', *Worldviews: environment, culture, religion*, 1: 37–55.

Szerszynski, B. and Toogood, M. (1999) 'Global citizenship, the environment and the mass media', in S. Allen, B. Adam, C. Carter (eds) *The Media Politics of Environmental Risks*, London: UCL Press.

Taylor, J. (1994) *A Dream of England*, Manchester: Manchester University Press.

Taylor, P. (1997) 'Izations of the world: Americanization, modernization and globalization', *Globalization Workshop*, University of Birmingham Politics Department, March.

Temourian, H. (1995) 'Iran bans Baywatch with purge on "Satan's dishes"', *Sunday Times*, 23 April.

Tester, K. (ed.) (1995)*The Flâneur*, London: Routledge.

Therborn, G. (1995) *European Modernity and Beyond*, London: Sage.

THES (1997) 'Smarten up those baggy notions now', *The Times Higher Education Supplement*, 30 May.

Thomas, J. (1993) 'The politics of vision and the archaeologies of landscape', in B. Bender (ed.) *Landscape, Politics and Perspectives*, Oxford: Berg.

Thompson, E.P. (1967) 'Time, work-discipline and industrial capitalism', *Past and Present*, 36: 57–97.

Thompson, J. (1995) *The Media and Modernity*, Cambridge: Polity.

—— (1997) *Scandal and Social Theory*, Mimeo, SPS, University of Cambridge.

Thoreau, H. ([1854] 1927) *Walden or Life in the Woods*, London: Chapman & Hall.

Thrift, N. (1990) 'The making of a capitalist time consciousness', in J. Hassard (ed.) *The Sociology of Time*, London: Macmillan.

—— (1996) *Spatial Formations*, London: Sage.

Toogood, M. (1998) *Globcit Image Database: description and categorisation of images*, Mimeo, CSEC, Linguistics, Sociology Departments, Lancaster University.

Touraine, A. (1998) 'Culture without Society', *Cultural Values*, 2: 140–57.

Tuan, Y.-F. (1979) 'Sight and pictures', *Geographical Review*, 69: 413–22.

—— (1993) *Passing Strange and Wonderful*, Washington DC: Island Press.

Turkle, S. (1996) *Life on the Screen*, London: Weidenfeld & Nicolson.

Turner, B. (1986) *Citizenship and Capitalism: the debate over reformism*, London: Allen & Unwin.

—— (1993a) 'Contemporary problems in the theory of citizenship' in B. Turner (ed.) *Citizenship and Social Theory*, London: Sage.

—— (1993b) 'Outline of a theory of human rights', in B. Turner (ed.) *Citizenship and Social Theory*, London: Sage.

Urry, J. (1990) *The Tourist Gaze*, London: Sage.

—— (1995) *Consuming Places*, London: Routledge.

—— (1996) 'How societies remember the past', in S. Macdonald and G. Fyfe (eds) *Theorizing Museums*, Oxford: Sociological Review Monographs.

Van den Abbeele, G. (1980) 'Sightseers: the tourist as theorist', *Diacritics*, 10: 3–14.

Van Hear, N. (1998) *New Diasporas*, London: UCL Press.

van Steenbergen, B. (1994) 'Towards a global ecological citizen', in van Steenbergen (ed.) *The Condition of Citizenship*, London: Sage.

Virilio, P. (1986) *Speed and Politics*, New York: Semiotext(e).

—— (1988) 'The work of art in the age of electronic reproduction', Interview in *Block*, 14: 4–7.

—— (1994) *The Vision Machine*, Bloomington, IN: Indiana University Press.

Walby, S. (1996) 'Women and citizenship: towards a comparative analysis', in *University College of Galway Women's Studies Centre Review*, 4: 41–58.

—— (1997) *Gender Transformations*, London: Routledge.

—— (1999) 'The new regulatory state: the social powers of the European Union', *British Journal of Sociology*, 50: 118-40.

Wallace, A. (1993) *Walking, Literature and English Culture*, Oxford: Clarendon Press.

Wallerstein, I. (1987) 'World-systems analysis', in J. Turner and A. Giddens (eds) *Social Theory Today*, Cambridge: Polity.

—— (1991) *Unthinking Social Science*, Cambridge: Polity.

—— (1998) 'The heritage of sociology, the promise of social science', *Presidential Address, 14th World Congress of Sociology*, Montreal, July.

Walvin, J. (1978) *Beside the Seaside*, London: Allen & Unwin.

Ward, N. (1996) 'Surfers, sewage and the new politics of pollution', *Area*, 28: 331–8.

Wark, M. (1994) *Virtual Geography: living with global media events*, Indiana: Indiana University Press.

Waters, M. (1995) *Globalization*, London: Routledge.

Weber, M. ([1904–5] 1930) *The Protestant Ethic and the Spirit of Capitalism*, London: Unwin.

Weiss, L. (1998) *The Myth of the Powerless State*, Cambridge: Polity.

Wheeler, M. (ed.) (1995) *Ruskin and the Environment*, Manchester: Manchester University Press.

Whitelegg, J. (1997) *Critical Mass*, London: Pluto.

Williams, R. (1972) 'Ideas of nature', in J. Benthall (ed.) *Ecology: the shaping enquiry*, London: Longman.

—— (1973) *The Country and the City*, London: Chatto & Windus.

—— (1988) *Border Country*, London: Hogarth Press.

—— (1989) 'Mining the Meaning: Keywords in the Miners' Strike', in *Resources in Hope*, London: Verso.

Wilson, A. (1992) *Culture of Nature*, Oxford: Blackwell.

Wilson, E.O. (1980) *Sociobiology*, Cambridge, MA: Belknap.

Wolff, J. (1993) 'On the road again: metaphors of travel in cultural criticism', *Cultural Studies*, 7: 224–39.

Wolff, V. (1938) *The Three Guineas*, London: Harcourt, Brace & Ward.

Wood, K. and House, S. (1991) *The Good Tourist: a worldwide guide for the green traveller*, London: Mandarin.

Wordsworth, W. ([1844] 1984) *The Illustrated Wordsworth's Guide to the Lakes*, ed. P. Bicknell, London: Book Club Associates.

Worster, D. (1980) 'The intrinsic value of nature', *Environmental Review*, 4: 43–7.

Wright, P. (1985) *On Living in an Old Country*, London: Verso.

WTO (1997) *Yearbook of Tourism Statistics (1996)*, 49th edn, vols 1 and 2, Madrid: World Tourism Organisation.

Wynne, B. (1991) 'After Chernobyl: science made too simple', *New Scientist*, 1753: 44–6.

—— (1994) 'Scientific knowledge and the global environment', in M. Redclift and T. Benton (eds) *Social Theory and the Global Environment*, London: Routledge.

Young, H. (1995) 'Democracy ditched in waves of escapism', *Guardian*, 22 June.

Yuval-Davis, N. (1997) *National Spaces and Collective Identities: borders, boundaries, citizenship and gender relations*, Inaugural Lecture, University of Greenwich.

Zerubavel, E. (1988) 'The standardisation of time: a sociohistorical perspective', *American Journal of Sociology*, 88: 1–23.

Zimmerman, M. (1990) *Heidegger's Confrontation with Modernity*, Bloomington, IA: Indiana University Press.

Zohar, D. and Marshall, I. (1994) *The Quantum Society*, New York: William Morrow.

Index

164–6, 167–8, 170, 187; nature as part of 204–5; notions based on societal model 5, 5–6, 9, 11; remaking 160; rights and duties 2, 19, 162, 163, 164–5, 166, 167, 168, 172, 185, 186–7; and societies 164–5, 166, 168–9, 186, 203; *see also* global citizenship; national citizenship

city-states: in global world 14

civil societies: and automobility 59, 189, 190–3; cyberspatial 74–5; and demand for rights 162; effect of new forms of dwelling 147; global 73–4, 211; and the nation-state 195

Clare, John 85–6

Clarke, D 100

Clarke, T. 198

Classen, C. 95, 96, 99

classes: and European-ness 156; relations in nineteenth-century cities 94–5; as societally structured 8, 9, 164; *see also* social class

Cleator Moor: leisurely walking experience 53

Clifford, J. 26, 28, 29, 133, 155

Clifford, Sue 136, 158–9

Clinton, Bill 181, 182

clocks: biological 120; invention and growth in ownership 110, 112, 114; measurement of time 105, 106, 107, 108, 109, 110–11, 112–14, 115, 118, 191, 192; as metaphor 123

coal-miners' strike (UK) 28–9

Cobbett, William 95

Coca-Cola 13, 37, 185

Cohen, G. 24

Cohen, J. 179, 180, 181, 211

Cohen, R. 154, 156, 157

Cold War 41

Coleridge, Samuel Taylor 52, 85–6

collective enthusiasms 5, 143–4

collective memory 116, 135, 137

collective powers: of societies 9–10

collective representations 26, 27, 175

colonialism: and cultures 154; nature of male power 93; powers of north Atlantic rim countries 11

Colson, F. 108

COMECON (Council for Mutual Economic Assistance) 41

commemoration: and collective memory 116, 137

commodities: development 83; exchange of 108; and labour times 108–9; as networks or chains of exchange 19–20, 64

Common Ground 136, 158–9

communications: computer-mediated 40, 74–5; facilitation of mobility of dispersed peoples 155; flows 14; processes necessary for citizenship 178–9; technologies 125, 126, 129, 146

communion: among the *bund* 142, 144, 145; community as 73, 132, 134, 136; formed in communities hostile to intruders 145–6; mobile 142

communism: collapse in Eastern Europe 41–2

community and communities: conscious and freely chosen 143; different senses of 73, 133–4; dwelling in 4, 5, 132; experiencing through imaginative travel 69; false implication of 139–40; importance of the car 59; landscapes 135; metaphors of 134; notions of 73; and slowing down of place 159; *see also* global communities; imagined communities; local communities; virtual communities

complexity: and global capitalism 208; notions of 130, 190; social systems 205–6; theory 77, 120–1, 122–3, 205

computers: case study of systems in France and the US 39–41; and communication 74–5, 134; databases and information-gathering 76, 196, 198, 200; de-materialisation of the medium 70; and development of new cognitive faculties 73; and instantaneous time 126; mobilities of dwelling 132; and virtual communities 71, 72–3

Comte, Auguste 123

concepts: Durkheim's view 26–7; generated by motor car 57

conflict theory 23, 24

Connerton, P. 116

Constable, John 85–6; *The Hay Wain* 150